CLARENDON LAW SERIES

CLARENDON LAW SERIES

LAND LAW

ELIZABETH COOKE

University of Reading

OXFORD
UNIVERSITY PRESS

OXFORD
UNIVERSITY PRESS

Great Clarendon Street, Oxford OX2 6DP

Oxford University Press is a department of the University of Oxford.
It furthers the University's objective of excellence in research, scholarship,
and education by publishing worldwide in

Oxford New York

Auckland Cape Town Dar es Salaam Hong Kong Karachi
Kuala Lumpur Madrid Melbourne Mexico City Nairobi
New Delhi Shanghai Taipei Toronto

With offices in

Argentina Austria Brazil Chile Czech Republic France Greece
Guatemala Hungary Italy Japan Poland Portugal Singapore
South Korea Switzerland Thailand Turkey Ukraine Vietnam

Oxford is a registered trade mark of Oxford University Press
in the UK and in certain other countries

Published in the United States
by Oxford University Press Inc., New York

British Library Cataloguing in Publication Data

Data available

Library of Congress Cataloging in Publication Data

Data available

Typeset in Ehrhardt
by RefineCatch Limited, Bungay, Suffolk
Printed in Great Britain
on acid-free paper by
Biddles Ltd., King's Lynn, Norfolk

ISBN 978-0-19-926899-3

3 5 7 9 10 8 6 4 2

'Leaf and branch, water and stone; we put the thought of all that we love into all that we make.'

J. R. R. Tolkien

Preface

I have written this book because Peter Birks asked me to.

Peter's vision for the Clarendon series was that they should be accessible and useful to three audiences: to students; to judges, academics and other lawyers; and to folk who are not lawyers but would like to know what the law is about. A tall order indeed. I have had all three in mind. I would be particularly pleased if I could pass on to a student readership some of my love for this subject, with its ancient roots and modern blossoming, its structure, and its messiness.

To the student: this is not an exposition of the law designed to enable you to solve problems. It is intended to be useful as an introduction before you begin detailed study, and again when you have finished that analysis, to draw together the threads, to show you the bigger picture, and to show you where it is all going. There is much more to land law than a set of rules about land transfers. The subject goes to the heart of social policy and plays a part in determining what sort of society we live in.

I have had a lot of help. Parts of the draft have been read by two lawyers and two physicists: I am so grateful to Martin Dixon, Sarah Worthington, Jonathan Gregory and Phil Wolf, who have given their time and their comments generously, and have helped me to see more clearly what I am trying to do. Each has made a difference to the book in its final form. The bad bits are all my own work. I should like to thank Michael Croker, Registrar at the Land Registry's Stevenage Office, for information and enlightenment. The conventions of the Clarendon series prevent my giving proper acknowledgment in the text to all the writers whose work is central to my thinking about land law. To all of them, my thanks for all they have taught me; to borrow Sarah's words from the preface of her wonderful Clarendon, they will recognise their footprints in what I have written. My dear husband, John, has read the whole manuscript at a late stage, and has made a lot of important points; he, Gillian, and Dominic have kept me sane and jolly.

I have endeavoured to state the law as it stands in mid-March 2006, and a few days after the House of Lords delivered its judgment in *Kay and others v London Borough of Lambeth, Leeds City Council v Price and others* [2006] UKHL 10. There has therefore not been a great deal of time to reflect on that decision. Nor do we know the outcome of the UK's application for leave to appeal to the Grand Chamber the decision of the European Court of Human Rights in *Pye v UK* Application no. 44302/02 (2005). Interesting times.

Lizzie Cooke
March 2006

Contents

Table of Cases

Table of Statutes

International Legislation

Statutory Instruments

I

What is Land Law?

We belong to the earth. We are made of it; we are tied to it by gravity; indirectly, we eat it. Without it, there is no human race. In the end, we return to it: dust to dust, ashes to ashes.

Until then, the earth belongs to us. Or so we say. English land law has grown from our deeply entrenched habit of saying 'mine!', a word that all toddlers learn quickly and shout often. We say it not only of our toys and our food and our houses, but also about bits of the earth. English land law is the product of people who say they *own* land. Some communities do not have this habit of thought. But we have, and our land law is shaped by that fact. A while after we learn to say 'mine!', we learn to share; and we have to do that with the earth too. The Englishman's house is his castle, but no man is an island; he is more like a spaghetti junction or a spider diagram. Land is so rich and complex, and so helpfully permanent (usually), that owning it is not like owning a piano. 'My' land is a home and a source of income for me, a pathway for my neighbour, a sort of hostage for the bank, a place to stay for my lodger, and an investment for my landlord.

Land law is about the connections between people and land. It is also about the relationships between people, jostling for space and allocating resources. It is as fascinating as people themselves, and as dynamic. As people change, so do the ways they use and think about land, and land law today looks different, even on this one small island, from how it did fifty years ago, and in another generation's time it will have changed again.

The land law in this book is the law of part of a small island. It is the law of England and Wales; not Northern Ireland, which has adopted some but not all of English land law; nor Scotland, which has inherited the Roman law of property, in common with most of Europe and in contrast with England and Wales. English land law is based on the 'common law', developed here after the island was invaded and conquered in 1066 and to some extent separated from the continental legal heritage. Today that separation seems more disturbing than it did in the days before the European Union; it is no longer possible to write a book like this without at least glancing at the civil law systems across the channel.

But the land law in this book is also the law of a significant part of the world. As a colonial power, up until the mid-twentieth century, we exported English law to the nations we conquered. It was often an inappropriate gift. But the result is that nowadays, absent the British Empire, we can identify a 'common law world' with which we share a legal tradition. Much of what is found in this book would not be especially foreign to a lawyer in Australia, New Zealand, parts of North America or of Africa; and developments in the law of those jurisdictions are nowadays enriching our understanding of the assumptions underlying English land law.

So what is land law? A great deal of law that involves or regulates land and its use—planning law, environmental law, the law of construction contracts, and many others—is not part of the core discipline with which we are concerned here. Land law is the law concerning property rights in land, also known as the law of real property. So what are property rights? What is real property? What is land?

WHAT ARE PROPERTY RIGHTS?

'Property' in everyday language has a range of meanings. Think of 'the property of a gentleman'; 'the properties of carbon dioxide'; or the description of God in the Book of Common Prayer, 'whose property is always to have mercy'. Property for a lawyer means rights, rights that people have in, or over, things, tangible or otherwise. A very wide range of things can be the subject of property rights—everything from socks to shares, from ideas to animals. Things that belong are important to me in monetary terms, or because I like or enjoy them, and even in terms of my identity, my status, and my relationship with other people. There are a few things in which the law states that there cannot be property rights, for a range of reasons. Among them are people, for moral reasons; so we do not have slaves, and 'my' children are not mine in any proprietary sense. The fresh air we breathe cannot be property, because if a thing can be property it must be in some sense scarce. There is no point in having property rights in something that everyone has more than enough of. Contrast bottled oxygen. The view from my window cannot be my property in this jurisdiction, even though it is unique. The reason for that may be convenience; a view is something that English law does not want people to litigate about.

There are many different property rights. There is ownership, the most important and extensive property right; ownership enables you to say 'this is mine'. There are lesser rights which we can call non-ownership rights. They are sometimes called third party rights, because when land is bought, the former owner transfers it to the new owners (two parties to a deal) and there may be third parties who hold non-ownership rights in the land such as rights of way, or a mortgage or a tenancy. Such rights are property rights—or, as we say, they are proprietary[1]—even though they are not ownership rights.

All these property rights can be thought of as bundles, or collections of abilities. The bundle known as ownership is the most extensive. Think of something of yours: a potted plant or a bicycle. You can do a lot of things with it; 'can' in the sense not merely that you are physically able to, but also that you are entitled to. You can use it; hide it; care for it; neglect it; destroy it; lend it to someone; give it away; sell it. There is a problem if you try to do any of these things with my property. You will find either that you physically can (use it, destroy it etc), but will be in trouble for infringing my rights; or that however hard you try (to lend it, give it away, sell it) you will not succeed.

Is there a core to the ownership bundle, one essential ingredient? One suggestion is alienability, meaning that if something is mine, I have the power, legally, to make it yours. This seems to be almost always true; although there are counter-examples. Much of the nation's heritage property belongs to the National Trust, which is able to acquire land and then to declare it inalienable. It is property nonetheless. A more truly core concept is the power to exclude others. My piano is mine, and therefore I am entitled to stop you playing it; my land is mine, and so I can keep you out. There are counter-examples: I cannot keep you out, for example, if you are a policeman with a search warrant. But outside those exceptions, I can keep you out because I have the key; more importantly, I can keep you out because I am entitled to do so. The law gives me 'trespassory protection'.

The lesser property rights are also bundles, though smaller ones. If I am the tenant, rather than the owner, of a house, there are things I can do with it. I can invite guests in. I can, in most tenancies, choose what to plant in the garden. I can sell my tenancy. I can close the door on anyone, the landlord included, during the term of the tenancy. And of course there are lots of things I cannot do, such as demolish the house. The

[1] The word 'proprietary' is here used interchangeably with the adjective 'property'.

holder of a right of way can walk along it (or drive, or whatever are the terms of the easement), and the courts will help him prevent anyone, including the owner, from interfering with his right. But his right of way does not authorise him to dig up the track, or to build on it.

Notice the complexity being described here. Land is so useful and flexible that lots of people can have different sets of rights in it; land may be 'mine', while other people may have property rights in it. Indeed, land law does not always make a rigid distinction between ownership and non-ownership rights; if I grant you a 999-year lease of my land, that lease is an ownership right (both of us can reasonably say that the land is 'mine'), and it is also a non-ownership right held by you in *my* land.

We have to think about the strength, or enforceability, of these bundles of rights as well as their content. Being legal rights, property rights are enforced by society, or the state, and ultimately by force. And property rights, by contrast with personal rights, are special because they are good against everyone. Personal rights, by contrast, are only good against one person or a few individuals. It works like this. Rights involve other people. If I have a right to do something, you have an obligation not to prevent me; if I have a right to payment for something you have bought from me, then you have an obligation to pay me but no-one else has. Property rights are much stronger. This is my lap-top, and it remains my lap-top whoever steals it from me. I can demand it from anyone who has it. By contrast, I have a contractual right to a salary from the University of Reading; that is only a personal right because I cannot demand it from anyone else. There can be personal rights over land: I have a personal right to spend time in my office, and that right arises from my contract of employment. If Reading University sells its land, including my office, I will no longer have a right to spend time in my office. My right to be on/in this bit of land is a personal one, known as a licence. A licence may be contractual, or it may be gratuitous, such as you give to a guest when you invite him in. A lease or tenancy, by contrast, is a property right; it gives exclusive possession of land, usually in return for a money payment to the freehold owner. My lease of a flat gives me a right to be there and to shut everyone else out. I have that right vis-à-vis my landlord, who owns the freehold of the building (these terms will be explained later; they are used here on the basis that most of us have at least a colloquial under-standing of them). And if my landlord sells his freehold I will still have that right against any future owner of the building, for as long as the lease lasts. The traditional lodger, living in part of a house with its owner, paying for lodging and perhaps food but without the right to shut the front door on his landlord, has a personal, contractual right to be in the house—a contractual licence—and not a proprietary right.

WHAT IS REAL PROPERTY?

Land law is a department of property law, known technically as 'real property'—the term is less familiar than 'real estate', which is derived from it. Why the term (are pianos not real?), and why does this form of property require a special area of law?

The term 'real' is easy. It derives from the medieval law of remedies. The law of property protects our rights to exclude, and therefore provides a remedy when property has been taken away from us. At a fairly early stage a division of remedies was evolved; the courts came to the view that for most things, money was an adequate remedy, but not for land. If I took away your falcon or your suit of armour and disposed of it, I would be ordered to pay you damages; but if I deprived you of your land, the uniqueness of that land would demand that the land itself be returned to you. 'Real' derives from the Latin *res*, a thing; for land, the remedy is the thing itself.

All property that is not real is personal. There is an unpleasant overlap of terminology here. The law enforces personal rights and property rights; within the law relating to property rights, the law distinguishes personal property and real property. The distinction between real and personal property used to be vital, because it determined which rules of inheritance would be applied to the property. The heir of one's real property might be different from the heir of one's personal estate. Now there is no difference so far as inheritance is concerned. And the law of remedies, the origin of the distinction, is today much more flexible, so that there is no firm rule that real property attracts real rather than monetary remedies. Nevertheless the term 'real property' is still used, partly out of lawyers' habit, as a convenient way of delineating land law.

Historically, the law of real property was special. Why? The answer is a mix of both current and outmoded concepts. To some extent it arose from the special value of land, in a bygone era when nothing else was so valuable or so significant to the individual. That is now no longer the case; one's pension, perhaps, or other investments may have taken over that importance. What remains is the other reason: the public aspect of land ownership. The state has an interest in the protection of all forms of property (this used to be the province of the legal philosophers, but is now expressed more visibly in the Human Rights Act 1998); arguably, if

rights in land become chaotic the resulting social disruption is greater
than if other forms of ownership are threatened. The state has a role in
ensuring the certainty and the publicity of land ownership, for everyone's
sake. The flip side of that particular coin is taxation. Land is a source of
revenue, and many of the fluctuations in English land law have happened
when the state has felt the need to assert or increase its ability to cream off
some of the value of land.

   At any rate, real property continues to be governed by rules different
from those that apply to cushions or copyrights. Perhaps the most convincing reason for this today is complexity. In land, but not in most items
of personal property, it is possible to have numerous different bundles of
rights—numerous interests, as we say—organised amongst themselves
according to importance, and also across time. Some rights can be exercised now, while others can only be used later, like a theatre ticket bought
now for a performance next week.

WHAT IS LAND?

Land law is about property rights in land; and we have to say what 'land'
means, for it refers not merely to the earth. Land is defined in section
205(1)(ix) of the Law of Property Act 1925:

... includes land of any tenure, and mines and minerals, whether or not held
apart from the surface, buildings or parts of buildings (whether the division is
horizontal, vertical or made in any other way) and other corporeal hereditaments;
also a manor, an advowson, and a rent and other incorporeal hereditaments, and
an easement, right, privilege, or benefit in, over, or derived from land; ... and
'mines and minerals' include any strata or seam of minerals or substances in or
under any land, and powers of working and getting the same, ... and 'manor'
includes a lordship, and reputed manor or lordship ...[2].

This is wordy and off-putting. It is also an unhelpful mix of things and
rights. The important points to take from it at this stage are, first, that
land includes the buildings on it; and it includes buildings separated from
the earth, so that the owner of the top-storey flat is still a landowner.
Secondly, that 'land' also includes intangible things: 'incorporeal hereditaments' are rights, such as rights of way. The owner of a typical English
mid-terrace house needs access to his garden from the street. As well as

---

[2] Some words have been omitted here: some no longer appear in the statute because they
have been repealed, and are represented there by dots; others remain in the statute but are
not quoted here because they are obsolete but have not yet been repealed.

owning his house and garden, therefore, he is likely to have a right of way across his neighbours' gardens from the end of the terrace. That right of way is land. It is a right that relates to a different piece of land from the house and garden itself; and it cannot be exercised by anyone who does not own that house and garden. It can be thought of as an item of intangible property, attached to physical property. Thirdly, land includes some rights that are not attached to physical land. An advowson is the right to choose a priest to be rector of a church; we shall not be saying any more about that. The lordship of a manor is a medieval survival, a collection of rights stripped of any useful content and likely to be meaningless or irrelevant now.

It is a peculiarity of English land law that easements (useful rights over another's land, such as a right of way) come into the second category rather than this third one; they have to be linked with physical land, and cannot be enjoyed as stand-alone rights. By contrast, a public right of way, over a street or a footpath, is not regarded as a property right and does not fall within this definition of land. This is difficult to explain, because the public right of way is certainly a right to do something on land; but it is easy to see that my right to walk down the pavement does not increase my personal wealth because everyone else has it too. It has no scarcity value. The law will defend my use of it; but it does not give me the power to prevent others from doing the same. There is no trespassory protection which, as we have seen, is an essential element of ownership and is important in some form for the non-ownership rights.

The statute does not give a complete answer to 'What is land?', and the courts have filled in some detail. Ownership of land includes, unless the contrary is stipulated, most of what can be found on it. Most importantly, buildings and everything fixed permanently to them, and crops and plants growing on it. It includes anything buried in the ground; but Roman coins and other historical items buried in or found on the land count as treasure trove and must be surrendered to the state. The rule is 'finders keepers' for anything found on land, rather than buried in it, whether the finder is the landowner or his visitor (but not a trespasser). Buildings themselves are ambiguous; what about the garden shed, wired up and perhaps plumbed in? What about the fixed but removable features of the building, such as the fitted kitchen or the light bulbs? The law has sorted things out as they have arisen, looking at the extent to which these potential 'fixtures' are actually fixed to the building, and the purpose of their being fixed. Were they intended to be taken away again? Were they intended to make the house a better house, or were they nailed up, as a picture might be, simply as a secure place to put something which was not meant to form part of the house.

There is a collection of rather dry rules here. They should never be needed at all when land is sold because a properly written contract will leave nothing to litigate about. They may become relevant in a dispute about inheritance (does 'my house' include my pictures?). One of the leading modern cases about the nature of land was about a mobile home,[3] and its purpose was not to determine ownership but to decide whether or not the building fell within the limits of rent control regulation. It could only do so if it was part of the land; and the court held that it was. In doing so, the court solved one small practical problem for one individual, and as a by-product added a paragraph to explanations of what land is.

TENSIONS AND THEMES IN LAND LAW

Land law is the battle ground for a struggle between competing categories of rights and competing values. Is the law to respond to complexity by simplifying, so as to make land as marketable as possible; or is it to respond by preserving as many rights as possible, at the expense, if necessary, of marketability? Do we safeguard the interests of those wanting to buy land or do we safeguard those who already have rights in it? A shorthand for this set of questions is to ask: is land law to tend towards dynamic security, or static security?

The trend, for a couple of centuries or more, has been to move towards dynamic security. Much of this book is devoted to the story of that trend. Major steps have been taken, sometimes by Parliament and sometimes by the courts, to simplify title to land—'title' meaning here the whole complex of rights owned by different people in one piece of land. This is done not by taking rights away but by adjusting their enforceability. So although property rights are in principle distinguishable from personal rights in land by their universal enforceability, that principle has been tweaked, particularly in the last century and a half. Today, property rights vary in their enforceability, and the most important tool used to achieve this has been the registration of title to land.

Registration creates a public record of ownership and of third party rights. It also exerts control over those rights by making the fact, or the form, of registration the crucial element in enforceability. Unregistered rights may have no, or very little, proprietary effect. This has

---

[3] *Elitestone Ltd v Morris* [1977] 1 WLR 687, HL.

happened even though, at the same time, the law is constantly adapting to provide new protection for those for whom formally created and publicly registered rights are unavailable or unsuitable. The latter trend has become increasingly important as home ownership has become more widespread, and as family relationships have become more complex and informal. So we have seen over the last century something of a tug of war between static and dynamic security, between protection and marketability. Dynamic security has tended to win. Will that still be the case once human rights, including the right to protection for our home and our possessions, have made themselves thoroughly at home in our legal system?

PROPERTY RIGHTS AND HUMAN RIGHTS

The Human Rights Act 1998 brought into our domestic law the European Convention on Human Rights and Fundamental Freedoms. It introduced new ways of enforcing human rights: re-interpreting legislation so as to be compatible with the Convention rights, where possible, and declaring legislation to be incompatible with the Convention as a last resort. It therefore brought into new prominence the need to consider all aspects of law in the light of human rights, including property law.

The Convention is not, in the main, about property. But Article 1 of the First Protocol provides:

Every natural or legal person is entitled to the peaceful enjoyment of his possessions. No one shall be deprived of his possessions except in the public interest and subject to the conditions provided for by the law and by the general principles of international law.

The preceding provisions shall not, however, in any way impair the right of a State to enforce such laws as it deems necessary to control the use of property in accordance with the general interest or to secure the payment of taxes or other contributions or penalties.

Article 8 of the Convention provides:

1. Everyone has the right to respect for private and family life, his home and his correspondence.
2. There shall be no interference by a public authority with the exercise of this right except such as is in accordance with the law and is necessary in a democratic society in the interests of national security, for public safety or the economic well-being of the country, for the prevention of disorder or crime, for the protection of health or morals, or for the protection of the rights and freedoms of others.

The human rights affirmed by the Convention are not themselves property rights; they do not, by themselves, give anyone a right over a particular piece of land. Having property is not, under this Convention, a human right. This is not a necessary truth. The South African Constitution, for example, gives all its citizens the right to a home. The European Convention gives you the right not to be deprived of a possession or of your home only if you already have the possession, or the home, in the first place.

The issue for land law is whether or not the Convention rights force a re-examination of the property rights we already recognise. When a landlord has a statutory right to evict a tenant from the landlord's property purely because the tenancy has come to an end and without giving any other reason, is that compatible with the tenant's human rights to respect for his home and to peaceful enjoyment of his possessions? When the law has given a long leaseholder the right to 'enfranchise' that is, to buy the freehold of his leasehold property at a price that reflects the value of the ground but not of the buildings, is that a justifiable interference with the freeholder's right to enjoy his possessions? When a bank repossesses a house because mortgage repayments have not been kept up, is that an infringement of human rights? Where a landowner has lost his title to a squatter, who has gained ownership of the land by treating it as his own for a number of years, is that compatible with the landowner's human rights?

Putting that dilemma more generally: does the Human Rights Act 1998 force us to re-examine established property rights on the basis that they might *not* be in the public interest or that, if they are, the means taken to enforce them might not be proportionate to the interest protected? If for example the law states that you must leave your home because it is someone else's property and that you have no proprietary or contractual right to be there, can you complain that your human rights have been violated? Until very recently the answer given by the courts has been 'No, never'. A few days before the manuscript of this book was delivered to the publisher the House of Lords held that, as a result of a decision of the European Court of Human Rights in Strasbourg, the answer has to be not 'never' but 'hardly ever'. Moreover, the issue about the squatter's title has now been the subject of a decision in Strasbourg, and the answer given is not a comfortable one for the common law tradition. We shall have to look at this in more detail later. For now, the point to be made is that lots of rights and remedies in land law are wide open to challenge on the basis of human rights, and that a number of well-established principles may have to be re-examined over the next few years.

Those, then, are the concepts necessary to an understanding of land law. In the next Chapter we look at the way property rights in land have been developed over centuries in order to reach the position we see today.

BIBLIOGRAPHY

P. Birks, 'Before We Begin: Five Keys to Land Law' in S. Bright and J. Dewar, eds, *Land Law: Themes and Perspectives* (Oxford, Oxford University Press, 1998).

S. Bright, 'Of Estates and Interests: a Tale of Ownership and Property Rights' in S. Bright and J. Dewar (eds), *Land Law: Themes and Perspectives* (Oxford Oxford University Press, 1998) 529.

K. Gray, 'Land law and human rights' in L. Tee, ed., *Land Law: Issues, debates, policy* (Cullompton, Willan, 2002) at 211.

K. Gray and S. Francis Gray, *Elements of Land Law* 4th edn, (Oxford, Oxford University Press, 2005), 100–52.

J. W. Harris, *Property and Justice* (Oxford, Oxford University Press, 1996).

T. W. Merrill, 'Property and the Right to Exclude' 77 *Nebraska Law Review* 730 (1998) at 730–9, in B. Ziff, *A Property Law Reader* (Toronto, Thomson, 2004).

S. Panesar, *General Principles of Property Law* (Harlow, Longman, 2001).

J. Penner, *The Idea of Property in the Law* (Oxford, Oxford University Press, 2000).

2

Property Rights in Land

The first chapter of this book explained some of the central concepts of land law. This chapter introduces the building blocks, namely property rights in land, and explains how they evolved by a mixture of design and accident. It is in four parts. The first is about ownership rights. The second introduces the systems of law and equity and the contrast between legal and equitable ownership rights. The third considers the range of non-ownership rights, both legal and equitable. The result is a heap of rights which may all be found in one piece of land. The fourth part of this chapter explains a little about the enforceability of the different elements of this heap. How the heap is organised, and enforceability managed, is the subject of Chapter 3.

OWNERSHIP OF LAND

TENURE: HOW IS LAND HELD?

English law differs from the civil law tradition found in Europe, in that it expresses ownership rights as relationships. Ownership may be freehold or leasehold; these labels can be seen in estate agents' windows. Both forms of ownership imply a connection; for the freehold owner, with the Crown, and for the leaseholder, with a landlord. Both forms are known as 'tenure', that is, ways of holding land, because they were not originally ownership rights. Both evolved, more or less directly, from the landholding system of the Middle Ages, known as the feudal system, in which the king allowed his subjects to hold or control land in return for services rendered to him.

There is a case for ignoring the feudal system. Most English land-owners go through life in ignorance of it, and their landowning activities are unaffected by it. It may, in any event, be abolished. But it remains part of the English land lawyer's mental furniture; it retains some practical effect; and the consolidation of the feudal system under the Norman kings is the first stage in the story that has to be told in order to explain where we are today.

The feudal system was a feature of medieval life. It was a network of relationships, whereby the powerful gave protection, in the form of material assistance and the use of land, to the weaker, who gave their service in return. The system seems to have existed before 1066, both in Anglo-Saxon society and in continental Europe. It has been claimed that the French developed it as a way of strengthening their defence against the Viking invaders, who nevertheless settled and put down strong roots in Normandy in the tenth and eleventh centuries. When one of those Vikings, William of Normandy, won the throne of England, he needed a way to control his conquered country, and the feudal system was one of the means he used. His genius may have been in adapting what had in essence been a series of local networks and converting it into a nationwide system of governance; or it may be that the picture we have today, and the story we tell, is in part the result of the success of the propaganda of later monarchs, in particular of Henry VIII.

The story goes like this. When William took the crown, he took the whole of England; he became, as contemporary legal documents describe him, *Dominus Rex*—'*dominus*' is the Latin term for an owner as well as a master. Then, while remaining owner of the whole of the country, he parcelled out the land and bestowed it on his followers, not as a gift but as something to make use of. One of his followers might be given, for example, a manor near Reading to have and to hold. 'Manor' in that context means simply an area of land; the word has come to mean land with feudal rights attached to it. He is described as a tenant (from the Latin *tenere*, one who holds), and was obliged to provide a service for the king in return. The service was defined as a particular activity. If it was knight service, then the tenant would be obliged to provide a specified number of knights for the king to command in each campaigning season. If the service demanded was religious, known as *frankalmoyn*, then the tenant was obliged to provide prayers for the king's soul (a reasonable arrangement if the tenant was the abbot of a monastery: Battle Abbey near Hastings, founded in order to give thanks for the king's victory, is an obvious example).

This left the tenant with a great deal of land and a weighty obligation. In order to meet it, he would do the same again: he would grant part of the land he held—he would *subinfeudate*—to someone else to hold it in return for services, not to the king but to him. The service would be knight service, but whereas the tenant-in-chief holding the land directly from the king (or 'of the king' as it is usually put) might owe the king 50 knights each summer, *his* tenant might owe *him* 5 knights.

And of course he parcelled his land out to a number of individuals on these terms, in order to fulfil his own obligation. But *these* men would, again, subinfeudate, and so on. Further down the feudal pyramid, the service was less likely to be knight service and more likely to be agricultural; and at the bottom layer of the pyramid was the villein, who held land in return for agricultural service on his own lord's land, and who was not free. He could not leave that land, and he had very few rights.

William did not wipe out all pre-conquest landownership and impose a feudal structure from the top down, even though the story has often been presented in that way. Such an upheaval would have been neither practical nor necessary. It is likely that the lower rungs of the existing Anglo-Saxon feudal ladders would have been left intact (being occupied by people too insignificant to trouble the new king and his henchmen), with the conqueror's friends slotted into the higher levels. The structure was unified by the king's rank as ultimate lord, and made visible in the ceremony of homage, in which the tenant had to do homage to his lord — he had to kneel, to give his hands to his lord and express loyalty and dependence. Here lie the seeds of many a later war. Would the king of England do homage to the king of France for his cross-channel holdings (as William the Conqueror himself did)?

Although the structure of the feudal system is easy to grasp, the detail of its operation is more subtle. There were far more services than are mentioned here. It is an entertainment to go through them—grand serjeanty, petty serjeanty, socage, gavelkind, copyhold—many of them expressed in the law-French that remained the language of the courts until the sixteenth century; but we get no more from it now than historical diversion. While they lasted there was a wonderfully colourful range of relationships, generating an immense amount of law.

But the feudal system slowly imploded after the enactment of a statute called *Quia Emptores* (simply the first two words of its long title in Latin: 'Because buyers [of land] . . .') in 1290, which forbade further subinfeudation. Thus when a lineage died out, the internal rungs of the feudal ladder disappeared. The end result of the process, all these centuries later, is that there is only one remaining layer of feudal tenancy, held directly from the Crown. Therefore all land in the United Kingdom is either held by one feudal tenant directly from the Crown, or retained by the Crown as Crown land. The Crown land we have all seen is the beach; most of the foreshore of England and Wales is still held by the Crown, but there are other areas too.

The feudal services themselves have lost their colour and variety. A series of statutory provisions, from the 17th century to 1925, abolished them or converted them into money payments, which rapidly became valueless because of inflation. Today all freehold owners remain feudal tenants, but almost all hold on socage tenure—in theory a form of agricultural service, in practice a nullity. A handful of very distinguished folk who hold their land by statute do something more interesting; the Duke of Marlborough, for instance, holds the Blenheim estate in return for the presentation of a fleur-de-lys flag at Windsor once a year. For the rest of us, the practical significance of the feudal system is very limited indeed. Our land reverts to the Crown if the tenant dies without heirs or a will; and if a tenant becomes bankrupt (or insolvent, in the case of corporate landowners) the land will ultimately pass to the Crown by a process known as escheat. There remain large areas of Crown land, of course, that have not been granted to feudal landholders.

Over the border, in Scotland, feudalism has only just died. The Abolition of Feudal Tenure etc (Scotland) Act 2002 took effect in 2004 and removes the Crown's position as *dominus*, or ultimate lord of the land. It also removes a whole system of conveyancing and landholding relationships; for the Scots had no *Quia Emptores* and therefore have been free to subinfeudate—and have kept on doing so. Thus landownership remained in the feudal, ladder-like pattern, with numbers of intermediate tenants receiving feudal services, invariably in monetary form. That pattern has now been wiped out, with compensation where necessary; and with no sign, so far, of any challenge from a human rights point of view despite the fact that, technically, it could be seen as an expropriation of property. The reason multi-layered feudalism survived for so long in Scotland was that it had become a form of planning control; if land was subinfeudated rather than sold outright, the feudal superior could impose services that effectively controlled how the land was used. These obligations have been reorganised as a consequence of the abolition of the feudal system, and the important ones preserved as obligations attached to land, sometimes for the benefit of the former feudal superior and in some cases for the benefit of neighbouring properties.

Further out in the common law world, feudalism remains a live and crucial issue. The processes of settlement and conquest led to the export of English land law; sometimes by agreement, as in New Zealand, more often by imposition as in Australia. The result was that the land of the colonised jurisdiction vested in the Crown, as surely as it did here in 1066, and the Crown was free to make grants of land—which it did, not in large parcels to military cronies, but in little, marketable/farmable/mortgageable/mineable lots to settlers. A modern New Zealander may well be able to trace his title (that is, a chain of ownership) back to a named grantee in the nineteenth century; scarcely anyone in England can trace their title back to the military henchman of 1066. So the colonies took on a fresh, although one-layered, feudalism that independence has not always changed. In Australia and New Zealand, for example (though not in America) land is still held from the Crown.

One of the wonderful developments in land law worldwide in the twentieth and twenty-first centuries has been a re-examination of the position of those who were deprived of land in the process of colonisation. Aboriginal title is an important issue now in the common law world, and various different methods have been found of giving, or giving back, or recognising land rights. And this has led to a fresh look at feudalism. One of the routes to the restoration of land rights in Australia has been the re-examination of what actually happened when land vested in the Crown, and a re-think of the traditional theory. The principal stimulus for this was a case brought by aboriginal Australians living on land which had never been the subject of a feudal grant.[1] It was one of those rare and happy instances where circumstances conspired to produce a test case where the issue in question was clear and isolated. The upshot of this and other cases in Australia was a new view, that the Crown is not literally the owner of ungranted land; it has the right to make feudal grants, and meanwhile the Crown's role pertains more to taking care of the land than to having dominion over it. It has responsibility rather than ownership. Therefore, in these quite unusual circumstances, aboriginal title survived colonisation; and legislation followed the decision in *Mabo* to give a marginally better deal to aboriginals. The consequences of these decisions for Australia, in constitutional law even more than in land law, are still being worked out; and we may see reflections of the Australian developments in English land law when steps are taken, as is surely likely, to abolish feudalism here.

ESTATE: FOR HOW LONG IS LAND HELD?

In land law, then, the feudal relationship is always there, quietly in the background. Tenure is one aspect of the feudal system: it tells us how (i.e. from whom, and for what service) land is held, as discussed above.

---

[1] *Mabo v Queensland [No 2]* (1992) 175 CLR 1.

A landowner is said to be a tenant[2] who holds land on, or for, a particular tenure. But there is another aspect; the tenant is also said to have an 'estate'. 'Estate' here means a right that is limited in time. A tenant's estate tells us how long his land is held for, because in the feudal system landholding is not supposed to be permanent. When the king and his cronies granted land to those lower down the feudal ladder (or, as discussed, imposed the relationship of their choice on conquered subjects without actually changing the occupation of the land), they granted the land for a particular length of time. Why part with it forever? Why not grant land just for the lifetime of a particular tenant, so that when he dies, his immediate lord retrieves the land and can grant it afresh to someone else. He can then choose whether to grant it to the current tenant's son, or to someone who, at the relevant time, might be more useful to him; he can review the services for which it is held; he can perhaps extract a price for the grant. If that was the lord's preference, he would grant a life estate. A more magnanimous approach was to grant the land for an estate not just for life, but 'in tail': the term comes from Norman French, *taillé*, meaning limited. Such an estate (called a fee tail or an entail—the word 'fee' denotes something that can be inherited) lasts for the lifetime of the current tenant and the lives of his direct descendants: thus it can pass from the tenant to his son, to his son's son, etc; but it reverts to the lord when the lineage fails. Much more secure for the tenant was the fee simple estate. This was an estate in fee, again, but the fee was simple: anyone could inherit it. It could pass to the heirs of the tenant, or to anyone else to whom he chose to bequeath it. It was possible for the tenant to prevent it ever passing back to the lord or, ultimately, to the Crown, although it might do so if the tenant had no family and failed to make a will.

As may be imagined, complications arose when the heir was female; also when the heir was a minor, in which case he became the ward (almost the property) of the feudal lord until his majority: there, rather surprisingly, lies the origin of the courts' modern powers in their wardship jurisdiction to protect children. In any event, the lord was usually able to extract a price at the point when the estate changed hands on the death of a tenant.

That sort of thing is long gone, but the different estates remain. Today, virtually all land is held in common socage tenure from the Crown for an

---

[2] We are still using the word in the ancient sense of one who holds land, not in the modern sense to denote a leaseholder.

estate in fee simple. But in some cases the different estates co-exist; and we can say that another difference between English land law and the civil law tradition found in the rest of Europe is that English law is comfortable with the idea that there may be more than one different ownership right coexisting in one piece of land. Imagine a will made by Ham, leaving his home to his second wife Pam for her lifetime (she therefore takes a life estate), and leaving the fee simple to the son of his first marriage, Sam—a not unusual arrangement. During Pam's lifetime, she holds an estate *in possession*, while Sam's estate is held *in remainder*; both she and Sam have an item of property that they can give away or sell (there is a market in life estates; the property purchased lasts just as long as the original holder lives), although only Pam is entitled to make use of the land right now. When Pam dies, her estate disappears and Sam's fee simple becomes an estate in possession.

Estates can be rather more complex than just described. For example, they can be subject to termination on the happening of specified events, either automatically or at the grantor's option. There is of course a huge volume of law as to which is which, and, in any event, as to what sort of condition is legally acceptable. What is the effect, for example, of a gift of land in fee simple to X provided she never marries? (The answer in that particular instance is that the gift is made unconditional, and the proviso has no effect; but some other clauses aiming to control lives through land have been effective). A fee tail can be limited to the estate owner's male heirs, or his female heirs, or his heirs born of a particular wife, and so the land may pass from one branch of a family to another. Such is the background to Jane Austen's *Pride and Prejudice*. Then there are rules about the characteristics of the estates, and the behaviour of those who hold them. Given the possibility of 'owning' land, if we can call it that, for one's lifetime only, there have to be rules about what one is allowed to do with the land during that time. This is known as the law of waste. Given that these limited estates are nevertheless items of property, there have to be rules about whether, and under what conditions, they can be marketed. Readers of Victorian novels are referred to *Felix Holt* (and for a modern twist, to Charles Paliser's *Quincunx*); an estate that will last until the death of the last of A's descendants *can* be sold to B, but it will still come to an end on the death of the last of *A*'s descendants, and the potential for that as a narrative device in fiction is delightful, however inconvenient the real-life practicalities.

However, that vast range of law is going to be left untouched here. Very few people indeed now own life estates or entails—indeed, since 1996 it has been not possible to create new entails. And all but the 'fee simple absolute in possession' (quoting from the Law of Property Act 1925) have, since 1925, been demoted. They still exist as property rights which can be owned; but they exist in less robust form (i.e. they can more easily be destroyed) than the fee simple absolute in possession, normally just referred to as the fee simple. To understand what that means, we have to look at another layer of complexity, the relationship between law and equity.

But before we do so we have to look at a different form of ownership, where one word describes both tenure and estate: the lease.

LEASEHOLD OWNERSHIP

Common socage is a freehold tenure, one of those feudal tenures that could be held by free men. The freehold tenures were originally contrasted with the unfree tenures, the estates that could be held by those who were not free to move around or to dispose of their land; they disappeared as the unfree folk became free, gradually over the course of the Middle Ages, one or two rights at a time. But another contrast can be made. There are the freehold tenures, and there is something less than freehold: leasehold. The word 'freehold' has lost its original meaning (the tenure of the free man) and nowadays tells us simply that the land is not leasehold.

Unlike a feudal relationship, a lease is a contract. It is based, not upon homage and the reciprocal feudal obligations of service and protection, but rather upon an explicit contract, made on terms the parties choose and lasting for a period that they decide upon (although choices may be one-sided, depending upon their respective bargaining power). In its early days it was not an estate in land at all; it was just a contract. The freehold estates were personal relationships which indicated one's status in society, whereas a lease was a commercial transaction. If the freeholder improperly evicted the leaseholder, the leaseholder's remedy was monetary compensation, not the return of his land. From the mid-fifteenth century the leaseholder became entitled to recover his land in those circumstances—he became entitled to a proprietary remedy, so that what he held could be regarded as real property. But because this was not so in the thirteenth century, *Quia Emptores* did not apply to leases. A leaseholder for 99 years could grant a sub-lease to another for, say, 70 years, who could grant a sub-underlease to another for, say, 21 years. Ladder-like arrangements of leasehold estates continued, and continue, to be possible and useful. And while the relationships upon which the freehold estates were founded eventually lost virtually all their content, the leasehold relationship did not. So although I hold my fee simple estate[3] in freehold (common socage) tenure direct from the Queen, the relationship has no substance. The lease is quite different and altogether more complex. It has been said that the lease has made the transition from contract to estate to tenure; but it has not lost any of its contractual features on the way. The lease is tenure, because the lease tells us from whom land is held and on what terms; it is estate, because it is ownership of land for a defined length of time; and it is a contract with extensive content in the form of substantial obligations.

The length of a lease is infinitely variable. There is nothing to prevent a freeholder granting a lease of a million years, although in practice 999 is about the longest seen; equally, a lease may be for an hour or two. And there are two ways of defining the time given by a lease; it may be for a fixed term—a single period of time—or it may be periodic. A periodic lease is known as a tenancy; it is defined by a minimum period, such as a week, a month or a year, and it will continue for as long as both parties want it to, subject to the ability of either party to stop it at the end of a period.

A lease is an ownership right—the holder of a 999-year lease can certainly say that it is *his* house. It is also a non-ownership right vis-à-vis the landlord; the landlord can say that the tenant has a lease of (i.e. a property right in) *his*, the landlord's, house. The shorter the lease, the more difficult it is to describe it as an ownership right. Can a weekly tenant say that he owns his own home? Almost certainly not, although he might refer loosely in conversation to 'my house'. A periodic tenancy is potentially among the shortest of all; yet it may last for decades, because the length of a lease may be changed by the law: special categories of tenant may be entitled to stay in their property at the end of their lease (when the fixed term ends or, in the case of a periodic tenancy, even if notice is given) because the law gives them protection beyond that given by their own contract. This used to be the case for most residential tenants but is no longer, except for some public sector housing; it is still the case for many business and agricultural tenants. This makes it difficult to say where the divide lies between ownership and not-ownership; it is probably determined not by length, but by whether the tenant pays just a rent for the property, or has paid—to the landlord or to the previous tenant—a capital sum; and this will never be the case for a periodic

---

[3] It may seem odd to say that I have an 'estate' in a rather average terraced house in Reading, but there it is. The estate is my bundle of rights, not the land.

tenancy, however long it in fact goes on for. It seems that in our sort of society, in order for something to be seen as truly *my land*, we feel it must be not only a place to do things in—a home or an office or a farm—but also a capital asset, and potentially an inheritance for the next generation.

FREEHOLD, LEASEHOLD AND COMMONHOLD

Today's landowner, then, may have a freehold or a long lease; the price would be much the same for either. The fee simple is, more precisely, a holding in freehold tenure for an estate in fee simple; we tend to mix them up and refer interchangeably to freehold land or to a, or the, fee simple. Houses tend to be freehold; parts of buildings, or flats, are almost invariably leasehold because of the peculiar characteristics of the rules about creating mutual obligations between landowners, for example, to maintain a shared road or stairway: in freehold land it is difficult to create positive duties that will stick to the property rather than disappearing when it is sold, but this is straightforward if the property is leasehold. We shall have more to say about land obligations later, and about the newly invented status of commonhold, which is one way of solving this problem.

LAW AND EQUITY

THE BEGINNINGS

Now for another dimension. While feudalism is nearly obsolete, equity is not, and it remains fundamental to English land law and to the jurisdictions that incorporated it. To the rest, the non-common law systems, it is a stumbling block, a headache, a nuisance, an incomprehensibility. Yet we cannot, it seems, do without it.

For there are two types of property right in English law, legal and equitable. We might as well call them category A and category B, or more helpfully grade them by strength, like coffee: strong and not so strong. Legal rights are more robust than equitable ones. The motto or maxim (or magic spell) that, historically, distinguished them was the phrase 'legal rights bind all the world, equitable rights bind all except a *bona fide* purchaser for value without notice', which will be explained in due course although it has lost much of its relevance now. It meant that equitable rights in land were not so well protected as legal ones and were more likely to disappear when land changed hands. Legal and equitable property rights also differ in their public-ness. As we shall see, much of English land law is now dictated by the rules of registration. Legal estates must be registered, and are therefore open to public inspection. Equitable ownership rights in land must be kept off the register, although equitable non-ownership rights may be partially protected on the register.

Why should these two different forms and strengths of property right have evolved in our legal system? Until 1873, England had two court systems, the courts of law and the courts of equity. Legal rights are those that were recognised in the courts of law, equitable rights were enforced by the courts of equity. Although now both systems are operated in all courts, legal rights are the ones that were formerly protected only in the courts of law, and equitable rights those that were formerly protected only by the courts of equity. Despite the merger of the two court systems, we have retained the two forms of property right because they have different characteristics.

But the explanation based on the court systems begs a rather longer story. Again we have to go back to the Middle Ages; the classic version of the story involves a knight going away on a crusade, unsure of his return, concerned for the safety of his family and his property in his absence. To secure both he conveys his lands to his friend, to keep for him. He might also hand over his jewellery and his spare horse; but the land cannot just be handed over, and so the knight carries out all the formalities of transfer of legal ownership, so that his friend can truly hold the property for him.

On his return, his friend refuses to re-transfer the land to him. The knight therefore seeks justice from the king, but the judge in the king's court will not assist him; his 'friend' holds the legal title to the land, and the judge does not have the power to go beyond that. However, by the fourteenth century the king has begun to delegate some judicial functions to the Lord Chancellor, and *his* courts, known as chancery, are an alternative recourse for our deprived knight. The Lord Chancellor holds ecclesiastical office, and his view of things is rather different. His concern is for matters of conscience, and he is prepared to look past the legal title and to order the friend to return the property, for in reality—in conscience, in equity—it belongs to the knight. The dating of all this is obscure, but it seems to be established by the early fifteenth century.

Once all this has evolved, ownership of land looks different depending upon which court is dealing with a dispute. 'At law' in the king's courts, it belongs to the transferee; 'in equity' it belongs to the knight who transferred it to be held on his behalf or, as the language of the time had it, 'to his use'. The earliest label for what we now call a trust was a 'use', and here is the distinctive feature of common law landholding.

Another question had to be resolved by the courts of equity; what if the friend had sold the land during the knight's absence? The purchaser might not know anything about the knight; should the knight be able to claim it back from him? The courts of equity evolved a rule for this; they took the view that the purchaser should not have to give the land back to the knight unless his conscience was touched by the knight's claim; and his conscience was affected if he knew about that claim. In other words, although legal rights bind all the world, the knight's equitable ownership was enforceable against all except a *bona fide* purchaser of the legal estate for value without notice. There is the rule mentioned earlier; while contemplating it in this chapter it is helpful to bear in mind that it is no longer accurate today because of the effect of title registration, to be explained below and in the next chapter.

The trust was remarkably useful, and not only for long absences. Friars, debarred by their vows from holding property, had no problem occupying and taking the profits of land held for their use. Feudal tenants anxious to avoid the problems of wardship—whereby the feudal overlord will hold land while an heir is a minor, and then receive a fee for transferring it back to him when he reaches his majority—would transfer land to an adult friend to hold until the child came of age. Restrictions on the ability to pass on one's land by will could be evaded by making the desired arrangement behind a trust, known at that date as a 'use' because it involved land being transferred to X 'for the use of' Y. We now call X the trustee and Y the beneficiary; Y's equitable ownership of the land is also known as a beneficial interest. Henry VIII, anxious to reap all the profits of his feudal overlordship, did his best to wipe out that particular device by a law called the 'Statute of Uses' but it was nowhere near sufficiently tightly drafted, and lawyers soon found ways round it by contorted conveyancing devices. The trust was now well-established as a way of organising entitlement to land.

THE DEVELOPMENT OF THE TRUST

The need to keep the reality of land ownership away from feudalism and its associated liabilities died away along with feudalism itself. But other uses were found for the trust, more comprehensible to us now even if remote from most of our experience. The landed gentry, who until the nineteenth century owned most of the land in this country, adopted the trust as a structuring device in order to control the ownership of land for future generations. Combine the trust mechanism, whereby land or money can be held by one or more individuals with responsibility to look after it for the benefit of family members, with the potential of the doctrine of estates for the planning of ownership over time, and it is possible to create a structure (known as a 'settlement') in which land is held on trust for some generations. The terms might be that Ed shall own it for his lifetime, then Fred for his lifetime; then it is to pass to Ted and his male heirs; failing those heirs, Samantha is to have a fee simple. Ed gets the land now; he has an estate in possession. Ted knows now that he will get the land later; he has an estate in reversion, which he already owns, although it will not become an estate in possession until Ed's death. Samantha has an estate in remainder; again, that is something she owns now. (The usual analogy is with a theatre ticket, which is now your property, although you cannot enter the theatre until the night of the performance). Note that normally we are talking about vast tracts of land, most of it tenanted; so the organisation of ownership into time-slices was a way of organising, not so much who lived in the family home/mansion (several generations might live there, irrespective of ownership) but who took the income from the land.

Trusts were also useful as ways of managing the property of married women, who could not hold a legal estate in land until 1882 (a problem for the rich but not for the poor), but could have land held on trust for them. Trusts could also be used, and still are, to enable land to be managed on behalf of an irresponsible beneficiary. This all generated a vast amount of law. What, for example, were the rights of the beneficiaries of the land among themselves and vis-à-vis the trustees? Could the beneficiaries deal with their equitable property rights, or interests? If so, how? Could they sell them? Could they mortgage them? And what of the public interest? The settlement was designed, in large measure, to ensure that land stayed in the family, whereas the industrial revolution demanded a market in land. How might the government ease the aristocracy's stranglehold on the countryside? This problem was to some extent managed by a device called the rule against perpetuities, which states that land may not be settled too far into the future; but death duties proved a far more effective way of getting land out of the hands of the gentry.

The aristocracy and the vast estates have largely gone now, and trusts are important in other areas of life; wealth management, investment vehicles, and pensions, rather than family landholdings. Trusts may be set up when the intention is, explicitly, that one person (or, for technical reasons to be explained, more usually two people) shall look after and manage property, such as a pension fund or a nominee shareholding, for another or others. And there will be a trust of land, whether or not the people involved intend it or are even aware of it, in a number of situations. It may happen deliberately, where it is intended that one or more trustees look after land for the benefit of one or more others. There is a trust (whether intended or not) whenever the ownership of land is structured over time. Ham's will, discussed above, creates a trust, whereby the house is held for Pam for her lifetime and then passed on to Sam. During Pam's lifetime, the legal fee simple must be held by trustees for Pam and Sam's benefit. This is because the freehold estates other than the fee simple can only now be equitable. There are no legal life estates. Where there is a life estate, *someone* must hold the fee simple, and he will hold it as a trustee. In this case, Ham may appoint trustees in his will, but if he fails to do so his executors will find that they have a continuing role as trustees of the house. Finally, and very importantly, there is a trust whenever land is owned jointly, by two or more people at the same time, for reasons to be discussed.

Why there is a trust in all these cases, and why the trust is so vital to land law, will become clearer when the legislation of 1925 is understood. For now, note that whenever there is a trust, there is a split in ownership, so that one or more trustees hold the legal fee simple, and one or more beneficiaries hold equitable ownership rights. Conversely, whenever legal and equitable (or 'beneficial') ownership is split between different people, there is a trust.

NON-OWNERSHIP RIGHTS

THE POSSIBILITIES

Whether land is freehold or leasehold, the owner is likely to be subject to the rights of others; these are the legal, rather than physical, limits of ownership. The most important one is likely to be a mortgage.

The major change in patterns of home ownership during the twentieth century has been the rise of owner-occupation. This has been referred to as the property-owning democracy; or, more realistically, as the property-mortgaged-to-a-building-society-owning democracy. For we cannot afford the capital value of our homes, any more than most people could 150 years ago; but what has changed is the availability of finance. It is now normal in this country—far more so than in most of Europe—for the homeowner to be a freeholder or long leaseholder, having borrowed the money for the purchase from a financial institution, and therefore subject to the obligation to repay that loan. Obligations are easily broken, and can be lost forever when the borrower goes bankrupt; a mortgage is a security right which attaches the loan to land. If the loan is not repaid by the borrower, the lender can take the land itself and can sell it and have first call on the sale proceeds to repay his loan. If the land is sold by the borrower and the loan is not repaid, the mortgage (if properly created) sticks to the land, and the lender keeps his rights no matter who the owner is. Thus the mortgage is a non-ownership right in land to which most landowners, whether domestic or commercial, are subject at some stage.

Land is more than just a place, in which to live or work; like all other items of property it is an asset, a piece of wealth with a market value. And it is a source of credit. A mortgage may enable the acquisition of the home or business premises; a mortgage of a home already owned may secure a loan for the improvement of that home, or for the financing of the homeowner's business. Once in place, it imposes restrictions on the owner's powers to deal as he wishes with his property. And when these arrangements go wrong, the law must regulate the competing claims of the homeowner, one or more mortgagees, the homeowner's other creditors if any, and her family.

There may well be other non-ownership rights attached to land, apart from those of the mortgagee. Neighbouring landowners may have rights, either to use the property (e.g. a right of way) or to restrict the owner's use (e.g. to ensure that he does not carry on a business from his home). This is the law of easements and covenants, which other jurisdictions call land obligations. Easements and covenants are property rights. As indicated above, one of the big issues to which they give rise is the potential for them to stick to the land when it is sold. They are property rights, but they exist as attachments to other land. They can be transferred from one person to another, but only where those people are the successive owners of the land to which they are attached. They can be thought of as pieces of string, tied at one end to the burdened land and at the other end to the benefited land.

A further external constraint lies in the law of town and country planning. Any development or change of use of land requires, in principle, the permission of the local planning authority. This is potentially far more restrictive than any constraints arising from the private law of land obligations. It is not discussed in detail in this book because it is not part of the law of real property, for the technical reason that the planning authority does not have property rights in our land; but it is a significant and inescapable aspect of land ownership.

LEGAL AND EQUITABLE NON-OWNERSHIP RIGHTS

We have already seen that equity gives proprietary force to the rights of the beneficiaries of trusts. Our deprived knight found that his moral ownership right was enforced by the courts of equity. He has an equitable ownership right, which is not as strong as a legal ownership right because some purchasers will not be bound by it. Equity also recognises a whole range of non-ownership rights, giving them proprietary force (albeit not as strong as that of legal rights) in circumstances where they did not qualify as legal rights.

Easements (i.e. rights of way and other third party rights over land), leases and mortgages were originally recognised and enforced by the courts of law. But the courts of equity would also recognise them, and would do so on less stringent conditions than those imposed by the courts of law. To be recognised by the law—to be legal—a mortgage must be created by deed (an especially formal piece of paper); but the courts of equity would enforce one created in writing or by an oral agreement, and such a transaction was therefore an equitable mortgage. Similarly with easements and leases. Historically, the courts of equity were kinder than those of law; they would recognise arrangements which *ought* to be enforced, even though formalities had been missed. A key concept of equity is unconscionability: a claimant's informally granted lease, say, would be upheld because it would be unconscionable for the landlord to deny the deal. In modern times there are strict limits to the level of informality that will be tolerated even for an equitable property right to be created, on which more later.[4] Today, of course, equity is no longer operated in separate courts; but the courts will enforce both law and equity, and will recognise both forms of property right.

In addition, there are some non-ownership rights over land recognised only by the courts of equity and not at all at law, and therefore existing today as equitable rather than legal interests. The two most significant examples are the estate contract and the restrictive covenant (the genetics of the two are closely similar, as both are forms of contract).

First, estate contracts. I make an enforceable agreement with you, that I will buy your land, say, in a month's time. What are my rights, if any, meanwhile? If you sell the land to C before the month is up, I can get

[4] Chapter 5.

damages from you for breach of contract; but can I instead enforce the contract against C, and therefore get the land? If I die before the month is up, can my right under the contract be inherited? The answer to that is as follows: the courts of equity were prepared to enforce contracts for the purchase of land (outright, or for the purchase of some interest in it such as an easement) by an order for specific performance, i.e. an order that the contract be performed, rather than merely an award of damages. From that fact there follow a number of steps, although with not entirely water-tight logic. Because he could obtain specific performance, the courts of equity regarded the purchaser as in some sense the owner of the land before the contract was completed. So he was, to some extent, an equit-able owner; and therefore the seller held on trust for him until completion of the contract. And from that it follows that the answers to the two questions above are 'yes' and 'yes'; the purchaser's pre-completion rights could be inherited; and, like any other equitable interest in land, they can be enforced against a purchaser with notice of them.

This is important not merely for straight sale-and-purchase contracts, but also for other contractual arrangements: for example options to buy (I can buy the land at my option, i.e. if I choose to do so, for a certain period), or rights of pre-emption (I have first refusal if you choose to sell). These are useful devices for structuring transactions and their finance; and they are robust devices because equity has turned these contractual rights into property rights.

Second, restrictive covenants. A covenant is a promise in a deed. It is common, when selling part of one's land (to someone who is therefore going to become one's neighbour) to require the buyer to make promises in the deed that transfers the land to him. Nowadays, he might be asked to promise not to use the land for anything other than a private residence. In the nineteenth century, before statutory planning control, and in an era where large areas of land were being sold to provide urban housing, covenants were vital.[5] They would typically include covenants not to build a house in front of a line on a plan (so as to create a pleasant street with front gardens); not to build a house of less than a certain value; not to build more than a certain number of houses; not to use the land for business purposes etc. I have sold my land to you and you have made these promises. You now sell the land to someone else (or perhaps in small pieces to lots of people); can I enforce those promises against

---

[5] It will be recalled that this was achieved in a different way in Scotland, by the use of feudal obligations.

the subsequent owners? If not, they are valueless. At law, the promises generate only personal, contractual obligations. But again, equity rides to the rescue, regarding them as far more substantial.[6] Substantial enough to cling to the land, so that subsequent buyers who have notice of them must also observe them. Where title to the land is registered, they can be recorded on the register so as to make them enforceable against purchasers.[7]

Equity's capacity to rescue the covenant was limited by one factor; the covenant must be negative. Positive covenants—those which, however worded, involve a promise to do something rather than to refrain from doing something—do not cling to freehold land.[8] If you promise to maintain the fence between your property and mine, and then sell your land, I cannot make my new neighbour keep your promise. We have already referred to this problem as the reason why flats, and other interdependent properties, are generally leasehold but may now be commonhold.[9]

THE ENFORCEABILITY OF LEGAL AND EQUITABLE PROPERTY RIGHTS

Most property rights in land, then, can be legal or equitable; just a few can only ever be equitable. We began the second section of this chapter by saying that legal and equitable rights in land are of different strengths. What does it mean to say that legal rights are stronger than equitable ones? We saw the answer to this when we looked at the deprived knight and the early form of trust. It involves a modification of what was said in Chapter 1 about the nature of property rights; we said there that while a personal right is good only against the one person with the corresponding obligation (to repay a debt, for example), property rights are good against the whole world. My car is my car, and no-one is exempt from that fact. And the same was originally true of legal property rights in land. If I held a legal easement over your garden, I would continue to hold it no matter who bought the land. But that was not quite true of equitable interests. The courts of equity, when they began in the Middle Ages to enforce, as property rights, claims which the courts of law would not recognise, had to decide how far they should go. We have seen the conclusion they came

---

    [6] *Tulk v Moxhay* (1848) 2 Ph 744.

    [7] See below, p. 42.

    [8] *Rhone v Stephens* [1994] 2 AC 310, HL; affirming the law as understood since *Tulk v Moxhay* (above). Positive covenants in leases are different, as we shall see.

    [9] See further in Chapter 7.

to: that equitable rights would not be effective against—would not bind, as the jargon puts it—all the world, but only some people; namely, those who knew about them, or should have known about them, or who took the land without giving value for it (e.g. someone to whom the land is given). They would bind all except the *bona fide* purchaser of the legal estate for value without notice.

Thus if I held an equitable easement over your garden, and you then sold the land, the buyer would only be bound by my easement (i.e. would have to let me keep on using the pathway, or whatever it was) if he knew about it, or if he didn't know but should have known (e.g. because there was an obvious path leading from my garden across yours to the road). Only if he bought the legal estate in the land in good faith, completely innocent of any rights I might have, would he be able safely to ignore my easement in the future, and I would lose my right. If you give the land away, the new owner is not protected from my right; only a purchaser, who gives value for the land, is protected. Legal rights bind all the world; but equitable interests bind all except the *bona fide* purchaser of a legal estate in the land, for value, without notice of the right claimed. The term 'purchaser' is a wide one and is used of anyone taking any interest in land, whether ownership or a lesser right such as a mortgage, in exchange for something of value, usually money, but not necessarily a market price.

Such was the original distinction between legal and equitable rights; they are good against different classes of people, the equitable ones against a smaller class. The distinction depended upon the operation of the rules about notice, which dictated who knew, and who didn't know but should have known and therefore is deemed to know. This is constructive notice: what you should have known about if you had not put the telescope to your blind eye, and if you had made the proper enquiries that any purchaser must make. And that itself became much less simple than it sounds, so that it was terribly easy for a purchaser of land to be caught by equitable interests that he really did not know about and could not, practically, have expected even though legally he was deemed to know about them. It was largely as a result of this difficulty and complexity that land law was thoroughly reformed in 1925.

Following that reform, the distinction between legal and equitable rights survives in its historical form only in the context of land that is not registered. Where land is registered—or, to put it correctly, where title to land (i.e. ownership of land) is registered—the distinction has become a different one. The modern significance of the legal/equitable distinction is still concerned with enforceability, but is closely linked with registration: legal estates and interests are registrable and are given the full protection of registration, in that registration makes them both valid and enforceable. Equitable interests may have their priority protected by registration, so that they are enforceable against the whole world, but their validity is not guaranteed by the registration system. What this means is that the distinction is in some ways less important than it was; the registration system can make equitable rights just as robust as legal rights, provided they are valid and actually appear on the register.

Now we need to examine how we moved from the old world, in which equitable property rights were enforceable against all except a specially favoured class of purchaser, to the new, where enforceability is determined by registration.

BIBLIOGRAPHY

S. Anderson, *Lawyers and the Making of English Land Law 1832–1940* (Oxford, Clarendon Press, 1992).

George Elliot, *Felix Holt, the Radical* (Oxford, Oxford University Press, 1988).

A. Hudson, *Equity and Trusts* (London, Cavendish, 2001), Chapter 1.

R. P. Meagher, J. D. Heydon, M. J. Leeming, *Meagher, Gummow and Lehane's Equity, Doctrines and Remedies* (Chatswood, Butterworths LexisNexis, 2002), Chapters 1–3.

C. Palliser, *The Quincunx* (Ballantine Books, 1990).

K. G. Reid, *The Abolition of Feudal Tenure in Scotland* (Edinburgh, LexisNexis, 2003).

A. W. B. Simpson, *A History of the Land Law* (Oxford, Clarendon Press, 1986).

3

Land Law and Registration Today

This chapter endeavours to give a portrait of land law today, in the light of the 1925 reforms and of the developments of the last 80 years. It is the central pivot of the book, describing the way in which the title registration system governs and structures the enforceability of property rights in land.

This chapter explores the heart of land law. It is in four parts. The first explains how the reforms of 1925 addressed the problem of complexity by redefining legal and equitable estates and interests. The second shows how the 1925 legislation managed the enforceability of property rights in land, particularly by registration. The third elaborates on this by showing how the law has managed the problem of hidden, undocumented ownership rights in land. The final part completes the picture by exploring the reliability of registered title to land, otherwise known as 'indefeasibility'.

1925 AND THE MANAGEMENT OF COMPLEXITY

THE BACKGROUND TO 1925

Chapter 2 gave an impression of the complexity of the rights that can be attached to any piece of land. Picture an office block, a house or a farm. There will always be someone with an ownership right, and there may be more than one. Someone will hold a fee simple (unless this is Crown land); there may also be one or more people with an ownership right that is limited in time—either a freehold estate (a life estate, for example) or a lease (long or short), so that the fee simple owner's right to use the property is suspended for a while. There may also be people who do not own the land, but have more restricted rights over it: a mortgage, or a right of way. These rights will be a mix of legal and equitable ones. A word for all this is fragmentation. Fragmentation can be a weakness and a strength. It is a strength because it means that many people can have rights, of some degree of permanence, in land; fragmentation may therefore be seized on deliberately, as something to be embraced and developed rather than something that grew up by historical accident. But it is a weakness because it brings complexity. Complexity is a problem if there is no reliable source of information about the rights in a piece of land. The problem is compounded if the system for enforceability is unreliable so that rights may be unexpectedly unenforceable (a problem for the right-holder) or unexpectedly enforceable (a problem for a purchaser of the land).

Complexity is particularly problematic for those who hold rights in land if the enforceability of their rights depends upon the purchaser knowing about them. How can they be sure that a potential purchaser will find out about them? Equally, potential purchasers are at risk; if there are too many interests in land, the purchaser may simply be unable to find out about, let alone physically find, all the people he needs to settle with in order to buy it. If he misses someone, and buys the land or a property right over it, he may find that what he bought is worthless because someone else's right trumps it, particularly if this was a right that the law deemed him to know about even though he did not.

Penny the purchaser buys land from Simon the seller. Before she buys, she (or, more likely, her conveyancer) looks carefully through the title deeds and checks whether or not Simon or his predecessors have granted any rights over the land. Is it mortgaged, for instance? If it is, she will not hand over the purchase price without ensuring that it is first applied in payment of the mortgage debt; otherwise, the land will still be mortgaged after her purchase.[1] She also inspects the property for signs of other interests in the land; someone else living there, perhaps, or a track across the garden from a neighbouring property to the road. Note that the law assumes that Penny will inspect, whether or not in practice she does so. Having checked in this way as much as she can, Penny buys the land. Then a stranger claims to have an interest in the land. If the right claimed is a legal one, perhaps a legal easement, Penny is bound by it in any event, even if the deed that created it was lost—ignorance is irrelevant. If the right is equitable, perhaps a mortgage created informally, it will not be apparent from the deeds, and the purchaser is bound only if she had notice of it, but it *may* be—depending on the circumstances—that the law deems her to have known, because she should have known—the evidence was available but she missed it, perhaps. In that event the interest is

---

[1] This is done by obtaining an undertaking from the seller's solicitor that the money will be so used; the procedure remains the same today. Undertakings are super-enforceable promises, in that the solicitor will be subject to professional disciplinary action if he breaks one.

enforceable against her. This is disastrous. Simon should have paid off such claimants, but he did not, and he has now disappeared.

This scenario was the nightmare of the nineteenth century conveyancer; if the risk of it occurring did not actually make land unsafe to buy, it certainly made conveyancing very expensive.[2] The problem was so great that one of the proposals in the nineteenth century was to reduce all equitable interests in land to the status of personal rights, so that they could not bind a purchaser. It is unsurprising that that idea did not get off the ground, given the wealth tied up at that time in land of which ownership was structured over time in complex family trusts. The fact that such a dramatic solution was mooted shows how serious the problem was. If land cannot safely be bought or used as security for money, or if the costs of a safe transaction are too high, the value of land falls. The eventual reform package, originally enacted in 1922 and now found in the statutes of 1925, hit upon a dramatic solution. It did not explicitly make equitable property rights into personal rights; but it limited the proprietary effect of equitable ownership rights (i.e. their enforceability) so that in most cases a purchaser would be safe from them, even if he knew about them. In Chapter 1 we mentioned the tension between static security (the protection of existing interests in land) and dynamic security (the protection of a purchaser); in the management of enforceability in the 1925 reforms we see a huge preference for dynamic security.

The shape of land law today, and the way we manage the problems of information and enforceability arising from the complexity of rights in land, depends upon the changes made in 1925. To English lawyers they seem so essential to land law that we tend to forget that the rest of the common law world live happy and useful lives without at least some of them. The 1925 reforms were not the only possible ways to solve the problems of complexity.

Six property statutes were enacted in 1925.[3] By now, they are much amended and to some extent replaced, but the Law of Property Act 1925

---

[2] One suspects that nineteenth and early twentieth century conveyancing was very much dominated by the need to take disproportionate steps to guard against very small risks, as are many quite different activities today. The likelihood of actually being 'fixed', as conveyancers put it, with constructive notice of something one knew nothing about, was quite small, but conveyancers had to take extensive steps to guard against it for fear of their own liability. This is conjecture.

[3] The Law of Property Act 1925, the Settled Land Act 1925, the Administration of Estates Act 1925, the Trustee Act 1925, the Land Charges Act 1925 and the Land Registration Act 1925. Of these, the latter two have been repealed by later Acts of the same names.

remains fundamental to our land law. It is not an easy Act to read, as it is
not a code, not a fresh start, but presupposes a great deal of very elderly
law; and the 1925 legislation as a whole is difficult to summarise. The
most fundamental steps taken in the management of English land law
are as follows. First, the creation of a hierarchy of legal and equitable
interests in land which severely cut down the number of legal estates.
Secondly, existing legislation for title registration was improved, and
preparations were made for the extension of the system. That extension
is now nearly completed; and it is through title registration that the
law now organises information and enforceability. Thirdly, the 1925
legislation established the use of the trust to structure joint ownership
and to complete the management of enforceability through the doctrine
of 'overreaching'. This was intended to be a reliable method of safeguarding purchasers from unexpected equitable ownership rights. It
has not worked as intended, because of social changes that the 1925
reformers could not have predicted, but conveyancing techniques have
supplied the necessary additional protection, reinforcing dynamic security. The result is a system of land law that provides robust protection for
purchasers of land and that therefore helps maintain the value of land. It
needs only a little knowledge of Western society to see how important this
is to us.

LEGAL AND EQUITABLE INTERESTS IN LAND: THE 1925 HIERARCHY

Section 1 of the Law of Property Act 1925 is a defining moment of English
land law. It sets up an organisation, or hierarchy, of three ideas: legal
estates, legal interests and equitable interests. This is actually the nearest
we get to a distinction between ownership rights and non-ownership
rights, though there is no one-to-one correspondence with those terms.
The aim is to limit the number of legal rights that a purchaser has
to think about, so as to make land safer to purchase. The trade-off is
that certain rights can only be equitable, or second-class, so that those
who hold them are less secure because their rights are less widely
enforceable.

Section 1 states that there are just two legal estates: the 'fee simple
absolute in possession' and the 'term of years absolute'. The fee simple
is the freehold estate described at the beginning of this chapter: and it
must be absolute, that is, not subject to conditions which make it liable
to disappear, and it must be in possession rather than in remainder or in
reversion. The term of years absolute is a lease; but despite the reference

to years, it means a lease of any length, even the humble weekly tenancy. Thus a number of rights were demoted in 1925: it is no longer possible to have a legal life interest.[4]

Next, section 1 defines legal interests. Parts of it have been repealed, and for practical purposes now the legal interests are mortgages, easements and rentcharges. The first two we have met, and are pervasive; the latter we shall say very little about. A rentcharge is a payment imposed on a freeholder, used now very rarely and only as a way of enforcing some forms of covenant. These two groups, the legal estates and legal interests, correspond approximately to ownership rights and non-ownership rights (not exactly, because leases can be both).

Section 1 ensures that a purchaser, checking for the legal rights in land—that is, for the ones most likely to be enforceable against him—need check only for a limited number of different kinds of right. Another provision of the same statute ensures that no more than four people can hold a legal estate in land—again for simplicity's sake. So if a farm is bought by the ten trustees of a charity, say, or by a business partnership of six, or is bequeathed to ten brothers and they decide to keep it rather than sell it, only four of them can hold the legal fee simple and be registered as owners at the land registry (the first four named in the transfer if it lists more than four), but all of them hold an equitable fee simple in the land.

The third part of section 1 states that everything else—any other property right in land—is an equitable interest. This includes everything from the restrictive covenant—that is, an obligation not to do something on the land, for example not to run a business on it—to an ownership right that is less than a fee simple absolute in possession, such as a life interest.

Section 1 therefore simplifies legal and equitable ownership in a rather basic and numerical way. It sets the filing cabinet in order and makes a decision as to what goes in each drawer, enabling us to categorise any interest in land that we may meet. But that alone does not, of course, sort out complexity; for the real problems of complexity are information and enforceability and (therefore, as explained above) the safety of the market. For that, we must look to registration.

---

[4] The modern lawyer instantly thinks: human rights, deprivation of possessions. But there were transitional provisions to ensure that individuals who actually held, at 1 January 1926, interests that were demoted from legal to equitable, nevertheless retained their status as if they held legal interests. The transitional provisions are quite hard to find because of course they are long repealed as obsolete.

REGISTRATION AND THE MANAGEMENT OF ENFORCEABILITY

WHAT IS TITLE REGISTRATION?

Now we come to the second of the 1925 changes; the management of the enforceability of property rights in land. From today's perspective, the central plank of the management plan is title registration, although it would not have looked that way in 1925.

In order to explain how title registration works, we have to digress a little and explain the word 'title'. It has two legal meanings. Lawyers use them without explaining, relying on the context to show which is intended. First, it means the whole collection of property rights in a piece of land. The title to my house comprises, typically, the fee simple ownership, burdened by the rights of a mortgagee and perhaps those of a neighbour who has an easement over the back yard. It can be paraphrased as 'entitlement'. Its second, subsidiary meaning is the *evidence* of title. If I am asked to show my title to my land, I am going to point to the register of title held at the land registry. The register displays a portrait of the property rights in my land, and also *is* my title in the sense that it proves my ownership.

This is a change. Read any novel, ask most folk, and you will be told that the way to prove ownership of land is to produce your deeds; and that your deeds are precious, to be kept in the bank or in a deeds box. Traditionally this was true; 'my deeds', or 'the deeds' of the house, would comprise a stack of documents, of which the top one was the conveyance to me, the one underneath that was the conveyance to my predecessor, and so on, going back a couple of generations or so and demonstrating my right to the land by telling the story of its ownership. But the advent of title registration means that this story is no longer needed to prove entitlement, because title registration replaces deeds.

If registration is a way of tackling complexity, there are a number of ways of doing it. One way is to register deeds centrally. It is possible to make an official copy of every deed connected with a piece of land, so that it does not matter if the original gets lost. That is a start. In addition, there can be a sanction for not registering a deed. The system can decree that unregistered deeds are ineffective. Or it can state that unregistered deeds are effective between the people who made them but do not have priority, so that they do not affect anyone buying the land later. Either of these measures will protect purchasers by ensuring that they are unaffected by anything they cannot see on the register. Equally, the holders of non-ownership rights are protected against later owners of the land, provided they register the deed that created their right. Such a system is called deeds registration; it operates very successfully in South Africa and in all the American states, for example. In order to work well, it needs an efficient indexing system so that deeds can be readily found; some sort of insurance system against mistakes in the register; and clear rules as to the effect of deeds which are not registered, but which a purchaser knows about. Middlesex and Yorkshire had deeds registries from the early eighteenth century. The system was never extended nationwide; new registrations ceased after 1925 and the deeds registries closed in 1976. Deeds registration is worth mentioning here in order to make clear what title registration is not: it is *not* merely a record of what the deeds to a property say.

Deeds registration has two weaknesses, both linked closely to complexity; first, it does not take away the work of examining a title. The buyer of land must still find and read all the deeds to a property and work out what their effect is. Second, it does not protect a purchaser against rights that were not created by deed. The latter is important in a system which recognises equitable property rights in land: equitable interests do not need to be created by deed (often they are equitable just because a deed was not used). So the problem of purchasers being tripped up by unexpected equitable interests is not eliminated by deeds registration.[5] Enter title registration, which does something different.

Title registration is a central record of title to land. Instead of copying the deeds, the registry sets out their effect in a single document. When a transaction takes place the deed or other document is sent to the registrar who reads it, interprets it and records its effect. The deed itself is thrown away. The vision is that the purchaser should be able to find out all he wants about the property rights in a piece of land just by looking up the property in the register, making land transfer as simple as is the transfer of shares in a company.

Title registration can be thought of as a collection of cards in a filing cabinet (as it originally was), or of electronic documents (as it now is). Each document represents, not a piece of land, but a legal estate in land (a fee simple or a lease for more than seven years);[6] so there can be more

---

[5] In America, the risks are managed through a pervasive commercial system of title insurance.

[6] Some other estates, listed in s. 2 of the Land Registration Act 2002, generate an individual register; they are ancient, unusual and not discussed here.

than one document for a given piece of land. Each document, known as an individual register, describes the estate, and tells us about any non-ownership rights over other land (such as easements) that are attached to this estate; it states who owns it, and occasionally gives a little more information about the owner, in particular any restriction of his ability to deal with the land; and finally it sets out rights to which the estate is subject, such as rights of way and mortgages. The individual register is not as simple as a share certificate; but it is at least a translation of that idea into a representation of land ownership. The purchaser no longer has to look back at the history of ownership, whether through a stack of deeds or through the folios of a deeds register—indeed he is not allowed to look at history. Title is all in the present tense.

Registration of title was devised in the middle of the nineteenth century, by Sir Robert Torrens in South Australia. Similar registration statutes were enacted throughout the common law world and are now known as the 'Torrens systems'. English title registration began in 1862, just four years after the South Australian statute (The Real Property Act, 1858), and, in contrast to its Australian counterpart, worked very badly. So it was not a concept for which all lawyers were enthusiastic in 1925. Today, after the replacement of the rather nervous Land Registration Act 1925 by the confident and assertive Land Registration Act 2002, it is central to land law and is unchallengeable as the way in which information and enforceability are controlled.

In 1925 about 300,000 titles were registered. Today, over nineteen million titles are registered. It is not known what proportion of registrable titles are registered, but it is perhaps startling that the Land Registry's current estimate of the proportion of land in England and Wales that is registered, by area, is only about 55%. The extension of registration was achieved gradually, by bringing new areas into the system every few years and providing that, in areas of compulsory registration, certain transactions triggered an obligation to register—the principal triggering events today are sales, first legal mortgages, the transmission of land on death and the creation or sale of leases longer than the seven year registration threshold. Today, the whole of England and Wales is an area of compulsory registration; and it is hoped that at some stage the register will be complete—although as things stand it cannot be, because some land is never sold, mortgaged or leased (consider Buckingham Palace). The 2002 Act has sought to address this difficulty by making registered title more attractive than unregistered, so as to encourage voluntary registration; the Act has made it almost impossible for title to be acquired against a registered owner by adverse possession—squatters' rights, or squatters' title, as it is known.[7] There are signs that this is working, as a number of local authorities have registered their landholdings. The 2002 Act also makes it possible for Crown land to be registered, by the rather strange device of enabling the Crown to grant to itself a fee simple, which can then be registered. This is because only estates in land can be registered, and the Crown, as the feudal overlord, is the one person who does not have an *estate* in land.

Once title is registered, any transactions involving that legal estate or any legal interests derived from it are ineffective until registration has taken place (with the exception of leases for seven years or less).[8] A deed must be executed in order to transfer a legal estate or create a legal interest, but the registration system has taken away the power of the deed. In cases where a deed is necessary, it is no longer sufficient. When that deed is sent to the registry and the register is updated, a legal estate or interest is transferred or created, depending on the nature of the transaction. Where necessary, a new individual register, with a fresh title number, is created, for example on the grant of a lease of more than seven years. It is therefore useful to refer to legal estates and interests as the 'registrable estates'. And the landowner does not have an estate created or transferred by deed, but a registered estate, emanating from the fact of registration. Even where the deed transferring land from Ned to Ted, say, is void because of fraud or mistake, registration of the deed makes Ted the owner of the land. This is startling and we shall have to explore more of its implications later.[9] For now, note that registration involves a guarantee of title. Registered estates are guaranteed valid and enforceable, and if there is a mistake on the register which causes loss to an innocent party the latter will be compensated. Equally, someone who has a registered estate and loses it because of the correction of a mistake in the register will be compensated. Again, more of this later.

The register has thus taken control of title. Registration is said to operate on the mirror principle, namely that the register is a mirror of the title. This is true provided we understand that what the register is mirroring is not a stack of deeds, but the truth about a title to a piece of land. The deeds are irrelevant except for that short period between what the estate agents call completion, when signed documents are handed

[7] Discussed in Chapter 9.
[8] Discussed in Chapter 4 at p. 71.
[9] Section 58 of the Land Registration Act 2002; p. 56 ff.

over, and their registration. Even that few days in the limelight will vanish
when we move to a system of electronic conveyancing, so that the parties'
own act of completing the transaction will update the register.

Title registration takes a big swipe at complexity by not only central-
ising and safeguarding information, but also reducing the number of
documents, and the amount of interpretation, involved in examining title.
The examining and summarising is all done by the registrar, and all
irrelevant bits of history are swept away. As well as keeping information
safe, it makes it succinct and eliminates all or most of the work of examining title. However, it also goes one step further: it defines very closely
what interests can bind a purchaser of land.

THE MECHANISM FOR ENFORCEABILITY

The Land Registration Act 1925 provided a list of those interests that
are to have priority over the purchaser—that is, the interests that are
enforceable against him—when a disposition is registered. The Land
Registration Act 2002 does the same, in section 29.[10] The idea is that a
prospective purchaser can check down this list and see all the types of
interests that will burden the land when he owns it. The old rules, that a
legal estate binds all the world and an equitable interest binds by notice,
no longer apply.

The list contains three items. Taking them out of order: first, if the
title is leasehold, the purchaser takes the land subject to any obligations
laid upon the tenant by the lease itself. This is easy and uncontroversial.
So is the second item, namely, anything appearing on the register. This
refers in particular to burdens on the registered title, that is, non-
ownership rights which have been protected by being entered on the
register. We know that any legal interests in the land to which the title is
registered (e.g. legal easements or mortgages) can only be created
by registration, so they simply cannot exist unless they appear on the
register. Moreover, most equitable interests—but not beneficial interests
under trusts, for reasons to be explained—may be, but do not have to
be, entered on the register. This form of registration is optional, and
is known as recording rather than registration. It does not guarantee
validity, but it does guarantee priority. The holder of an equitable easement, or of the benefit of a restrictive covenant, must record his right
against the owner's title if he wants his rights to be effective after the

---

[10] Section 30 contains the same list adapted for use when what is being transferred is a
mortgage rather than an ownership right; see Chapter 6, p. 129.

owner sells on. (He *must*, because the old rules of notice are disapplied by the registration statute, so there is no other form of protection for him).

Why can trust interests not be entered on the register as other equitable interests can? Quite simply because the 1925 reformers intended them to be ineffective against purchasers. They sought to operate a 'curtain', whereby trusts could not be seen on the register, and were irrelevant to conveyancing. There is more to be said about the protection of purchasers from trust interests, as we shall see.

Back to the list: the third item is 'interests that override a registered disposition', listed in a schedule to the statute. And here we have a big disappointment, because overriding interests are ones which bind a purchaser even though they are not on the register. The mirror tells the truth, but not the whole truth.

Consider the good reasons for allowing some such interests to be enforceable. First, there are some transactions which are so short-lived that the legislature considered them unsuitable for registration. At present, leases for seven years or less are not registrable. A tenant under a six-year lease cannot point to a register which shows his title; he can only display his lease, and the transfer of the lease to him if he is not the first tenant to hold that lease, and so on. But his lease is an overriding interest vis-à-vis his landlord's title; if his landlord (be he a freeholder or a leaseholder) sells the land the tenant's lease survives and is enforceable against the buyer. Second, some legal interests can arise without any formality at all. Leases for three years or less (including, therefore, a periodic tenancy) can be created without using a deed and without even putting anything in writing; equally, in some circumstances legal easements can be created without documentation.[11] In these cases there is no document to register; but the legal interests created are enforceable against the title they depend upon. Third, there are some transactions which the legislature wished to privilege; in particular, interests of the state. So a local land charge (an obligation imposed by a local authority, such as a compulsory purchase order or a tree preservation order) is enforceable against the land (i.e. against anyone who owns it) without the authority having to register it.

A further policy concern is seen in what is now the most significant of the overriding interests:

An interest belonging at the time of the disposition to a person in actual

---

[11] See Chapter 8, p. 183.

occupation, so far as relating to the land of which he is in actual occupation, except for—

. . .

   (c) an interest—

     (i) which belongs to a person whose occupation would not have been obvious on a reasonably careful inspection of the land at the time of the disposition, and

     (ii) of which the person to whom the disposition is made does not have actual knowledge at that time . . .[12]

This category is listed as paragraph 2 of Schedule 3 to the Land Registration Act 2002; but all the significant case law on it was pre-2002, so they refer to section 70(1)(g) of the Land Registration Act 1925. Its aim was to protect the rights of those who lived in a property, even if it did not belong to them, and even if their rights were not registered. The provision means that an equitable lease, even though unrecorded,[13] is enforceable against a purchaser if the landlord sells, provided that the tenant is actually living or working at the property. Similarly, someone who lives at the property and happens to have an option to purchase it will find that his option is enforceable against a future owner of the land. The policy operating here is the protection of the home. And if someone is in actual occupation as described in the schedule, a purchaser who goes to look at the land (generally buyers do but mortgagees do not) cannot claim to have been taken by surprise; the right is only enforceable if the occupation is obvious. The 2002 statute states this; the 1925 one did not, but the draftsman's intention was probably the same.

So there are good reasons for allowing some unregistered rights to be enforceable, and the list of such rights was designed so as to be harmless to purchasers. Of the examples we have given so far, all but short legal leases are going to be pretty rare in any event. However, the overriding interest for those in actual occupation—paragraph 2 of Schedule 3—has turned out to be a minefield. For reasons to be explained, the 1925 legislators did not anticipate that beneficial interests under trusts could be overriding interests in this category. That was true in 1925, but it ceased to be true early in the 1980s, so there is more to tell of the story of actual occupation interests, and we shall do so below, in the context of the enforceability of beneficial interests in land.

---

[12] There is more to this paragraph, but these are the parts relevant to this discussion.

[13] Recall that this is not a legal interest and so not a registrable estate, so it cannot be registered but may be recorded; the difference is that validity is not guaranteed.

SECTION 29 AND THE REGISTER'S NEGATIVE WARRANTY

Section 29 is part of the register's guarantee of title; writers on the Torrens system have called it (or its equivalents in other statutes) the 'negative warranty' of registration: the promise that there are no other interests in the land that could affect a purchaser. So how watertight is section 29? Are these three categories the *only* interests that can possibly bind a purchaser? In particular, what of the old conundrum, the unregistered interest that the purchaser knows about? The old deeds registration systems had to address this, and came up with more than one answer. It is actually extremely difficult for a court to hold that a purchaser is unaffected by an interest about which he knew, but which happens to be unregistered. Knowledge is very persuasive, which is why the courts of equity came up with the old rules of notice. But part of the point of title registration is to disapply those rules because they involve so many pitfalls for the purchaser. In fact, one decision under the Land Registration Act 1925 did hold that a purchaser was bound by notice—in effect, though not in so many words.[14] The decision was made possible by an unintended quirk in the drafting of the 1925 statute. A definition of a 'purchaser' required him to be 'in good faith', which enabled the court to find that, since he knew about the unregistered interest, he could not *in good faith* seek to escape from it. But the case is widely agreed to have been wrongly decided, and the definitions used in the 2002 statute make it impossible for it to be replicated under the new statute.

Section 29 is therefore designed to be truly watertight. However, consistent with that is one further possibility. This is that a purchaser might, by his own conduct, make himself liable to a third party who had an interest in the land immediately before the disposition. This is a fresh liability arising, in effect, after section 27 has done its work, and not a burden passed on from the former proprietor through the filter of . section 27. The one case where this is agreed to have happened is *Lyus v Prowsa*.[15] Mr and Mrs Lyus contracted to purchase a house on a housing development, and protected their contract by recording it on the register. However, the site was already mortgaged to a bank. The developer went into liquidation and the bank sold the development. A mortgagee sells the title as it stood at the date of the mortgage, and is not bound by an option registered at a later date. So the bank's purchaser took free from the option in accordance with the then equivalent of section 29. However, the

---

[14] *Peffer v Rigg* [1977] 1 WLR 285.
[15] [1982] 1 WLR 1044.

transfer stated that the purchaser took the land 'subject to' the option insofar as it was enforceable—a step taken out of caution by the bank—and, significantly, the purchaser paid a reduced price because it was believed that the option would be binding. Accordingly it was found that the purchaser held the land on constructive trust for the prospective buyer of the plot, who could therefore exercise the option. The decision is the subject of some scepticism. Comments made in the Court of Appeal in *Ashburn Anstalt v Arnold*[16] confirm the authority of the decision, but stress that its application will be very narrow indeed. But the principle is in line with much more developed case law on the point in most Torrens registration systems, where it is known as the *in personam* exception to the guarantee of title that the register gives. '*In personam*' means 'against the individual', because it is the enforcement of a liability against an individual, by making him a trustee. It has to be regarded as a concept that could be operated in extreme circumstances, where otherwise the operation of section 29 would produce too grave an injustice for the courts to swallow. A deliberate plan by a seller and buyer to defeat a third party's interest would probably be an example.

LAND CHARGES REGISTRATION: THE DYING ALTERNATIVE

Before we go on to explore the enforceability of beneficial interests in land under the land registration statutes, we have to mention the management of enforceability of interests in land, the title to which was not registered. This accounts for a small proportion of titles today, but in 1925 most titles were unregistered. For these, the legislation introduced a new form of registration designed to manage the enforceability only of non-ownership rights in land: land charges registration. It is not yet obsolete but should one day become so when title registration has become universal. Where the title to land is *not* registered at the land registry, some but not all non-ownership rights may by registered on the register of Land Charges. If not registered, they are void against very nearly, but not quite, all forms of purchasers for value.

Investigation of the title to unregistered land therefore involves two jobs: the purchaser must examine the deeds, to discover the legal ownership of the land and most legal interests in it; he must also search the Land Charges Register to discover the interests listed in the Act (some legal, most equitable; for example some types of mortgage, contractual interests, and equitable easements). Some interests, in particular those of

---

[16] [1988] 2 All ER 147.

beneficiaries of trusts, will not be found either in the deeds or on the Land Charges Register; they bind the purchaser by notice in the usual way unless the conditions for overreaching are met, as described below. Land Charges Registration is not a good system and none will weep when/if it finally becomes obsolete. In 1925, the intention was that in ten years' time there would be a review of the two systems: registered title on the one hand, and on the other the Land Charges Register, to see which was working better. At the time, many would have placed their bets on Land Charges registration and unregistered title. The review never took place, and title registration has gradually become pervasive as more and more title became registered. Today, every Land Charges search done by a purchaser of unregistered land is the last; once the purchase is completed, the purchaser's title must be registered. So land charges registration is alive, but dying. Whether or not it will ever become decisively and properly dead depends upon whether or not compulsion is eventually applied so as to make title registration complete in England and Wales.

THE ENFORCEABILITY OF BENEFICIAL INTERESTS IN LAND

TRUSTS

Equitable ownership rights, or beneficial interests, were a major concern of the reformers. One of the risks that prompted reform was the danger for purchasers of being bound by constructive notice of beneficial interests. And the 1925 reforms actually proliferated trusts, making the management of enforceability all the more urgent.

How did the 1925 legislation proliferate trusts, and how was enforceability controlled?

Section 1 of the Law of Property Act 1925 reduced the number of legal estates in land. The corresponding increase in equitable ownership rights meant more trusts, because whenever there are equitable ownership rights in land there must also be someone holding the legal estate, which is held in trust for the equitable owner(s). That is not a necessary truth, but it is one of the principles upon which English land law happens to operate. So by making limited ownership rights equitable, section 1 proliferated trusts.

But there is more. The 1925 legislation ensured that there is a trust of land in every case where there is joint ownership of land, concurrent as well as successive.

A trust arises where the equitable owners outnumber the permitted

legal owners; if ten brothers own a farm, the first four are trustees of
the land for all ten (themselves included). It is easy to see the point of
trusteeship in that case; the four legal owners must have a responsibility
to use their ownership powers for the benefit of all ten, and must not be
permitted to take advantage of their position. The real surprise is that
all cases of concurrent co-ownership involve a trust. When a commercial
partnership of four accountants, say, buys an office, or a couple buys a
house, the land is automatically held on trust, the joint owners being both
trustees and beneficiaries. The couple buying a home will probably never
know this.

  Whatever is the point of having a trust in such cases? Where land is held
for Pam for life with remainder to Sam in fee simple, the beneficiaries
actually have competing interests (short-term enjoyment versus capital
value), and trustees have an obvious management and decision-making
role. But where trustees and beneficiaries are identical and the position
and powers of both/all are equal, trusteeship is not going to solve any
problems if there is a dispute. Most of the common law world does not
use a trust structure for ordinary joint ownership like this; so why does
English law do so? The answer is that the cases where legal and equitable
ownership match may cease to be such, because equitable ownership may
diversify over time. The accountancy partnership may grow; one of the
couple may die and leave her share in the property to two children. If
the legal estate is held on trust, it can stay simple, even where equitable
ownership diversifies. And the caring/management function of trustees
becomes necessary and useful, as does the court's power to intervene in
cases where trustees and/or beneficiaries are in dispute.[17] These factors
do not make a trust *necessary*; both purposes could be managed by other
means. But the 1925 reformers were confident in their employment of
trusts. A major reason why they seemed such a safe device was the availability of a device known as 'overreaching' to control the enforceability of
beneficial interests.

OVERREACHING

Now, we have seen that where title to land is registered, beneficial interests
could not be entered on the register. And, for reasons to be explained, it
was not supposed in 1925 that trust interests could be overriding interests. Where title to land was not registered, beneficial interests bound

---

[17] Sections 14 and 15 of the Trusts of Land and Appointment of Trustees Act 1996; the
job was originally done by s. 40 of the Law of Property Act 1925.

a purchaser by notice just as they always had done because they were not registrable on the Land Charges Register. But the doctrine of over-reaching meant that, despite this, beneficial interests would never trouble a purchaser.

Overreaching is a form of magic. It is a doctrine that says that when land is purchased, if and only if certain conditions are met, certain equit-able interests cease to affect the land. The rights that can be overreached are equitable ownership rights; thus not equitable leases, equitable mort-gages, equitable interests, nor the contractually-based interests such as options. Overreachable interests include life interests in land, or a fee simple which is subject to a current life interest so that the holder cannot access the land until the life interest ends (he does not have a fee simple *in possession*). They include the fees simple of brothers 5 to 10 of the group mentioned above. Overreaching means that when land is sold, the only claims the holders of those interests can have is against their trustees who sold the land and now hold the proceeds of sale; they have no claim on the purchaser.

Overreaching applies only on purchase. The protection given here is for buyers, not for anyone taking the land as a gift. The aim is to protect the market. But the main condition for the operation of overreaching, set out in section 2 of the Law of Property Act 1925 (the position of the provision, next to s. 1, reminds us just how central it was to the reform-ers' thinking), concerns the identity of the seller of the land. In order for overreaching to happen, the purchase money must be paid to at least two trustees of the legal estate.[18] In other words, all the purchaser has to do is to be careful about who he pays his money to. Provided the conditions are met, the rules of notice (where title was unregistered) did not apply, and overreaching took place even though the purchaser knew of the existence of beneficial interests.

The upshot is that if a purchaser is buying from two or more legal owners then he knows, with absolute certainty, that even if the land is held on trust he will take it free of any equitable interests. If sale is offered by a sole owner, and the purchaser knows that the land is held on trust, he must insist that it is conveyed to him by two individuals, not one. Again, if he does so, the purchaser is safe. Doing it is quick and easy; the transfer document simply takes two steps: it consists, first, of an appointment by the sole owner of an additional trustee of the legal estate, and then proceeds to be a sale by those legal owners. The proceeds of sale of the

---

[18] Or to a trust corporation (a commercial organisation set up to operate trust funds).

land are then held on trust by the two trustees, and the existence of *two* trustees is supposed to afford some protection to beneficiaries. And the 1925 reformers' expectation was that trusts would in any event be properly managed so that they normally had two trustees.

Overreaching was not invented by the 1925 reformers; it was extended and given fresh importance as a major mechanism for the protection of purchasers. It was intended to be a fail-safe mechanism. The expectation was that where there was a trust of land, there would be more than one trustee, and that overreaching would take place. Purchasers were safe.

HIDDEN BENEFICIAL INTERESTS: THE PROBLEM AND THE SOLUTION

As it turned out, purchasers were not safe. Overreaching did not prove to be the fail-safe that the 1925 reformers had expected.

The problem was that the reformers assumed that in all cases where overreaching was actually needed, those involved would be aware of the need and would ensure that the two trustees requirement was met. A quick trawl through the different types of trust shows that this appeared to be a safe assumption in 1925.

First, there were formal, family settlements of land. These were almost always governed by the Settled Land Act 1925. That statute is now virtually obsolete because it has not been possible to create new settlements under it since 1996, but in 1925 conveyancers were familiar and comfortable with it. Conveyancing rules ensured that the existence of the trust (though no details of its provisions) was obvious from the deeds, and the purchaser was therefore alerted to the need to pay his money to two trustees. The trustees themselves could normally be relied upon to ensure that this would happen in any event. It was unlikely that title to land held on this sort of trust would be registered (registration is required when land is sold, and such land tended to remain in families), but if it was, overreaching was not even needed: the beneficiaries' interests could not be protected by registration, and the statute provided that beneficial interests in a Settled Land Act settlement could not be overriding interests by virtue of the beneficiaries' occupation of the land (now replicated in paragraph 2(a) of schedule 3 to the 2002 statute). They could not therefore bind a purchaser.

Most other trusts were implied ones, arising by virtue of joint ownership, whether joint purchase or as a result of inheritance. These trusts, by contrast, were governed by provisions in the Law of Property Act 1925, not the Settled Land Act. The fact of joint ownership would be readily apparent to a purchaser, from the deeds or the register; if all but one joint owner had died so that the legal estate was held by a sole survivor, the purchaser would know that he had to insist on the appointment of an additional trustee.[19,20] Moreover, if title was registered then, again, overreaching was unnecessary because of the safeguards built into the registration system. One was that beneficial interests could not be protected on the register. The other was that these trusts, governed not by the Settled Land Act but by the Law of Property Act, derived their structure and rules from nineteenth century investment practice and the management of land bought only for its value and not as a home. They were therefore known as trusts for sale. If it sounds strange to label ordinary joint ownership as a 'trust for sale', recall that where land is inherited by, say, five brothers they will normally sell it, sooner or later; and that joint ownership of the family home by husband and wife was extremely rare. And because of that derivation from investment practice, interests under such trusts were regarded not as interests in the land itself, but in the proceeds of sale of the land. And that meant, according to the then current interpretation of the Land Registration Act 1925, that they could not be overriding interests in registered land. They could not therefore bind a purchaser.

Just a few trusts did not fall within either of these categories, in particular cases known as 'bare trusts' where a trustee held land for someone who was entitled to the legal estate, but chose to have it held for him by a nominee. Outside these narrow exceptions, beneficial interests virtually lost their proprietary status. By sleight of hand the reformers achieved what had been proposed and rejected earlier in the reform process.

Social changes made this tidy structure break down. One was the rise in owner-occupation. In 1925 more than 70% of the population—the less wealthy end of the social scale—rented their homes. Nowadays, over 70% of homes are owner-occupied; we are a 'property-owning democracy'. Another was the change in the economic status of women. In 1925 few were economically independent or had means of their own; during the following forty or fifty years that changed radically. Add to this the rule that is the foundation of another type of trust, the resulting trust: that if I finance the purchase of land by someone else, he will hold it on trust for me, to the extent of my contribution. The result was a case which badly

[19] The land register was at that date a series of typed cards; former proprietors were struck out when they sold on or died, but the deleted entry remained visible.

[20] There is a further point to make about the survivor of joint owners, discussed in Chapter 5 at p. 113.

frightened conveyancers. In *Williams and Glyn's Bank Ltd v Boland*[21] Mr Boland was sole legal owner of the house. He mortgaged it, post-acquisition, to the bank to secure a loan. The bank did not appreciate that Mrs Boland had paid a substantial part of the purchase price and therefore owned a proportionate share of the house. Mr Boland defaulted on the loan and the bank sought to re-possess, only to be met by Mrs Boland's claim that she was a part-owner of the house. She was in actual occupation of it at the time the mortgage was granted and therefore at that point her interest bound the bank, and the mortgage did not affect her share. The bank argued that Mrs Boland's interest was held under a trust for sale, so that her interest was in money and not in land and she could not have an overriding interest. This was rejected by the House of Lords as an unrealistic way of regarding home ownership. The bank also argued, following earlier precedent, that she was not in actual occupation of the house because her presence was simply an extension of that of her husband. That argument was equally robustly (and inevitably by that date) rejected. She won, and the bank could only take Mr Boland's share of the value of the house, and in any case could not, at this stage, get possession of the property because of Mrs Boland's right to live there.[22]

Thus it is clear that overreaching is not the guaranteed safeguard that it was supposed to be. Trusts with a sole trustee could arise where there was no clue for the purchaser that overreaching was needed, and no professional trustees involved to ensure that it happened. And registration was not the safeguard it was intended to be in these cases because of the re-conceptualisation, in *Boland*, of the trust for sale.

The danger for purchasers was intensified by two other developments. One was the rise in unmarried cohabitation. The advice given to the writer as a student, 'never take a conveyance from a sole married vendor', does not cover the multitude of relationship possibilities. The other was the development, in equity, of additional means for those who are not legal owners to acquire, informally, a share in the property. Principal among these is the common intention constructive trust, to be discussed at length later.[23] Briefly, it enabled non-owners to acquire a share, on a much more generous basis than did the resulting trust, and without such stringent requirements for direct contribution. A spouse or cohabitant

---

[21] [1981] AC 487.
[22] The eventual solution for the bank would be to take insolvency proceedings against Mr Boland, since under the insolvency legislation the wife's right to occupy would be subordinated to the bank's right to possession. See Chapter 5 at p. 109.
[23] See Chapter 4.

who had contributed just a few hundred pounds to the acquisition of the property might be discovered, later, to own a half share in equity.

CONTROLLING THE ENFORCEABILITY OF INFORMAL TRUSTS

So it is clear that overreaching is not the guaranteed safeguard that it was supposed to be.

What could be done to protect banks and buyers? One proposal, made by the Law Commission[24] was that the land registry should compensate any purchaser who suffered loss because of an overriding interest. The proposal was not followed up. The land register provides a guaranteed title to land, largely in the interests of purchasers, but the system is designed to ensure that the registry very rarely has to make any payment in support of that guarantee.[25] Instead, the answer devised to the problem of unexpected occupiers is simple, conceptually unsatisfying and reasonably effective. Standard conveyancing practice introduced soon after *Boland* is for the purchaser (whether buyer or mortgagee) to ask the owner to disclose the names of all adult[26] occupiers of the property. Each of those occupiers is then asked to consent to the disposition and to give up, as against the purchaser, whatever rights, if any, they have in the land. This is unsatisfying because it does not protect the purchaser if the owner lies; the purchaser is left with a personal remedy only, i.e. the right to seek damages from the owner for misrepresentation. Yet it seems to have laid the *Boland* problem to rest. Either misrepresentation has not happened, or it has done so seldom enough for the institutional lenders to regard it as an acceptable risk. Equitable ownership rights in land do not generally pose a problem for purchasers—which is what the 1925 reformers intended, although it has not been done anywhere near so tidily as they planned.

And the upshot, curiously, is that provided that normal conveyancing safeguards are observed, the holder of an equitable ownership right in land is unprotected against a purchaser. The result is the same as if the equitable interest were not proprietary, provided that either over-reaching takes place or the post-*Boland* safeguards are observed and no misrepresentation takes place. A complex route has been taken to achieve a very simple result.

---

[24] The Law Commission is a statutory body charged, by the Law Commissions Act 1965, with keeping the law under review and considering its development and reform.

[25] See below, at p. 55 ff.

[26] It has been decided that children cannot have an overriding interest under Schedule 3, paragraph 2.

OVERRIDING VERSUS OVERREACHING

One final point about overreaching. Where a trust interest has overriding status because of occupation, but can also be overreached, does overreaching trump overriding, or vice versa? The statute does not say because the issue was not supposed to arise. Settled Land Act interests were excluded from being overriding interests; and interests under trusts for sale were conceived as financial interests which could not therefore be interests *in the land* as required for overriding status. But *Boland* of course opened that door. Mrs Boland's interest could not be overreached because the legal estate was held by a sole trustee. But what if the conditions for overreaching had been met? The issue went to the House of Lords in 1988.[27] The case concerned a couple, Mr and Mrs Flegg, who bought a large house which included a 'granny flat'. Into the granny flat moved the wife's parents, Mr and Mrs Maxwell-Brown; in a not-untypical arrangement, they sold their own home and put the proceeds into this one, amounting to about a quarter of the price. The four of them were therefore joint owners in equity; but the Maxwell-Browns did not wish to be legal owners, because they did not wish to take on responsibility for the Fleggs' mortgage repayments. So the Fleggs bought as joint legal owners, holding on trust (they were probably unaware of this) for the four of them. Later, they re-mortgaged the property. Later still, they defaulted on that loan. The bank sought to re-possess the house. Up jumped the Maxwell-Browns, who lived there and owned a one-quarter share in the property. They were in actual occupation, and so their equitable ownership was an overriding interest which bound the bank. In answer, the bank claimed that it took its mortgage, as security for the loan, from two trustees of the legal estate. Any equitable interests should therefore have been overreached, and should not affect the bank. So which form of magic prevails: overriding or overreaching?

Perhaps surprisingly, the statute did not say. Arrangements like this, though normal now, were not thought of in 1925. Much was said in the judgments in *Flegg* about statutory interpretation and about the protection of the home. Nevertheless, in this writer's view the statute left the court a free choice as to which should prevail; there is simply no decisive provision. The case is an excellent illustration of the fact that a 'purchaser' can be either a buyer or a mortgagee, or indeed anyone acquiring, for value, an interest in land. And it is a good illustration of the courts' prevailing policy: to protect purchasers. The bank won.

[27] *City of London Building Society v Flegg* [1988] AC 54.

INDEFEASIBILITY AND THE REGISTER'S POSITIVE WARRANTY

WHAT IS INDEFEASIBILITY?

Most of what we have said so far about enforceability has tended towards dynamic rather than static security. Assuming an owner willing to sell, the purchaser is favoured by the system, in preference to those who hold interests in the land. A purchaser can be confident that he will not be bound by non-ownership rights unless they were protected (and were therefore visible to him) by registration or by actual occupation, and he can also be sure that in virtually all cases he cannot be caught out by unexpected equitable ownership rights. This, we said, is the negative warranty inherent in section 29: there is nothing else to worry about.

Writers on the Torrens system also speak of the register's positive warranty: it guarantees the validity of the registered title. This too is part of dynamic security. A system that gives a strong positive warranty tells a purchaser that what he buys will be stable, and cannot be taken away from him because of a defect in the transaction by which he acquired it. That guarantee is also known as indefeasibility. Different levels of indefeasibility are possible, and the English system's version is significantly different from either of the two found in the Torrens systems.

To see why this matters, consider some examples. In the first, X's registered estate is transferred to Y. Y forged the transfer. We can call this the 'straight fraud' case. In the second, Mr and Mrs X own a house. Mrs Y mortgaged it to the Y bank, by forging her husband's signature, and the Y bank now has a registered charge. This is the 'innocent Y' case. In the third example, there is a void transfer from X to Y, whether because of fraud or because of 'double conveyancing', that is, the sale of the same piece of land twice usually by mistake (this is far less likely to happen where title is registered). In a few years' time, it might be void because of the fraudulent use of the electronic conveyancing system. The land is then bought by Z, who is unconnected with and uninvolved in the void transfer. This we shall call the 'acid-bath' case, after the series of transfers made by Haigh, who forged the signature of some of his victims, transferring their land to him, and then sold the land on.

In all the examples there is a void transfer from X to Y. In the straight fraud case, Y is the forger; in the innocent Y case, he is not. And in the acid-bath case, the chain of title has gone from X to Y to Z, but the first link is void. In all cases, if title were unregistered X's title would be unaffected and he would not lose his legal estate, because the transfer is simply void. If title is registered, section 58 of the 2002 Act states that the registered proprietor, Y or Z as the case may be, has the legal estate. What should happen now? In the straight fraud case the register clearly should be altered to restore X's legal estate. Where Y is innocent of the fraud— be he a buyer or a mortgagee—it is not entirely obvious which of two innocent parties, X or Y, should benefit from the register's guarantee of title, but in the particular example we have used it seems very wrong for the mortgage to be valid so that Mr X is liable for mortgage repayments. If Y were a buyer who had moved into the property (perhaps the fraud was carried out while the Xs were away from home for a long period) then the answer would not be so obvious.

Moving on one step: if the land has passed to Z, should he be able to rely on the register, or is he in danger from the invalidity of a transaction once removed from his own? And one of the ingredients of the problem—one of the values to be weighed—is the security of the register, and therefore the confidence of the market.

INDEFEASIBILITY IN THE 2002 ACT

The theory of indefeasibility has been worked out in great detail in the Torrens registration systems. They all give security of title to Z. Some also give security of title to Y, always provided he is innocent of the fraud. Where Y's title is guaranteed, the system is said to be one of immediate indefeasibility. Where X is able to recover the land from Y, but not from Z, there is said to be deferred indefeasibility. In very nearly all Torrens systems there is a system of indemnity, or insurance, funded by the land registry fees system, which will compensate X.

By contrast, English law operates a compromise. It does not guarantee Y's title, but it makes Y's title secure if he is in possession of the land. It does so by using the concept of mistake. Schedule 6 of the Land Registration Act 2002 states that the register can be altered in order to correct a mistake. This is obviously needed for typographical errors, for example. But the schedule goes on to define a sub-set of cases where an alteration to correct a mistake prejudicially affects the title of a registered proprietor of the land. Such cases are called rectification. Rectification will not be ordered if a registered proprietor *in possession of the land* objects to it, unless he has caused or substantially contributed to the mistake by fraud or carelessness, or unless it would for any other reason be unjust not to order rectification. This gives a clear answer in our first two cases. In the straight fraud case, Y loses; but where Y is innocent, he keeps the land provided he is in possession of it. Moreover, possession is carefully defined, so that if land is in the possession of a tenant, the landlord is treated as being in possession; if it is in the possession of a licensee, it is deemed to be in the possession of the licensor; if in the possession of a beneficiary, it is deemed to be in the possession of the trustee. So Y is safe even if he is a buyer (unlike our example) and has let the land, or taken in a lodger, or declared a trust of the land. However, if land is in the possession of a mortgagee, it is deemed to be in the possession of the mortgagor. So in our example, the Y bank does not keep its registered charge, and Mr X does not have to pay off the mortgage.

Where Y *is* in possession, the Schedule gives the court a discretion to rectify nevertheless if it would be just to do so. A good example is where the land concerned is a tiny piece of land, of no benefit to Y, but important to X.[28] It would be unjust to allow Y to keep it and then demand a ransom price from X.

The English system has been described as qualified indefeasibility. It is kinder than immediate indefeasibility, because it tends to keep the land with those to whom it matters most: proprietors who are living on it or running a business on it. And the rules about rectification have to be read side by side with the provisions of Schedule 8 to the statute, on indemnity. It provides that in all cases where someone suffers loss because of the rectification of the register, or because of a mistake whose correction would involve rectification, he will be compensated. So in our second example, the innocent Y bank is compensated for losing the security of half the land (the loss will be whatever part of the debt Mrs X, or her share in the property, cannot pay). But if the innocent Y were a buyer from X under a void transfer, who kept the land because rectification could not be ordered against him, X would be compensated.

Under the Land Registration Act 1925 Z, too, was vulnerable and could lose his title unless he was in possession of the land. This was not a problem for the ordinary domestic purchasers in the acid-bath cases, but it left some purchasers, particularly mortgagees, insecure. The 2002 Act is not explicit on the point but the best view is that Z's title is secure, because there is no mistake in the transfer to him. He can rely on the title he sees on the register, provided the disposition to him is itself valid. There is thus qualified indefeasibility for Y, but true deferred indefeasibility for Z, as we would expect in a system so firmly orientated to dynamic security. And where Z gets to keep the land, despite the discovery

[28] *James Hay Pension Trustees Ltd v Cooper Estates Ltd* [2005] EWHC 36 (Ch).

of a mistake further back in the chain of title, again, X can look to the indemnity fund for compensation.

The 1925 provisions for rectification generated a number of awkward cases, some of them betraying serious misunderstanding of the operation both of registration and of indefeasibility. In some, the courts succumbed to the temptation to use a trusts analysis, on the basis that Y might hold the land on trust for Z following a void transfer. This is unhelpful. It cannot be correct in cases where Y is innocent. Where Y is guilty of fraud, the remedy should not depend on the existence of a trust interest which can be overreached. Much of the confusion arose from the poor drafting of the relevant provisions of the 1925 Act. The 2002 Act represents a great improvement; a consistent set of results can be achieved, for X, Y and Z, from the mechanism in Schedules 4 and 8, without the need to rely on concepts not intended for the purpose of defining indefeasibility.

The final chapter of this book reverts to the tension between legitimate acquisition of land and the value placed on possession, in the context of the law of adverse possession. We shall see that in that context the tension is under acute strain at present and that one of the problems is the absence of any provision for compensation in order to restore a balance.

BRINGING THE REGISTER UP TO DATE

Schedule 6 to the Land Registration Act 2002 also provides that the register can be altered in order to bring it up to date. Again, this covers some very simple cases in the 'oh, of course' category, for example where a street name or number has changed or where a death certificate is sent in to record the death of one of joint proprietors. It covers the registration of transactions carried out by the registered proprietor, and events subsequent to his acquisition such as the registration of an easement acquired by prescription (long use).[29] And it also covers two quite difficult instances.

One is what the Torrens writers call the *in personam* exception: where a registered title has been bought in circumstances which make the purchaser hold it on a constructive trust for another party. We discussed this in the case where a third party has an unregistered interest. Mere notice of this interest will not bind a purchaser. But if he has actively engaged in a deal whose object is the defeat of that interest, or otherwise behaved with serious dishonesty—the issue has not been explored in English

---

[29] See Chapter 8.

case law—a trust may be imposed. In such a case the register can be altered, for example to give effect to the unregistered interest. This is not rectification, because there has been no mistake on the registrar's part.

Second is the voidable transfer. This is a transfer tainted by a problem such as misrepresentation or undue influence, but not actually void. The party who is the victim of the wrongdoing can choose to *avoid*, that is cancel, the transaction, subject to rules about taking action within a reasonable time. Until he does so, he has an 'equity', that is, a right falling short of an equitable interest but which may nevertheless bind a purchaser if protected on the register or by actual occupation. So a purchaser of a registered estate may be bound by an earlier owner's right to avoid a transaction, one or more steps back in the chain of title. This leans rather more in the direction of static security than do the indefeasibility rules and the principles of rectification; it may arise from a particularly unfortunate decision under the 1925 statute.[30]

CONCLUSION

This chapter has explored the heart of modern English land law. We have seen why the law has to organise complexity: because it is a source of uncertainty to purchasers of land, and to those who hold rights in land. In organising complexity, the law has to make a choice: will it protect the holder of, say, an equitable easement or a trust interest in the land, or will it protect the purchaser who wants to be free of them? The draftsmen of the 1925 legislation were quite clear that they wanted to protect the purchaser. The legislation they drafted was not entirely watertight, but the decisions of the courts and the practice of conveyancers have filled in the gaps and the 2002 statute has largely followed the 1925 pattern. In cases of conflict the odds are stacked in favour of a purchaser of land. This is closely linked with our perception of what land is for; there is no getting away from the fact that we value it as capital. The buyer of land may or may not want to live there, but he certainly wants to have a marketable asset. It is in the interests of both purchasers and land owners to have a land law system that protects purchasers and maintains a brisk market in land, even at the expense of those who have rights in land but are not owners.

There is a contradiction inherent in this preference for dynamic security, in the effect upon long-term stability for purchasers. We have

---

[30] *Norwich and Peterborough Building Society Ltd v Steed* [1993] Ch 116.

seen that section 29 gives a negative warranty that is, in practice, robust.
The three items that it lists are all of the pre-existing interests that a
purchaser need be concerned with. The provisions on alteration of the
register control the register's positive warranty, the promise that the
registered title is secure. We have seen that, again, the odds are stacked
in favour of a purchaser insofar as his own acquisition is in question:
provided that he is in possession of the land, he will be able to keep it
despite any defect in the transfer to him, and provided the defect was
not his fault. This is splendid for a purchaser contemplating his own
acquisition of the land. But once he steps past that acquisition, it
makes him vulnerable to fraud in the future. The purchaser interested
in dynamic security has become the owner interested in static security,
and in that capacity he may find the registration system disappoin-
ting. But he will not find it disastrous, because of the existence of the
indemnity fund.

The chapters that follow explore further the acquisition of land and
of interests in it, and the nature of those interests. All are affected by
registration and by this tension between dynamic and static security.
The challenge for the system is to find a balance between the two and,
increasingly, to do so in a way that does not conflict with human rights.
For dynamic security may well involve people being deprived of their
possessions. In the context of indefeasibility, compensation provisions
provide that balance. In the context of adverse possession, as we shall
see in Chapter 9, the absence of compensation provisions have led to a
serious conflict between land law principle and human rights. For most
holders of non-ownership rights in land, registration provides a safeguard, and is consistent with dynamic security. For some, in particular
the beneficiaries of informally constituted trusts (to be explored in the
next chapter), there is little safeguard because their interests have little
proprietary effect. They might be said to be the main victims of our
purchaser-focused registration system.

BIBLIOGRAPHY

E. Cooke, *The New Law of Land Registration* (Oxford, Hart Publishing Ltd,
    2003).
E. Cooke and P. O'Connor, 'Purchaser liability to third parties in the English
    Land Registration System: a Comparative Perspective' (2004) 120 *Law
    Quarterly Review* 640.
M. Dixon, 'Proprietary and non-proprietary rights in modern land law' in

L. Tee, ed, *Land Law: Issues, Debates, Policy* (Cullompton, Willan Publishing, 2002).

A. Pottage, 'The Originality of Registration' (1995) 15 *Oxford Journal of Legal Studies* 370.

R. B. Roper et al, *Ruoff and Roper: Registered Conveyancing* (London, Sweet and Maxwell Limited, 2005), chapter 46.

P. Sparkes, *A New Land Law* (Oxford, Hart Publishing Ltd, 2003), Chapter 1.

4

Creating and Acquiring Interests in Land: Words and Intentions

This chapter is about the way the law controls the creation and transfer of interests in land, when we buy houses, grant a lease, acquire an easement, grant a mortgage in exchange for a loan and so on. To grasp this topic, we have to embrace a contrast. On the one hand, the law likes these things to be done unambiguously, deliberately and publicly. On the other hand, the law recognises that in some cases it would be oppressive, in some cases even discriminatory, to require this. Besides, some transactions are too trivial, in the sense of being short-term, for it to be worth insisting on formal procedures.

So how does the law deal with this contrast? We need to examine the formal requirements for the acquisition of interests in land. *Formal* requirements are rules about the practical, physical way in which such transactions are carried out, for example that they be done in writing or by deed. Then we need to look at short leases, where informality is not a problem, and at implied trusts and estoppel, which enable informal acquisition. These latter two ideas are closely linked, and in some cases are alternative responses to the same set of facts. A very different method of informal acquisition is adverse possession, to be considered in Chapter 9; its diminishing importance means that it is not discussed here alongside other methods of informal acquisition.

The impression that this chapter aims to give is one of a battery of rules about formality, a carefully-built wall of requirements, behind which we find a carefully limited area where there is scope for informally created interests. Here, again, is the land law dilemma of clean titles versus grace for the vulnerable, or of dynamic versus static security.

Land Law

FORMALITIES

The law requires that certain land transactions be done in writing; that some be done by deed; and that some be done by deed and then registered. The penalty for failing to comply with the rules is that the transaction does not work; in some cases it is wholly ineffective, in others partially so.

Why? The earliest statute imposing formality requirements for land transactions was the Statute of Frauds 1677. Its title explains its purpose and a principal motivation for all formality rules: the avoidance of fraud, because informal transactions are so easily concealed. More generally, we can say that the rules are imposed to protect people. One aim is to make sure that they know what they are doing; there is no 'cooling off' period for land transactions as there is for some consumer contracts, but making people write things down (as we used to: nowadays we type things up) serves a similar function, bringing the transaction itself and many of its details to the parties' attention. Another aim is to make sure that people can check what they have done, and that other people can see what they have done. Where formalities include registration, the evidence is made public so that it is hard to conceal. For the same reasons, publicity and registration requirements were introduced for marriages in 1753, although land transactions in this jurisdiction, unlike weddings, do not now have to be actually performed in public. Other purposes for formalities include the government's interest in seeing what has been done and, in some instances, in taxing it.

CONTRACTS

Contracts are not a necessary preliminary to the creation or transfer of property rights. If I am going to give, not sell, a plot of land to you, there would be no contract between us beforehand, and the formalities we would need to think about would be those necessary for the transfer of a legal estate. But most sales of land (leasehold or freehold) and grants of leases will be preceded by a contract. The context where most people meet land contracts is domestic conveyancing, where the contract has a vital role in practical and financial planning: it locks both seller and buyer into the deal and fixes the date of completion, enabling removal vans to be booked and mortgage arrangements to be finalised. It is of course possible to sell and buy land without a prior contract, but it is rarely convenient to do so.

Contracts are therefore a frequent preliminary to the creation or transfer of legal rights (usually ownership rights) in land, and the layman regards them as just that. But they play another role; they are fundamental to the creation of equitable rights in land.

We noted in Chapter 2[1] that a contractual right to buy land is an equitable interest in it. It was explained that this is because of the availability of specific performance of the contract. It means that the purchaser's pre-completion rights can be inherited; and, like any other equitable interest in land, they can be enforced against at least some purchasers of the land.

Other equitable rights can all be seen to have their roots in contract: a contract to grant a lease generates an equitable lease; a contract to grant a mortgage generates an equitable mortgage. Moreover, it has been explained that equity will rescue deals which are insufficiently formal to generate legal rights, so that equitable rights can be seen as a sort of consolation prize, or a rescue effort for those who have missed the boat by failing to complete the formalities required for an effective transaction at law. The reason for this is the readiness of equity to recognise the proprietary nature of rights arising from contracts. But it follows from this that if a deal fails to be a valid contract, it will not generate rights at law *nor in equity*.

With that in mind we turn to the formality requirements for contracts. With a few exceptions, contracts for the creation or transfer of any interest in land must be in writing; the document must be signed by both (or all) parties; and all the terms they have agreed must be written in the one document. The law implies some terms in some contracts, and these implied terms do not need to be written. For example, if the parties to an agreement to sell land do not state when they will complete the sale, the law implies that it will be done in a reasonable time (for what that is worth). The rules allow for transactions where contracts are 'exchanged', a practice familiar to anyone who has bought a house. In that case, two identical contracts are prepared, each party signs one, and the contract comes into effect when they swap copies.

These requirements are set out in the Law of Property (Miscellaneous Provisions) Act 1989—a relatively recent enactment. Until 1989, the requirements for land contracts were more subtle; they did not have to *be* in writing, but if there was no written *evidence* of a land contract, they were 'unenforceable by action'. For example, suppose you and I agreed, over a pint and a handshake, that you would buy my house, and you paid a 5% deposit. Nothing was written down. Come the agreed day for com-

---

[1] At p. 29.

pletion, you refused to complete; it would have been perfectly proper for
me to keep your deposit, because that is what a deposit is for—agreed
compensation for a failure to complete. But if you were ready to buy and I
refused to complete, you would not be able to retrieve your deposit; the
contract was unwritten and so you would not have been able to get a court
to order me to pay the money back. That is the consequence of the
contract's being unenforceable by [court] action.

This rule was difficult to understand, and could lead to inconsistent
results. The current law was constructed by the Law Commission with
the aim of better serving the protective purpose of formalities. And so it
does; it makes it unlikely, for example, that anyone will get trapped into a
land contract inadvertently, and therefore renders superfluous the 'Subject to Contract' slogan still used in conveyancing correspondence. It
makes the deal described above completely void: I would have to give
your deposit back because there would be no reason to keep it. Note that
the 1989 rules apply both at law and in equity; a deal that fails to meet
their requirements will create neither a legal nor an equitable interest.

What the new rule also did was to complicate some well-established
ways of dealing with land. It made the traditional analysis of options
untenable, for example. An option is a deal whereby I give you the right to
buy my land from me at any time you choose within a defined period, say
five years, at a price we have agreed or to be determined in an agreed way;
you exercise that right by sending me notification. Options are useful for
structuring transactions and their finance, and they are robust devices
because equity has turned these contractual rights into property rights.
The difficulty is that the option structure had always been analysed so
that the initial agreement was seen as an offer, to be held open for the
option period; the notification that the option is to be exercised was the
acceptance; together they made a complete contract. Clearly this would
not work in the new dispensation, as it was a contract that was not
comprised in one document. So were options now impossible? No, said
the court; they are to be re-conceptualised as conditional contracts, complete at the point of agreement, but activated by the notification. What
the courts could not save was the mortgage by deposit of title deeds; the
ancient and handy arrangement whereby A lends money to B on the
security of his land, and, instead of drafting documentation and then
registering a legal mortgage, A simply takes the title deeds. Such a transaction took effect before 1989 as an equitable mortgage, but cannot now
do so because the contractual basis that underpins all equitable property
rights has gone; for an equitable mortgage to take effect now the deal

must be written down in a single document complying with the terms of the 1989 Act. The same goes, of course, for equitable leases and equitable easements; these are still subject to less onerous requirements than are their legal counterparts, but the 1989 rules stand as a minimum for equity as well as for law. Despite its ancient role in rescuing deals that have not complied with the rules, equity has never been entirely insouciant about formalities; but the 1989 Act is rather disturbing in its restriction of equity's scope. It brings a loss in freedom and in time; a gain in lawyers' fees; a gain in certainty and evidence.

More generally, we can say that the 1989 rules make it easier for people to get things wrong. It is more likely now that people who seriously intended a transaction will fail to effect one. Should they be given any help in enforcing it? In order to answer that, we might ask whether or not we would have expected either party to take legal advice and therefore to get it right; we might also ask what are the effects, on either party, of their transaction being void. We shall have more to say about this later.

TRANSACTIONS: CREATING OR CONVEYING

As we might expect, transactions which actually create or transfer an interest in land are subject to more onerous formality requirements than are contracts to do so. We use the word 'transfer' now, to conform to the terms used in the land registration legislation, whereas the older statutes use the word 'convey', which was appropriate to unregistered land. But in this context, the terms mean the same thing. With some exceptions, section 53 of the Law of Property Act 1925 requires that interests in land, whether legal or equitable, can only be created in writing, and that a declaration of a trust of land (which creates equitable interests) must be evidenced in writing. Thus a declaration of trust is effective if done orally, provided there is written evidence of the declaration—a tricky distinction which has generated some tortuous case law. Section 52 goes a step further and states that to be effective at law—to create a legal interest with the extra strength that such interests have in the face of buyers or mortgagees—a transaction has to be done by deed. This takes us a step beyond mere formality and into the realm of ritual.

In medieval times, in practice until the mid-sixteenth century, land had to be transferred by livery of seisin. The transaction was carried out publicly, in the presence of witnesses (in an era before folk were willing to rely on mere documentation), and very physically: the parties stood on the land, and the transferor would hand a bit of it—a twig or a turf—to the tranferee. By the mid-nineteenth century the ritual was formally abolished, so that all legal estates in land could be transferred by deed. A deed was sealed writing; literally sealed, with hot wax (as much correspondence still was at that date).[2] As the use of wax and seals became obsolete, the seal was represented by a little circle of red, self-adhesive paper. The seal is a rite; a visible sign of something invisible yet deeply significant. A seal by itself did not do the job; the document had to be signed by the parties, witnessed, and then delivered, i.e. put into effect by the delivery of the deed to the party whose title it completed.

Another modernisation effected by the Law of Property (Miscellaneous Provisions) Act 1989 was a change in the requirements for a deed. A document is a deed if it "makes clear on its face that it is a deed", i.e. if it claims to be a deed. A heading will do; and the requirements for witnessing remain.

Originally, a deed was a sufficient condition for the transmission or creation of a legal estate; now it is only a necessary condition; in most cases (though not all) even the delivered deed will not do the job by itself. As we have seen,[3] it is not possible to transfer a registered estate in land, or to grant a legal lease of more than seven years out of it, or to create a legal interest in it (such as a mortgage), without registering the transaction. And the creation of a legal lease of more than seven years out of an unregistered estate (a fee simple or a lease) triggers a requirement that that new lease be registered as an independent title, on pain of its losing legal status.

Three rather mechanical, but crucially important, conclusions follow from what has been said above. First, transactions that should be in writing but are not will be wholly ineffective.

Secondly, that those that should be done by deed but are merely in writing will be effective in equity but not at law. A mortgage effected in writing (complying with s. 2 of the 1989 Act) but not by a deed will be an equitable mortgage; an attempt to register it, so that it has the benefit of guaranteed status,[4] will be unsuccessful (although the registrar will record it against the title of the mortgaged land so that its priority is protected). It is more likely, of course, that parties who do not get round to using a deed will also fail to get round to registering the deal, so that the mortgage remains unprotected and will not be of any effect against a subsequent purchaser of the land.

---

[2] 'He wrote with his own hand his love to his cousin William, and sent him half a guinea under the seal', Jane Austen, *Mansfield Park* (London, Penguin Books, 1966), 52.

[3] Chapter 3, at p. 41.

[4] Chapter 3, at p. 42–3.

Thirdly, a transaction that is done by deed but not registered works only in equity, consistent with the tradition of equity's rescuing transactions that miss the legal boat. A mortgage done by deed but not registered is an equitable one; a purchase of a house, done by deed but not registered, gives the buyer an equitable title only.

We can now build on what was said in Chapter 2 about the distinction between legal and equitable ownership, and non-ownership rights, using formalities to distinguish between the two kinds. Given a property right, for example a right of way, how can we tell whether it is legal or equitable? We have to look first at what it is: it may be something that can only be equitable. But a right of way is an easement, and easements can be either. Secondly, if it was created using words, whether unwritten or documented, it may be clear from what was said that the people involved may have deliberately created an equitable right when they could have created a legal one. There are reasons why someone might want to grant an equitable mortgage, for example. Thirdly, if the right is one that could be either and no deliberate choice is evident, then we have to look again, and more precisely, at the way in which it was created or transferred. If the legal requirements for its creation are met, then the right is legal; otherwise, if it has missed the boat by falling short of the formal requirements, then it is equitable.

A few examples may help.

First, the creation of a property right. Adam has been granted a ten-year lease of a shop. The requirements for a legal ten year lease are that it be written down in the form of a deed, properly executed (i.e. signed and witnessed), and registered at the land registry. If and only if this has all been done, the lease is legal. Contrast a weekly tenancy granted to Zoe, orally. Nothing is even written down, let alone turned into a deed or registered. Nevertheless Zoe has a legal lease, because for leases for a term of three years or less (provided that a full rent is charged), no formalities are required, so there is no boat to miss.

Secondly, a transfer. Bertha has bought a house from Colin, who was the registered proprietor, holding a legal fee simple. The transfer of the land to Bertha was in the form of a deed, and has been registered at the Land Registry. Bertha now holds the legal fee simple.

Third, a transfer that has failed to meet the requirements for legal validity. Adam sells his lease to Dennis, so that Dennis will stand in the original tenant's shoes and take over Adam's relationship with the landlord (just as Bertha took over Colin's relationship with the Crown, though that is far less important). The transfer of the lease to Dennis is done by deed, but Dennis (or his solicitor) forgets to send the transfer to the Land Registry. Unless and until he does so, he holds only an equitable lease. The legal lease is still held by Adam, on trust for Dennis, even though neither Adam nor Dennis knows of the trust.

ELECTRONIC LAND TRANSACTIONS

Notice how much less physical the formalities for land transactions have become. We have moved away from the era where we had to get earth on our hands in order to own it. Gone, too, is the ritual with hot drippy wax, and even the little red gummed paper circles that pretended to be seals. All that is needed now is paper and ink . . . but this book is being written without either. No sooner has the law become accustomed to a business world of printing on paper, than paper is *passé* and the law needs to work out how to manage electronic dealings without sacrificing the protection that formalities give.

The Land Registration Act 2002 lays the legislative foundation for electronic conveyancing, in provisions that have not yet been brought into force by statutory instrument.[5] The idea is that within the next few years the land register, which is already held in electronic form, and is already available for inspection online (for a fee), will become accessible and changeable from the conveyancer's PC. Completion of a land transaction will take place, not by signing and delivering a piece of paper, but by clicking a mouse and thereby, in one instant, creating or transferring a registered estate. (It is only fair to add that an instant may be a long time for a computer).

At the time of writing, the land registry is committed to a gradual implementation of e-conveyancing rather than a 'big bang' approach. The electronic discharge of mortgages is being piloted, but for true e-conveyancing much more complex systems are needed, and the necessary software is still under development. Issues such as the electronic transfer of funds, including the payment of Stamp Duty Land Tax, and the security of electronic signatures, are being explored. If and when the electronic dream becomes a reality, paper will disappear from conveyancing and the register will be more powerful than ever.

If the system takes effect as envisaged, the formality requirements explained here will become far more rigorous; it will become impossible to deal effectively with land without the use of a computer. The intention

---

[5] That is, orders laid before Parliament for approval but not subjected to the full rigours of debate there.

is that transactions that are not made electronically will be of no effect either at law or in equity; equity's rescuing role will be further diminished. Dispositions that have to be done electronically will include contracts. There may be a way of rescuing such transactions; we have to take a journey around a number of concepts before coming back to this.

INFORMAL TRANSACTING

So far, then, we have a relatively tidy picture. One statute regulates the formality requirements for land contracts; another sets out the requirement of writing for creating all interests in land, and the additional requirement of a deed for creating or transferring a legal interest; and in most but not all cases registration is a further requirement for legal validity. The rest of this chapter is about the exceptions to the formality rules, exceptions made because formality would be inconvenient or oppressive.

EXCEPTIONS FOR SHORT LEASES

All the statutory formality requirements make an exception for short leases. Leases are both contracts and estates in land. Yet most leases of three years or less, for which a market rent is charged, do not have to be created in writing, and are valid at law even though they are not made by deed. The 1925 and 1989 Acts provide this explicitly. This makes it unlikely, by the way, that a short lease will ever be equitable, unless the rent condition is not met or unless the grantor has only an equitable estate so that he cannot create a legal one. In the short leases category come all periodic tenancies, of course, where informal arrangements made on the doorstep or by telephone have always been commonplace and whose validity the law simply has to recognise. Trivial though it sounds, this deserves a paragraph to itself: it shows the law accommodating itself to the convenience of its users. For the same reason, auction contracts—complete when the hammer falls—are exempt from the formality requirements. The concession for short leases is thought to be a safe one so far as purchasers are concerned, because a tenant paying a weekly or monthly rent is likely to be in occupation of the property, and the law continues to make the assumption that a purchaser will actually inspect the property he is buying (as he probably will) or of which he is accepting a mortgage (yet in that case inspection is very unlikely). Short leases are also kept off the land register, partly at least to keep the register uncluttered, and to avoid an excessive workload for the registries. Notice that this paragraph had to start by saying '*most* leases of three years or less'; there are exceptions to the exception, where special factors make publicity desirable. One example is reversionary leases where possession is given at a date later than the grant of the lease and where therefore the tenant might not be readily discoverable by the purchaser.

It is odd, however, that the assignment of a periodic tenancy, whether as a gift or as a sale, is subject to the full rigour of the formality requirements; the periodic tenancy is a legal estate and so a transfer must be done by deed in accordance with section 52. Lawyers had not noticed this until it was exposed in a 1990s case;[6] the exception in the statute is only for creation. The fact that there was no scope for equity to come to the rescue, despite the hardship involved in that case, is a useful reminder of the nature of equity today.

The exception to the registration requirement is for leases of seven years or less; these can be created and transferred off-register. There is therefore a group of leases—for seven years or less, but for more than three years—where writing and a deed are required for creation and transfer, but registration is not, so that the deed remains a sufficient condition for the manipulation of the legal estate. It may be that this will be tidied up by moving the threshold for registration down to three years, to match the requirements for contracts in the 1989 Act and the requirements for creation and transfer in the 1925 Act. Whatever the eventual threshold for registration of leases will be will also be the threshold for the requirement of electronic dealing.

IMPLIED TRUSTS AND ESTOPPEL; INTRODUCTORY POINTS

The exception for short leases generates legal estates. So does the doctrine of adverse possession, the other exception to informality which we have already examined. A further provision found in the 1925 and 1989 Acts is for 'implied, resulting and constructive trusts' to be exempt from the requirements of writing. Here we move into equity and the creation of equitable interests in land. Note that it is generally accepted that resulting and constructive trusts are a subset of implied trusts, and this narrative proceeds on that basis.

When the exception for implied trusts was written into section 53 of the Law of Property Act 1925, it was expected to cover quite a narrow range of circumstances. Its importance has grown considerably, however, thanks to developments in the second half of the twentieth century. As we

---

[6] *Crago v Julian* [1992] 1 WLR 372, CA.

have already mentioned, the courts became very creative during that period in adapting quite ancient doctrines to modern contexts. Much of what we are about to discuss has been developed as a way of bringing ownership into line with the reality of a relationship. It does so in a very restricted way; it sets rules for itself, within which it can do justice but outside which it is powerless. But equity is not an 'it'; equity is a community of judges and a body of legal thinking. The fact that we do not have a system in which judges sit under a 'portable palm tree' (as one judge put it a few years ago) dispensing justice in the form of whatever is needed reflects not merely a respect for precedent but also an instinct for the balance between the courts and Parliament. We have legislation for the redistribution, on a very wide discretionary basis, of the property of divorcing couples; in the absence of statutory provision for cohabitants the judges have not felt able to give themselves an unfettered discretion. Couples who are, or have been, cohabiting have therefore formed a large proportion of claimants under the doctrines to be discussed. The common intention constructive trust was actually developed in response to their needs; resulting trusts and estoppel were not, although estoppel in particular has proved very adaptable for use in this context.

Two preliminary points have to be stressed. First, it follows from what has just been said that divorcing couples will not normally need to use any of the following doctrines; but some of the cases involve married couples because the trigger for litigation was not divorce but bankruptcy, and sometimes succession, when it is vital to know precisely who owns what. Even if, as is likely, the law is reformed during the next few years so as to introduce for cohabitants a discretionary jurisdiction to redistribute assets on the breakdown of the relationship, it seems inevitable that property law doctrines will continue to be needed for married couples, civil partners and cohabitants in cases arising on bankruptcy or death. Secondly, the courts have stated clearly that where a declaration of trust *has* been made, defining the beneficial ownership of a property, that declaration is the final word, and equitable ownership cannot be re-assessed using implied trusts or estoppel. Now to explain those doctrines.

RESULTING TRUSTS

Resulting trusts are ancient. The idea is that where one person supplies the money to buy a property which is purchased in another's name, then, unless it is clear that the one who provided the funds was making the other a gift, the buyer holds it on trust for the one who supplied the money. I send you a large sum of money and ask you to buy a house with it, and you do so; unless it is clear that this was a gift, equity regards you as trustee for me. The house is really mine. (The word 'resulting' is supposed to be a Latin derivation, because the equitable interest jumps back to the one who gave the money: *re-salire*). If I provide part of the money for the house purchase, we become co-owners in equity.

In a family context, the concept is skewed by the 'presumption of advancement'; in certain circumstances the law starts from the assumption that a gift is being made. A father buys a house in the name of his daughter for her to live in while she is at university; the house is presumed to be a gift to her unless (in the event of dispute) he can show that both parties regarded the daughter as holding the legal title on trust for him. The case law here is very old; it is probable that the courts would be reluctant today to hold that the presumption did not equally apply in a purchase by a mother.

The presumption also applies when a husband provides money for a purchase in his wife's name; but not vice versa—fortunately for women, because the resulting trust has been very useful in an era when the purchase of the family home was often done in the husband's name. When part of the funds for the purchase were provided by the wife, he was regarded as holding the house on trust for her to the extent of her contribution (she puts in 25%, she has a 25% share, etc). The courts are now very reluctant to apply the presumption of advancement, because of its sexist nature. If a resulting trust were claimed by a husband, it is unlikely that the presumption of advancement would stand in his way. Legislation is planned to abolish the presumption as between married and engaged couples.

The downside of the resulting trust is that the beneficiary gets exactly what he contributes to the property, in terms of proportion of value. A 5% contribution to the purchase of the family home, followed by years of hard labour, self-sacrifice, and devotion of income to the household bills, will only ever generate a 5% share in the value of the property. And contribution is rather closely defined: making mortgage repayments does not seem to be recognised for this purpose. The existence and extent of a resulting trust is fixed at the moment of acquisition of the property.

But equity can be much more creative than that.

COMMON INTENTION CONSTRUCTIVE TRUST

ORIGINS

The common intention constructive trust was invented in response to a failed attempt to create a discretionary jurisdiction for the assistance of married claimants. The story goes like this.

Lord Denning has become an almost mythical figure to law students in the last twenty-five years or so—starting from those of us who began learning the law just after he left the Bench. The 1960s and 1970s must have been exciting times. What would he come up with next? And would the House of Lords let him get away with it? There was something of a cat and mouse game going on. In 1967 Lord Denning, then a member of the Court of Appeal, invented 'deserted wife's equity', the doctrine that where the family home belongs to the husband, the wife automatically has a proprietary interest in it. The purpose of the invention was to give the wife a stake in the home when the husband defaulted on the mortgage, to save her from homelessness; had Denning's invention been allowed to stand, it would have had a most revolutionary effect on family property in this jurisdiction. It would have brought us into line with the European doctrine of community of property, whereby marriage automatically generates a form of joint ownership of the family home and some or all of the couple's other assets (the extent of co-ownership varies from one jurisdiction to another). But the House of Lords overruled Denning's efforts in this instance, being more anxious to ensure that the mortgage industry would function smoothly than to make a significant move towards European legal integration (this was 1967!).

As it turned out, the overruling was softened a little by a statute enacted shortly afterwards and in response to the House of Lords' decision: the Matrimonial Homes Act 1967. Its key provision is now found in section 30 of the Family Law Act 1996. It asserts the right of spouses to occupy the couple's home, even where they do not own it; and it enables that personal occupation right to be registered so that it can bind a purchaser. It thus takes on, through registration, a partially proprietary status. Only partially: the right can be made enforceable, as if it were a property right, but it is not alienable. It means that a wife who is aware that her husband is planning to sell or mortgage the house, against her wishes, can register her occupation right on the land register, just as if it were the burden of an easement or a lease. If title is unregistered the registration can be done through the Land Charges Registry. A potential purchaser, whether a buyer or a mortgagee, will not deal with the husband or make any commitment to the property in the presence of that registration. The statute has given the non-owning spouse a right to veto transactions. Its weakness is that very few individuals are aware of it and by the time the need for protection is known, it will probably be too late. The occupation right cannot be an overriding interest, and so in the absence of actual registration it gives no protection at all against third parties.

The swift suppression of the 'deserted wife's equity' left us with the system of separation of property, whereby marriage has no effect upon the property rights of the couples as individuals (until they divorce, that is). Separation was a considerable improvement upon the law before 1882, whereby a married woman was unable to own a legal estate in land at all. That disability was removed by the Married Women's Property Act 1882. And that statute provided the tool for Denning's next attempt to reform the law of family property. He took section 17 of the Act, which was intended to enable the court to declare the respective interests of the parties, and read it as if it enabled the court to determine, and therefore to redistribute. The statute enabled the court, said Denning, to declare that a contribution to the home, in labour and materials, entitled a wife or husband to a beneficial interest. His views prevailed in the Court of Appeal for a short period. But the House of Lords decisively overruled this use of the 1882 statute, in a case where a Mr Pettitt was claiming an interest in his wife's property by virtue of his contribution in work and materials.[7] Mr Pettitt was found to have no property rights. His contribution was not in fact substantial and he was perhaps not a claimant who prompted a great deal of sympathy. But the House of Lords made the principle very clear, that property rights are not granted merely because the claimant needs or deserves them.

That sequence of decisions triggered two responses. First, a small and little-used statutory provision,[8] to the effect that where someone carried out substantial improvements to his or her spouse's property, that person would acquire a share (or an enhanced share, if already a co-owner) in the property in equity. The provision is useful only to spouses (who do not normally need it); and it would not have helped Mr Pettitt, whose work was hardly substantial. A much more exciting response to the *Pettitt* saga was the case of *Gissing v Gissing*,[9] where the House of Lords, having

---

[7] *Pettitt v Pettitt* [1970] AC 777, HL.
[8] Section 37 of the Matrimonial Proceedings and Property Act 1970.
[9] [1971] AC 886, HL.

closed the door rather firmly on Lord Denning, opened a door of its own—the common intention constructive trust.

CONSTRUCTING A TRUST

Constructive trusts are nearly as ancient and respectable as resulting trusts. They arise in a number of contexts where the courts have concluded that there ought to be a trust even though one has not been formally set up. They may arise as a response to wrongdoing, for example when someone has received trust property and is then obliged to hold it as a trustee rather than for his own benefit because he knew about the trust. In the context of land registration, for example, a constructive trust may in exceptional circumstances be imposed on a purchaser whose conduct is so dishonest that he cannot be allowed the protection that registration normally gives a purchaser, but is obliged instead to hold the land for the benefit of someone else.[10] The common intention constructive trust harnesses the idea of a response to wrongdoing, and of the imposition of trustee status on someone who did not want or expect it. But it extends the conditions under which a trust may arise. The House of Lords held that where there has been an agreement (also called a 'common intention') between the landowner and the claimant that the claimant is to have an interest in the property, and she has acted to her detriment in reliance on that agreement, then the landowner holds the property as trustee for her—or, more usually, for the two of them together.

From this formulation we can construct a claim for a disappointed cohabitant. She can say: he promised that the house was as much mine as his; I relied on that and helped with the finances, or gave up my protected tenancy, or worked hard at renovating the property. The house should therefore belong, in part, to me. The House of Lords is doing something apparently quite close to what Lord Denning wanted to do. But it is doing so with better roots in precedent; and, as we shall see, within rather careful constraints. The result is a doctrine that will not help every claimant and does not plant palm trees; but is nevertheless very flexible and is something that the courts have worked with creatively, if not entirely consistently.

The introduction of this recipe (agreement, plus detrimental reliance generates an equitable interest) has given the courts scope to explore the ingredients. First, the agreement or common intention. If the parties made a verbal agreement, then there is no difficulty; but who does? The

[10] Chapter 3, p. 46.

business of falling in love and setting up home together does not generally involve cosy discussions about the beneficial ownership of the property, even if the parties know what that means. The cases are marred by squabblings over who said what and what it meant, when in fact, at the time, the words were not about property rights and may have been no more than pillow talk. The courts have even found express agreement in words which were actually lies and excuses, when he said to her that the house could not be put in their joint names because she was under 21 (at a time when the age of majority was 18), or because it would complicate her divorce proceedings. In these cases, the courts have found an express agreement, forcing the speaker to stand by what he said (compare the ideas behind proprietary estoppel, discussed below). So he should; but to label the conversation an agreement, or to say that the two shared the same intention, is ridiculous.

Then there are the cases where nothing was said. The courts are willing to construe or imply an agreement from conduct; and this is even more obviously a case where the court is simply making the agreement up. The idea is that if the parties have behaved in a particular way then they *must* have both intended that the claimant should have a share in the property. The behaviour from which the courts are prepared to make this leap of faith is actually very limited: only a direct financial contribution to the acquisition of the house will suffice.[11] But what counts as a financial contribution is considerably wider than the type of payment that would be regarded as a contribution sufficient to give rise to a resulting trust. The contribution may be in the form of a capital payment, or of contributions to the mortgage payments. It may be made at the time of purchase, or it may be made later; it may be the financing of an extension, rather than the purchase of the house itself; but repair and maintenance will not suffice. The 'contribution' may actually be the right-to-buy discount, that is, the reduction in the purchase price earned by a public sector tenant; this is important, as so often council houses are bought by the tenant who has earned a discount, and a family member who pays the rest or raises it as a loan. What will not suffice as a contribution from which a shared intention can be inferred is payment of household expenses alone. The most authoritative cases in this area are clear that paying the bills (as in the common arrangement: you pay the mortgage and I'll pay the bills) is

---

[11] *Lloyds Bank plc v Rossett* [1991] 1 AC 107, still the leading case on common intention constructive trusts, although the lower courts have been perhaps somewhat flexible in their interpretations of it.

too ambiguous, insufficiently closely linked to the acquisition of the house. However, there is real uncertainty as to the position where the claimant has paid the bills and thereby has actually freed up the other party's resources and enabled him to pay the mortgage; there are contradictory statements in the cases, but it is to be hoped that the courts would ensure that a claimant was not prejudiced by this very common arrangement, since couples so often decide more or less at random who is to pay which bills.

Given this constraint, many claimants will not get past the 'common intention' hurdle. Of those that do, many do so because they have put money into the property rather than because anything was said; as we shall see, what they get out is rather different from what is available to them on a resulting trust analysis. But before the claimant can succeed, she must prove detrimental reliance upon that common intention.

There are two issues here. Detriment is supposed to be something costly, or difficult; and reliance is about causation. The detriment suffered by the claimant is supposed to be something she would not have done but for the prospect of an interest in the property.

The easy example is financial contribution. The courts have no difficulty accepting that anyone who puts money into the acquisition or improvement of someone else's property must be expecting an interest in it. This is legally uncontroversial, although it may not match how non-lawyers think. However, in cases where there is no express agreement in the first place, but an agreement is implied from conduct, we may find that the same behaviour pattern does two jobs: the claimant's making mortgage payments may be the evidence for the claimed common intention, and it may also constitute the claimant's detrimental reliance on that intention.

Where the action or course of conduct alleged to be the detrimental reliance is not a money contribution, the courts have had more difficulty assessing the validity of the claim of detrimental reliance. Successful examples include giving something up, such as a protected tenancy elsewhere, or looking after the landowner or assisting his business endeavours. The courts have had difficulty with manual labour, and homemaking; they have looked for something more than a wife or partner would normally be expected to contribute to her home. So claimants are vulnerable to the personal ideologies of the (mostly male) judges, however innocent or unconscious, which may mean that the odds are stacked against female claimants.

OUTCOMES

How much does the claimant get? Again, the courts give primacy to an
express agreement; if the parties actually put into words how much the
claimant's share would be ('as much yours as mine'), that is what she gets.
If there was no express agreement,[12] the latest authorities[13] state that the
court will look at the whole course of the relationship and of the parties'
behaviour. If they have shared a common life, with its ups and downs, it is
likely that the claimant will get a half share. She is not limited to the
amount she put in; the constructive trust does not mirror the resulting
trust.

This section is labelled 'outcomes' rather than remedies because the
court does not see itself as awarding a remedy. The theory is that the
parties' own actions have generated a beneficial interest in the property, at
the time of acquisition or whenever the claimant's contribution was
made. What the court is doing is declaring the existence of that beneficial
interest and declaring the proportion of the property's value that it represents. This means that the outcome of a claim of an interest under a
common intention constructive trust is the discovery of something that
happened a long time ago. (Did it really? Does an interest under such a
trust have any reality at all until someone thinks about it and decides that
it exists?) If the claim is made in a context where someone else—a mortgagee or a buyer—is claiming ownership of the property, the claimant
needs to show that she has had an interest in it for some time and that it is
enforceable against that purchaser. Where the legal owner's title is registered, the story she needs to construct is something like: he bought the
house, I moved in with him, I paid off a substantial part of the mortgage.
So I have made contributions to the acquisition of the property which
demonstrate our common intention that I should be a joint owner of it.
The partnership in which we lived and the extent to which we shared our
lives indicates that I have had, in equity, a half-share in the property for
some time now, and certainly since before my partner mortgaged the
property to the bank. I was in actual occupation of the property so I have
an overriding interest in it under the Land Registration Act 2002;[14] and as
my partner is the sole legal owner my interest was not overreached when
the mortgage was created;[15] so my interest binds the bank. The bank can

---

[12] As there was, e.g. in *Crossley v Crossley* [2005] EWCA Civ 1581.
[13] In particular, *Midland Bank plc v Cooke* [1995] 4 All ER 562, CA.
[14] Chapter 3, p. 44.
[15] Chapter 3, p. 52.

take possession of the property and sell it, but it will have to give me a half-share in the value of the property as if there were no mortgage.

If the bank is lucky, and if the legal owner has been honest, the normal conveyancing safeguards of making enquiries of occupiers[16] will prevent this disaster. We have to contemplate it to understand the mechanics of the claim, and to appreciate the disaster that the conveyancing safeguards will normally prevent.

Where the claim is made only against the legal owner, it is a powerful weapon, if the claimant can fulfil the requirements of the doctrine—the 'recipe' discussed above. The courts have come a long way with the common intention constructive trust. Something like a concept of family property has been created; but only within rather narrow limits. We can say that what the courts respond to is either words or money. There must be an express agreement, or a direct contribution to the purchase of the house; given one or other of those, the court enjoys a wide and creative discretion; it can be generous. Without either, it will do nothing, however close, long-standing and familial the relationship between claimant and defendant has been, however much the claimant has given in terms of love and support, however pressing the claimant's needs. Moreover, the courts' generosity is constrained by the conveyancing safeguards; although the common intention constructive trust gives rise to a property right for the claimant, which in theory will bind a purchaser, in fact it will very rarely do so. As we saw in Chapter 3, equitable ownership in fact has very little proprietary effect. What looks like a protection of static security in fact has had very little impact on dynamic security.

PROPRIETARY ESTOPPEL

ORIGINS

Resulting and implied trusts are expressly contemplated in the statutory provisions that require formalities for land transactions, and are accepted explicitly as exceptions. Rather more on the edge of land law lies proprietary estoppel, which has the effect of enforcing informal transactions involving land but is rather different. Its origins are older than those of the common intention constructive trust. It is an amalgam of ideas rather than a deliberately constructed doctrine. It works in a wide variety of contexts meeting a number of very different needs, and its effect is not to generate a

---

[16] Chapter 3, p. 53.

property right automatically. It is a more unwieldy instrument than the common intention constructive trust, and rather more of a loose cannon.

Estoppel in its most basic form is a rule of evidence. It prevents someone from contradicting himself, in certain circumstances.[17] It has been extended to form part of the law of contract, as a result of the requirement for consideration. English law does not enforce promises, however serious, unless they form part of a bargain. Something most be given in return, whether a promise or an action, and that something is known as 'consideration'. The fact that a promise has been relied upon will not make it enforceable. It is still the law that if I promise to give you £10,000 next Monday and you, relying on my promise, spend £5,000 on a new piano, I am free to pay you nothing. (Whether or not that would actually be the law's answer would depend upon whether or not, after years of academic badgering, the courts were prepared to adopt American precedent; but that is another story). But occasionally one may be estopped, that is, prevented, from going back on a promise to let someone off a contractual obligation. The leading case on this concept, known as 'promissory estoppel', concerned a letting arrangement in the 1940s, when the landlord agreed to accept a lower rent for the duration of the war. After the war he was able, of course, to charge the full rent; but he was not allowed to recover for the arrears of rent that had built up during the war, even though the tenants had given no consideration for the promise to charge less.

Proprietary estoppel is older than this and it grew from the rather stronger requirements for contracts concerning land, already discussed in this chapter, and from the fact that where there are strict rules for formalities in contracts, there is bound to be demand for the law to enforce promises made less formally.

Although there are a number of more ancient precedents, the major inspiration for proprietary estoppel was a case in the 1860s.[18] The context is urban expansion following the industrial revolution. A landowner offered short-term tenancies to a large number of tenants, and encouraged them to build on the land, promising that they could have a long lease for the asking at any stage. Later, he tried to evict them on the basis that they just had short-term tenancies (this was long before the security of tenure legislation). The tenants pleaded the landlord's promise, upon

---

[17] The word comes from Norman French, and is derived from the word for a bung or stopper: c.f. those handy little things for stopping up open bottles of wine.

[18] *Ramsden v Dyson* (1866) LR 1 HL 129.

which they had relied. They failed; the majority of the judges in the House of Lords held that they could have succeeded only if they had been under an actual mistake about their title to the land. They knew they had only short-term lettings; the promise to give a long lease was simply unenforceable. Lord Cranworth said:

If a stranger begins to build on my land supposing it to be his own, and I, perceiving his mistake, abstain from setting him right, and leave him to persevere in his error, a Court of equity will not allow me afterwards to assert my title to the land on which he had expended money on the supposition that it was his own.

That in itself was a powerful authority, even though it did not help the tenants in this case. A modern application of it is where I build my garage 20 cm beyond my boundary and on your land, supposing that 20 cm strip to be my own, and you stand watching without correcting my mistake; you may be prevented from asserting your ownership of the strip, and indeed be ordered to transfer it to me.[19] The doctrine which developed from Lord Cranworth's judgment depended upon the idea of a statement, known as a 'representation', being made and relied upon (echoes of the common intention constructive trust spring to mind; but proprietary estoppel was the earlier doctrine). Debate has focussed on how much the defendant (the 'representor', the one who made the statement) must know about the claimant's state of mind: must he know that the claimant has made a mistake about the boundary; must he have intended the claimant to rely on his statement, etc? A body of law also built up about the way the statement could be made: as well as words, there might be actions, or even silence, provided there was communication. As Lord Cranworth envisaged, silence can communicate, in circumstances where the landowner might be expected to speak up (e.g. 'but he watched me building the garage; if I was on his land he should have said'), so that his failing to do so when he is obviously aware of the situation may speak volumes.

But there was more in *Ramsden v Dyson*. This being a House of Lords case, even a dissenting judgment is authoritative. Here is what Lord Kingsdown said:

---

[19] A different way of solving boundary problems in this form is adverse possession; see Chapter 9 at p. 208. The use of adverse possession in this context has been severely curtailed by the provisions of the Land Registration Act 2002, but the use of estoppel appears to survive: Chapter 9, p. 218.

If a man, under a verbal agreement with a landlord for a certain interest in land, or, what amounts to the same thing, under an expectation, created or encouraged by the landlord, that he shall have a certain interest, takes possession of such land, with the consent of the landlord, and upon the faith of such promise or expectation, with the knowledge of the landlord, and without objection by him, lays out money upon the land, a Court of equity will compel the landlord *to give effect to such promise or expectation*. [emphasis added].

This is much stronger; and although the majority of their lordships did not recognise it as the law in *Ramsden v Dyson*, a number of authoritative decisions later adopted this statement, placed it alongside Lord Cranworth's, and combined both as the foundation of the doctrine we now call 'proprietary estoppel'. It is estoppel because it prevents someone from going back on a promise, but it does much more than an estoppel because it has a positive effect. It results in the award of a remedy, which may (not must) be an interest in land.

CONSTRUCTING A FLEXIBLE DOCTRINE

The term 'proprietary estoppel' was not coined until the twentieth century. The controversial element was the idea of enforcing promises about future ownership, rather than just statements about current ownership. Expanded in this way, its scope is huge. The farmer who was promised an easement by the neighbouring landowner, and therefore goes ahead with a deal that leaves his field land-locked if the easement is not granted, will be able to claim the right to an easement;[20] the holder of an option to extend a lease, which seems to be unenforceable because it was not registered against the landlord's title, can claim that the option is enforceable anyway because the landlord assured him it would be.[21] A father with lots of land encourages his son to build a house on it, promising that he can have the land; the father's executors will not be allowed to build on the land.[22] And the cohabitant who was promised 'this house is as much yours as mine' can make a claim on the basis that so it should be, if she has relied on the promise to her detriment. She may be allowed to stay there for life; or she may be awarded a beneficial interest in the property so that it really is half hers. So proprietary estoppel has been used in a wide range of contexts, just one of which overlaps with that of the common intention constructive trust, namely the provision of an interest in property following cohabitation.

---

[20] *Crabb v Arun District Council* [1976] Ch 179, CA.
[21] *Taylors Fashions Ltd v Liverpool Victoria Trustees Co Ltd* [1984] 1 QB 133.
[22] *Inwards v Baker* [1965] 2 QB 29, CA.

The 'recipe' for proprietary estoppel is remarkably similar to that for the common intention constructive trust: there must be a representation (a broad term covering express statements but also other forms of communication) that the claimant has or will have an interest in land; and the claimant must have relied on that to her detriment, so that it is unconscionable for the representor to go back on his promise or statement. It does not take much imagination to see that a 'representation' may be made in a conversation which could equally found the inference of a common intention. Exactly what is meant by 'unconscionability' is simply not known—there is no consistent policy in the judges' use of the word—and so it is easy to build up theories about what it does mean. Sometimes it is used as a way of describing the rest of the recipe (representation + detrimental reliance); sometimes it is an extra ingredient, for example where the recipe ingredients are present but for some other reason the claimant should not be given anything (for example because she does not need the property and the defendant does).[23]

OUTCOMES: THE EQUITY AND THE RESPONSE

How much does the claimant get? Here there is a significant theoretical distinction between estoppel and the constructive trust. For the fulfilment of the recipe ingredients for estoppel does not of itself give rise to an interest in land. It gives the claimant an 'equity': that is, a claim, to which the court must respond in some way.

The 'equity' idea is a very unsatisfactory one. It is used in other contexts to indicate a very weak interest in land, rather less robust than an equitable interest. Here it seems to indicate even less than that, because the court's response to an equity by estoppel may be to do nothing. But it is more than just a right to seek relief, because anyone can go to court to seek relief. We might say that it is a *prima facie* case for relief, or perhaps a presumption that some relief will be given.

And there is in principle complete freedom for the court to grant whatever relief it thinks best; in doing so, the court is said to be 'satisfying the equity'. It might give the claimant precisely what was promised, whether that is an easement, or an interest in land, or simply permission to occupy a home (i.e. a licence). Or it might give the value of that in money. An award of what was promised, or its value, is known as 'expectation-based relief'. Equally, relief may be reliance-based, aiming to

---

[23] *Sledmore v Dalby* (1996) 72 P & CR 196, CA.

compensate the claimant, by a money award, for the detrimental reliance suffered. But any other basis of calculation is acceptable in principle. In fact, in the vast majority of cases up until the end of the twentieth century the award was expectation-based. This reflects the doctrine's basis in contract, where relief is almost always expectation-based; but it also reflects a very human factor. In almost all the cases, what the claimant wants is expectation-based relief. And once the court has been swayed by an argument to the effect that the claimant has an equity, and that it would be unconscionable not to give relief, the court is then pre-disposed to give the claimant what he wants.

The problem with this is that it may turn out to be a very severe penalty for admittedly unconscionable behaviour. In the last five years or so we have seen a swing in the courts' response to the estoppel equity; and one suspects that this has been motivated by a particular trend in the type of cases reaching the higher courts. We have seen a number of cases concerned neither with boundaries nor with cohabitants, but with carers to whom a promise of an inheritance has been made, and where the promise has failed to meet the formality requirements for wills rather than for contracts. Typical is the elderly person who is looked after by someone who is not a family member, who spends a good deal of time looking after her, perhaps undertaking personal care; and the elderly person promises to 'see them right'. Sometimes there is an explicit promise of a gift of a property in a will. Sometimes a more general promise of a gift of everything—the 'all this will be yours'-type of reassurance. Then the person dies without making such a gift in her will, and the claimant challenges the executors and the beneficiaries of the estate. And it may well be that the court can find a clear promise, relied on by the claimant to his detriment in time and money over a considerable period. To respond to this equity by the gift of a house, or perhaps of more extensive property, can seem out of proportion to the detriment suffered. So the courts in recent years have stressed the need for proportionality; and inevitably that means a move towards a more reliance-based response, at least in this context. In the context of cohabitants, we may expect this approach to be used with care, and that the relief given will be proportionate to need rather than just to the cost of reliance; this would be consistent with the courts' traditional approach to such claims, as well as ensuring a response that is consistent with what a claimant would get out of a common intention constructive trust.

IMPLIED TRUSTS, ESTOPPEL AND
FAMILY PROPERTY

Implied trusts and proprietary estoppel have been very fluid concepts. Until a few years ago there was some difficulty in distinguishing resulting and constructive trusts, until the courts made it clear that in the latter case, what the claimant gets out is not necessarily the same as what he put in. The generosity of approach seen in *Midland Bank plc v Cooke*[24] has opened up the scope of the common intention constructive trust, so that it can be an answer, not really to a type of transaction, but to a relationship.[25]

The same could readily be said of proprietary estoppel, and indeed in the context of the cohabitant claimant it is very difficult to distinguish the two. If he said to her 'the house is yours, darling', or 'you can live here for as long as you like' there is no point trying to decide whether that was a common intention or a representation.

The common intention constructive trust and proprietary estoppel are truly distinct in their consequences. The constructive trust is supposed to arise when detrimental reliance takes place, and so may have given rise—supposedly—to a beneficial interest long before any court order given in recognition of that interest. But only the court can determine the response to estoppel, which therefore crystallises, as it were, only at the point of the court order. This made the common intention constructive trust the obvious better choice for a cohabitant claiming *now* to have priority over a lender who took a mortgage a while ago. The effect of estoppel on a purchaser, by contrast, was unclear. If the representor—a cohabitant, say—sold the property while the claimant's equity by estoppel was still unsatisfied (she might not at this stage know that she had one), would the purchaser be bound by it? Various cases gave inconsistent and ambiguous answers to this; but section 116 of the Land Registration Act 2002 states that an equity by estoppel 'has effect from the time the equity arises as an interest capable of binding successors in title (subject to the rules about the effect of dispositions on priority)'.

The full implications of section 116 have yet to be explored. The principle remains that until the court makes a decision, we do not know what will be the response to the estoppel equity. If A has an estoppel claim against B, which is litigated after B sells to C, then if the response

---

[24] Note 13 above.
[25] The other leading case is *Oxley v Hiscock* [2004] EWCA Civ 546.

to the equity raised against B is a beneficial interest in the land that interest must be enforceable against C. If B is in fact two people, is it also overreachable? If the response is a licence to occupy the property, will that licence take on proprietary effect and bind C? What happens if the response is a monetary award—does section 116 transform an award of damages into a charge upon the property? These and other questions are still matters for speculation.

Section 116 is both generous and strict. It is generous because it makes clear that a purchaser can be bound by an estoppel equity before any determination has been made as to the appropriate response to the equity, and without any need for the purchaser to have actually done anything unconscionable. It is strict because it makes clear that this will only happen if the claimant has recorded her equity on the land register—which is highly unlikely—or if she has an overriding interest by virtue of her actual occupation of the land, as she probably will in the cohabitant cases only. That brings the estoppel claimant into line with the constructive trust claimant. And again, if a mortgagee took the normal conveyancing precautions, inquiring about the occupiers of property and obtaining their consent to the transaction, then, again, the cohabitant's right has no proprietary effect.

That does not make it valueless. In both cases, the claim remains good against the owning cohabitant. So the strength of these claims is their use when a relationship breaks down. They form a substitute for the discretionary jurisdiction of the Matrimonial Causes Act 1973—only, of course, for cohabitants who can meet the requirements of the trust or the estoppel. That makes them unhelpful as a tool for family law. They are not designed to meet need, nor to give compensation for economic disadvantage suffered because of a relationship, for example as a result of being the principal child-carer and home-maker. They are blunt instruments in this context. The Law Commission is working on the problem, and it is likely that a legislative solution will be found to the problem before very long.

ESTOPPEL AND THE RESCUING OF INFORMAL TRANSACTIONS

BACK TO LAND CONTRACTS

We began this chapter with an examination of the requirements for contracts to create or transfer interests in land; and we noted that estoppel grew out of the courts' need to find a way to rescue deals that did not meet the formal requirements for land transactions. The deals or arrangements where it has operated have been rather complex ones, often involving an ongoing relationship which adds an extra dimension beyond the failure to do the paperwork. Now we have to look at something which ought to be rather simpler and to look at the potential use of estoppel in the simple case of a contract for the sale and purchase of land; and it brings us back full circle to the beginning of this chapter.

The issue is this: if you promise to sell your land to me, and I rely on that promise to my detriment (perhaps by doing some building work), are you estopped from going back on it? There are a number of ways of analysing this. We can say you are estopped from denying a representation that there was a contract; or that you are estopped from going back on a promise to enter a contract; or estopped from going back on a promise to transfer the fee simple (i.e. the promise that would have been contained in the contract if formalised). However we choose to put it, the issue is the same: are you estopped, or prevented, from refusing to sell me your land even though you have not entered into a contract to do so? If so, what would be the courts' response to this estoppel equity?

When the Law Commission advocated the reform which is now section 2 of the Law of Property (Miscellaneous Provisions) Act 1989, discussed above, they assumed that estoppel could be used in that way, the courts' response being normally to enforce a sale. Clearly estoppel was a way of rescuing informal deals, and so surely the most basic form of such a deal—a straight sale and purchase contract—could be rescued in this way. There was no direct English case like this, but there was a powerful Australian precedent. Indeed, when the 1989 Act was debated in Parliament, reassurance was given to MPs that informal deals that had 'missed the boat' could be rescued in this way.

Two things were not noticed. One was that estoppel, as used to date, could not possibly be used to help a seller in such a situation, because it has only been used when there is an assurance that someone has or will have an interest in land—never where there has been assurance that someone will buy, or accept, an interest. That problem remains outstanding.

The other was that the courts have always felt something of a reluctance to use estoppel to contradict a statutory provision. It is not forbidden; there is no difficulty in using estoppel to avoid the formalities required in the Wills Act 1837, so as to validate a promise of a gift to take effect after death, even though the giver has not made the gift in a will.

But it is not possible, for example, for a tenant protected by the Rent Acts (and so having security of tenure) to be estopped from asserting that status; nor is it possible for a borrower to be estopped from claiming the protection given him under the moneylending legislation (which regulates who may lend, rates etc). The possibility for undue pressure in such cases is obvious; there is a tendency for them to be one-sided deals. So estoppel is not used 'in the face of a statute', as the courts have put it, if the statute is there to protect a vulnerable party. Given this policy on the part of the courts, can estoppel be used to rescue deals that have fallen foul of the 1989 requirements for land contracts? It is hard to say whether or not the requirements are there to protect the vulnerable; it is suggested that they are not, since sellers are no more vulnerable than buyers. But the courts have nevertheless been extremely reluctant to use estoppel in this way without direct statutory authority.

Initially, therefore, the courts avoided using estoppel to assist claimants whose agreements failed for informality. Instead they looked at the explicit provision in the 1989 Act to the effect that the operation of implied trusts was unaffected, and used a constructive trust instead of estoppel. The idea is that the defendant has behaved unconscionably in going back on the informal agreement; therefore he must hold his land on trust for the claimant, ready to transfer it as agreed.

There are a lot of problems with this. For one thing, it limits the court's choice as to remedy; it is not obvious that in all these cases there has to be a full expectation-based remedy given. For another, if a constructive trust is awarded in cases where estoppel has been pleaded, there is a tendency to confusion between the two doctrines which are, as has been shown here, distinct.

It has been suggested that estoppel can be used in these cases because in using estoppel the courts are simply responding to unconscionable conduct, they are not enforcing the failed deal. That seems a little disingenuous—it is obvious what the end result is. But it meets the problem of principle, and it gives effect to Parliament's intentions. There should really be no difficulty in using estoppel, and the most recent cases appear to recognise that. It is not contrary to principle to do so because it does not take away a protection from a vulnerable party in a deal that is naturally one-sided. Parliament itself accepted that estoppel would be used to rescue deals, probably in extreme cases where substantial injustice would otherwise be done.

But if it is always wrong to go back on a promise—or to renege on an agreement, to put it less emotively—then there will always be an argument about injustice and a case for enforcement. We need a tighter criterion. One suggestion is that estoppel will be used to enforce informal, and therefore non-contractual, promises when the promisor actually made an extra promise that he would stand by what he said, or that the deal would be valid, despite the lack of formality.

This would be a tidy solution, but it is suggested that it would not really work. People just do not make explicit extra promises along these lines, so we are being forced into the world of constructing promises that were not actually made. In most cases the parties are unaware of the provisions of the Law of Property (Miscellaneous Provisions) Act 1989, and made or understood the promise without reference to any legal requirements for formality. And even if an extra promise—a 'double assurance' as it has been called—can be spelled out of some discussions, there will then be cases of extreme injustice which cannot be rescued because it is perfectly clear that no double assurance was made. If estoppel is to be used to prevent injustice arising from the statute, one of the things it must do is to protect parties from ignorance, which it cannot adequately do if its use is limited to cases where a deliberate step has been taken by one of the parties. Least of all can it do so if its use is dependant on that step being taken by the promisor, when in fact it is the promisee that the doctrine is supposed to be helping.

It is suggested that the courts will have to take another look at their criteria for using estoppel to enforce informal promises, in the simple contractual situation when there are no factors to assist the court other than a promise to sell or create an interest. Factors that they might, and probably should use include: substantial financial detriment (compared, perhaps, to the value of the land); substantial personal hardship (in particular, homelessness); the abuse of a relationship of trust, where one party is particularly vulnerable to the other; and circumstances where the folk involved could not have been expected to take legal advice.

ESTOPPEL AND ELECTRONIC CONVEYANCING

It is imperative that the courts sort this out, because another demand for the use of estoppel is coming up. As discussed, the Land Registration Act 2002 makes provision for the introduction of a requirement that most transactions concerning land, including contracts, be carried out electronically. The intention is that transactions not so effected will have no effect, either at law or in equity.

If this happens, it will be startling. It will wipe out a large part of equity's role in land law, because whereas now a disposition that for some reason is not registered will nevertheless be effective in equity, under these rules it will be totally ineffective. The formality requirements for legal estates and interests are already such that the layman is ill-equipped to carry them out, and in that regard the addition of electronic conveyancing may do little harm; whether the further inroad into contractual freedom will be tolerated is open to doubt. It is not hard to imagine how hard the courts will be pressed to find a way of rescuing failed deals. Estoppel, again, is the obvious vehicle. There has been a prediction of an 'estoppel boom' if electronic conveyancing comes into force with the full rigour expected. Certainly if it does, there will be a 'boom' in failed deals.

Part of the answer to this is that electronic conveyancing may not be as thoroughgoing as was originally envisaged. It may be that fewer transactions than planned will be caught by the requirements. Computers have limitations, and there may now be a little less optimism, and a little more experience, behind the process.

Equally surely, electronic conveyancing will come into force in some form. And when it does, we shall have a fresh reminder of the power of formality requirements, which can make a nullity of the most sincerely-intentioned deals. And we shall have a fresh opportunity to examine how far the courts are committed to the formalities imposed by Parliament, and how far they will go to ameliorate the problems and injustice caused by those requirements.

BIBLIOGRAPHY

E. Cooke, *The Modern Law of Estoppel* (Oxford, Oxford University Press, 2000).

P. Critchley, 'Taking formalities seriously' in S. Bright and J. Dewar (eds) *Land Law: Themes and Perspectives* (Oxford, OUP, 1998), 507.

M. Dixon, 'Proprietary Estoppel and Formalities in Land Law and the Land Registration Act 2002' in E. Cooke (ed) *Modern Studies in Property Law, vol II* (Oxford, Hart Publishing Ltd, 2003), 165.

L. Fox 'Trusts of the Family Home: the Impact of *Oxley v Hiscock*' [2005] 56 *Northern Ireland Legal Quarterly* 63.

S. Gardner, 'Rethinking Family Property' (1993) 109 *Law Quarterly Review* 263.

S. Gardner, 'The Remedial Discretion in Proprietary Estoppel' (1999) 115 *Law Quarterly Review* 438.

A. Lawson, 'The things we do for love' (1996) 16 *Legal Studies* 218.

R. Probert, 'Trusts and the modern woman—establishing an interest in the family home' [2001] 13 *Child and Family Law Quarterly* 275.

R. Smith, *Property Law* 4th edn (Harlow, Pearson, 2003), 144–64 and 170–210.

P. Sparkes, *A New Land Law* 2nd edn (Oxford, Hart Publishing, 2003), 329–44.

5

Joint Ownership of Land

Chapter 4 explored how sole ownership can become joint ownership, in ways which may be unexpected and unwelcome to one of those involved. This chapter looks at the wider issues involved in the joint ownership of land; and we begin by recalling that for the most part, it is set up deliberately and is welcome to all concerned for a range of practical and emotional reasons. Mostly, joint ownership happens when a couple, married or not, buy their home in joint names. But there are other cases: the partners in a firm of solicitors will hold the lease of their office jointly, and the trustees of a charity are the joint owners of the charity's property.

We have already seen that whenever there is joint ownership of land, there is a trust, and that this is largely a way of keeping the title to property tidy for the sake of purchasers. In the cases we looked at in Chapter 4 there is one legal owner, and more than one owner in equity because shared ownership has been achieved informally. But in most deliberate joint purchases, trustees and beneficiaries are identical. When a married couple buys a house together there is simply no distinction between legal and equitable ownership; the same goes for, say, three business partners buying an office. When there are more than four owners, a maximum of four of them can hold the legal estate; but all are owners in equity ('beneficial owners' is another term).

Less common cases of joint ownership are the deliberately created trusts, set up as a way of sharing wealth across generations, or of looking after land for children. Such trusts are often created by will; but sometimes they are the result of a transaction *inter vivos*, as the jargon has it— 'among the living'. The person who sets up a trust is called a 'settlor', because when property is placed in a trust it is said to be 'settled'.[1] A deliberate settlement may involve successive or concurrent joint ownership or both; successive joint ownership is where more than one person holds an ownership right, but ownership is planned over time and not all have interests in possession. The typical case is when land is left to A for

---

[1] Even when, as in most cases nowadays, the Settled Land Act 1925 is not involved.

life, with remainder to B in fee simple. This type of settlement, with its many variants, used to account for the ownership of most of the land in this country, whereas today it is very unusual. A deliberately created trust might equally involve concurrent co-ownership; imagine parents buying an extra house and holding it on trust for their children for their use while at university.

A will may set up joint ownership on a temporary basis. Property may be left to a group of people—perhaps siblings—with no expectation that they will keep it. It is held on trust for them by the executors of the will—whether or not the will actually says so—until it is sold, and the proceeds divided. The same may happen under the rules of intestacy, where no will has been made but property passes automatically to, say, the parents of the deceased, or his brothers. Again, there is a trust, set up automatically; the trustees are the administrators of the estate, a task which falls to the nearest relatives of the deceased.[2]

So this chapter looks at four broad categories of joint ownership. Case one is the joint purchase, where ownership rights are concurrent and all or some of the beneficiaries are also the trustees. Such are the couple, or the business partners; in the former case, and sometimes in the latter, the parties may be unaware of their trusteeship. Case two is the Chapter 4-type co-ownership claimed or discovered, or perhaps agreed (at varying distances from the door of the court) when the relationship between the joint owners has broken down. Here it is likely that just one of the beneficiaries is also a trustee; and probably an unwilling one. Case three is the deliberate settlement, or 'express trust'—express because it must be set up expressly, deliberately, by a written declaration of trust. Case four is joint ownership set up by will, or by the rules of intestacy, just on a temporary basis for the sake of passing property along. Case four may become something that is functionally identical to cases one or three, if the siblings of the deceased (say) decide not to sell his house but to keep it and let it out. In that event the house is held on trust for as long as they keep it; the deceased's personal representatives[3] may retain the legal title for them, so that it looks like case four; or may transmit it to the three of them (or indeed the three of them may be the personal representatives), so that what looked like a temporary joint ownership becomes a deliberate joint venture as in case one. Or a will might leave land to the testator's children,

---

[2] These provisions are the subject matter of the Administration of Estates Act 1925.

[3] This means the executors of the will; or the administrators of the estate, where the will did not appoint executors or where there was no will.

and they are under 18 when he dies. Minors cannot hold a legal estate in land, and so the trust set up by the will must continue at least until the youngest child is 18, perhaps longer, depending on its terms. The trustees would often be the executors of the will, who might be close friends or family members; one might be the testator's solicitor. The will has set up for them a years' long relationship with the land and its beneficial owners.

In all these cases it does not matter at all, for the purposes of this chapter, whether the estate held on trust is freehold or leasehold—although it may matter a lot in the daily lives of the owners.

English law does not recognise the rather closer form of joint ownership used in some jurisdictions known as 'community of property', where the property of a married couple (and in some cases of registered partners) is automatically owned jointly (subject to contracting out) in such a way that the property can be taken by creditors in satisfaction of the personal debts of either, so that the way one of the couple conducts her business has a potential effect on her partner's share in the family home. In English law, and common law jurisdictions generally, this idea is unknown because our law of family property evolved in a different way from those of the civil law jurisdictions.

The issue for this chapter is the way the law manages joint ownership using the structure known as the 'trust of land'. Of its various sections, it will be noticed that not all are relevant to each of our four cases in equal measure. We begin by looking at an issue which concerns only concurrent joint ownership, which can occur in two forms.

LEGAL STRUCTURE OF CONCURRENT BENEFICIAL JOINT OWNERSHIP: JOINT TENANCY OR TENANCY IN COMMON

Take a Kit-Kat bar and give it to two people, X and Y, to own jointly; there are two bars, joined up and hidden in one wrapper; ask them to hold it in their hands (if not too warm). If they own it as joint tenants, then when X dies, both bars stay in Y's hand, still conjoined, still in their wrapper. There is nothing X can do about this, even if she has made a will leaving her share of the Kit-Kat bar to her son. But if they own it as tenants in common, then when X dies the two bars may separate. One will certainly stay in Y's hand; the other must go to whoever is entitled to it under X's will, or under the rules of intestacy if she has not made a will. It may actually be Y, in which case the two bars stay together; or it may be someone else, in which case they split up.

There are two forms of beneficial joint ownership of land. Where two or more people are joint owners in equity, they may be either joint tenants or tenants in common (for reasons to be explained, at law they can only ever be joint tenants). If they are joint tenants when one of them dies, then the other automatically becomes sole owner of the land. If they are tenants in common at that point then the share of the land belonging to the deceased goes to whoever is entitled to inherit it. It is possible for a joint tenant to change the form of ownership, and make it into a tenancy in common—this is known as severing the joint tenancy; but it cannot be done by making a will. So if a joint tenant makes a will leaving her share to someone else, this is of no effect; she remains a joint tenant and her co-owner takes the whole property when she dies.

The words 'tenant' and 'tenancy' in this context have their ancient meaning derived from the Latin *tenere*, to hold. They indicate landholding, in line with the feudal tradition whereby land is held but not owned, and have nothing to do with leaseholds and the law of landlord and tenant. Joint tenants may be co-owners in fee simple or of a lease, or, less likely but possible, of a life estate or an entail.

The theoretical distinction between joint tenancy and tenancy in common during the currency of the co-ownership is that tenants in common are said to have shares in the property while joint tenants own the whole without division. Tenants in common are said to have *undivided* shares, since the property is not physically divided and each is still entitled to possession of the whole. This is not a helpful distinction while the joint ownership continues although it may entertain the theorists. Its practical consequence arises when joint ownership ends on sale. In that event, joint tenants take half the proceeds each, whether or not they contributed equally to the purchase. Tenants in common will take the proceeds in whatever proportions they have decided, if they have actually made a declaration of trust and defined their shares; if they have not, they will take the proceeds in proportion to their contributions. Thus only tenants in common can take an unequal share of the sale proceeds.

That, in a nutshell, is the structure of beneficial joint ownership of land. The detail we need to look at includes: how do you tell what form of joint ownership is in operation in a given case? How can a joint tenancy be severed? Why do we have the two forms?

IDENTIFICATION

Equity is supposed to prefer tenancy in common. The point is that joint tenancy limits the parties' freedom (to dispose of their property effectively by will) and so the courts will discover a tenancy in common where possible. But it is not a default option; the default option is actually the joint tenancy in cases where the parties have not said which form of co-ownership they want, and where they have the same interest in the property, acquired at the same time, and in the same way. This will usually be the case with an everyday joint purchase by a couple: both take a fee simple or a lease, on the same day under the same transfer. These conditions are known as the unities; joint tenancy is said to have four unities, known as time, title, interest and possession; but possession, being the right to possess the whole property, is a feature of tenancy in common too, so does not help with identification. The couples who became joint owners in Chapter 4 by virtue of a common intention constructive trust or, if the court so decides, thanks to the operation of proprietary estoppel, will always be tenants in common because they came by their interests in different ways (one by formal transfer and one not) and, often, at different times.

Ideally, joint owners should address this question explicitly when they buy the land. A transfer to joint owners should transfer the land 'to X and Y as beneficial joint tenants' or 'as beneficial tenants in common', and if it does, that is the end of the matter. The courts have held that if the joint owners have done this, there is no scope for either of them to argue about the form of the acquisition subsequently (although of course either may claim that a joint tenancy has been severed subsequently, as we shall see). Where title is registered, or where the purchase triggers first registration, the land registry now requires that joint owners state, in their application for registration, which sort they are, so failure to state this explicitly should become an increasingly small problem. In our third type of co-ownership, the express trust, there will be a written settlement, whether a will or an *inter vivos* trust document, which should state how beneficiaries with concurrent interests will hold them.

However, if the parties have not stated which way they hold the land, and if the four unities are present, it may be possible for the courts to find that there is nevertheless a tenancy in common either from the words of the transfer (or will, etc) or from the surrounding circumstances. The words of the transfer will indicate that a tenancy in common is intended if its wording refers to shares or to any form of division, by transferring the land 'to X and Y in equal shares' or 'equally' or 'to be divided between them'. The use of such wording is now highly unlikely, and survives in the textbooks as examples of how not to draft wills. Circumstances that indicate a tenancy in common are: a business purchase (professional partners will not want the right of survivorship to operate); where the purchasers are in fact mortgagees (because their interest is financial and it is probable that neither would want the other to recover the whole debt secured by the mortgage); and where contributions to the purchase price are unequal. The latter is of course fairly usual, and we do not know just how unequal the contributions would have to be. The deposit is £10,000; X finds £4,500 from her savings, Y finds £5,500; and they split the legal fees equally as well as the subsequent mortgage payments; in the absence of other evidence, is this a joint tenancy or a tenancy in common? Joint tenancy does have the social utility of saving the trouble of making a will, and it is not obviously right for the court (in those extremely rare cases where the matter is disputed) to find a tenancy in common where there is only a slight inequality in contributions.

SEVERANCE

A joint tenant who no longer wishes to be one can take one of the actions specified in one case, *Williams v Hensman*[4] or in one statutory provision, section 36(2) of the Law of Property Act 1925. The statutory provision is that a joint tenant can sever by giving a notice. He must write to the other owner(s) and state that the tenancy is severed. There are no particular words prescribed. The courts have held that the notice is effective if it is received at the other's address, even if he does not read it, even if the sender, having changed her mind, picks it up and throws it away, even if the dog eats it. This is equity favouring a tenancy in common. That statutory provision preserves methods of severance invented before 1925, which means in effect that *Williams v Hensman* remains the law. It sets out three methods: severance can be done by one joint tenant dealing with his own share, by 'mutual agreement', and by a course of dealing. 'Dealing' means selling or mortgaging one's share; which is why it was said above that both forms of joint owners can do this. It points to the unreality of saying that joint tenants do not have 'shares' in the land. Bankruptcy is another 'dealing' that severs the joint tenancy. Agreement is self-explanatory; but it can be inferred from behaviour and so can merge with the other method, a course of dealing. In one of the leading cases[5] two people bought a house as beneficial joint tenants; the man intended that they would get married, and the lady did not. When the misunderstanding became apparent, the man agreed to buy his friend out; but then she

---

[4] (1861) 1 John & H 557, 70 ER 862.
[5] *Burgess v Rawnsley* [1975] Ch 429.

withdrew from that arrangement. Next, the man died; so now of course the lady argued that their discussions did not amount to severance. Did she take his share by survivorship? It was held that the course of dealing and/or agreement was sufficient to sever the joint tenancy. Note that the agreement does not have to be a valid contract. There is a large body of case law about attempts to sever; a fertile ground for dispute is the commencement of divorce proceedings; does a request for financial provision on divorce sever a joint tenancy?

A final and very effective way to sever a joint tenancy is homicide; if you murder your joint tenant, you will not take his share by survivorship: this is provided by the Forfeiture Act 1982. Where the homicide is manslaughter rather than murder, there is the possibility of relief from forfeiture; the court may decide that severance is not fair. It may be very unfair if the killer was a battered wife, for example, as happened in one case.

Severance by will, as already stated, is impossible. There is something to be said for making it possible; the argument against it is that severance is not only unilateral but unknown to the other party. This is a poor argument in view of the courts' policy of finding severance by other methods wherever possible. But severance by will, which presumably takes effect on the death of the testator, is peculiarly one-sided. It leaves the testator with the chance of benefiting by survivorship, while claiming the independence gained by severing in case he died first. This is perhaps the unwelcome aspect of this method of severance. The essence of joint tenancy is that it is a gamble, and to weight the dice in this way does not seem right.

POLICY

The difficulty with the joint tenancy is that it is an automatic decision; it takes a choice away. And folk are not always aware of its effect. They may not remember what their solicitor explained to them (if indeed he did); they may find that survivorship operates in an unwelcome way after a relationship has broken down; they may be surprised to find that joint tenancy means the two owners must take an equal share of the sale proceeds, no matter what their contribution to the purchase price— usually the survivorship point gets explained and this aspect is omitted. If joint tenancy becomes unwelcome, people may be unsure how to sever. Litigation may be needed to determine whether or not severance has taken place. And if a joint tenancy is severed, the resulting tenants in common hold the land in equal shares unless they explicitly agree otherwise; they do not hold in proportion to their contributions to the purchase, and this may be an unexpected, and unwelcome, feature of the joint tenancy.

Against those arguments are two in favour of its continued availability. The joint tenancy is known as the 'poor man's will': one rather weak argument in its favour is that it saves making a will. There is much to be said, on the other hand, for encouraging the tidy habit of doing so. If this became standard whenever property was purchased, equitable joint tenancy would be needless. The stronger argument is the rather fuzzy ideological one, that joint tenancy is appropriate to an intimate partnership arrangement. Recent research into community of property in Europe has shown that in those countries where community of property is more comprehensive—particularly The Netherlands—there is a strong feeling that it is fitting for married couples to share their property as deeply as possible. We do not have community of property; but joint tenancy has been described as a 'thorough and most intimate union of interest and possession'.[6] And it is worth noting that in California a new form of community of property has recently been introduced by statute: Community of Property With Right Of Survivorship.[7] In a jurisdiction where community of property is available and normal, there was popular demand for it to be strengthened by the addition of the characteristic of a joint tenancy.

THE STATUTORY FRAMEWORK FOR TRUSTS OF LAND

From a formal issue affecting only concurrent co-owners, we turn to a structural matter relevant to all forms of joint ownership: the nature of the trust of land. This is the domain of the Trusts of Land and Appointment of Trustees Act 1996, known as 'TLATA'.

TLATA's first task was the reform of the structure of the trust of land. From 1925, there was always a trust when land was owned jointly, whether deliberate or not; and prior to 1996 the vast majority of them took one of two forms: the 'trust for sale' or the 'Settled Land Act settlement' (also called the 'strict settlement'). The default form was the latter; the preferred form was the former.

---

[6] W. Blackstone's *Commentaries on the Laws of England* (1st edn, London 1765–1769), Vol II, p. 182.
[7] California Civil Code 682.1.

The trust for sale was adopted as a management tool by the 1925 legislation, borrowed from nineteenth century investment practice and designed for cases where land was bought as an asset and not as a home. It operated in all cases of concurrent joint ownership—our cases one, two and four—and in express trusts when expressly chosen, that is where the will or other trust document used the words 'upon trust for sale'. The legal estate in the land was held by trustees, who might or might not be identical with the beneficiaries, and who had the power to manage and control the property. The trustees were under a duty to sell the land, but had power to postpone sale. Where there was no agreement on postponement, the trustees had to sell.

Such a trust was ideal for our case four. It seems very strange indeed for the other cases, particularly where the property was a family home; and indeed, this was not the case that the 1925 reformers particularly had in mind, since at that date only a small proportion of homes were owner occupied and joint ownership by couples was unusual. But provided the trustees—the joint owners themselves—agreed to exercise their power to postpone rather than their duty to sell (and in their ignorance of the existence of a trust for sale, of course they would in effect do so), the trust for sale was a perfectly good structure for long-term co-ownership. Its theoretical basis was that the beneficiaries had interests in the sale proceeds rather than in the land, and it was not until *Williams and Glyn's Bank Ltd v Boland*[8] that the courts forced a change in this. Recall that the bank was taken by surprise by the enforceability of Mrs Boland's interest in that case.[9] Among the reasons for this was the fact that even if a wife might have an unexpected equitable interest, and even if, despite being a mere wife, she could be regarded as being in actual occupation of the property, she was not regarded as having an interest *in the land*. The House of Lords held that the theory of the trust for sale had to give place to the reality of modern joint ownership, and that of course she did have an interest in the land; but it was not until TLATA in 1996 that the doctrine of conversion—the converting of a beneficiary's interest into money—was formally abolished.

The Settled Land Act 1925 regulated a form of trust with a very different structure. Until 1925, and to some extent afterwards, the strict settlement was the normal vehicle for the settlement of land within a family. It worked like this. Take a gift of land by will to A for life, with

---

[8] [1981] AC 487.
[9] Chapter 3, p. 52.

remainder to B in fee simple. A gift in those terms before 1996, which did not use the words 'upon trust for sale', would create a settlement in which the legal estate was held by A. A, the tenant for life, had the power to manage and control the land. The settlement would have trustees, whose task was not to hold an estate in land, but to receive the proceeds of sale if the land was ever sold, and then to distribute or reinvest them (and, of course, to be the vehicle for overreaching, which occurs when purchase money is paid to at least two trustees).

The strict settlement was the vehicle intended by the 1925 reformers for our case three, the deliberate settlement; it would also arise automatically in some quite unusual cases, for example an attempted conveyance of land to a minor. It involved some difficult conveyancing documentation. In time, the fact that the trustees of the settlement did not actually hold the legal estate in the land became very counterintuitive, as did the principle that the tenant for life rather than the trustees managed the property. The fact that a gift by will 'upon trust for my wife for life with remainder to my son' generated a strict settlement became very unpopular.

So TLATA provides that no more strict settlements can be created; that all trusts of property that consist of or include land are, simply, trusts of land; and that a trust of land only involves an obligation to sell if the trust document says so. Trustees of land have all the powers of an absolute owner, subject to any restrictions imposed by the settlor of an express trust; those restrictions may include a requirement that they obtain someone's consent before selling, or may even take away the power to sell altogether. Statutory provisions dealing with joint ownership are all amended so that they speak of trusts of land, not trusts for sale.

So we can no longer enjoy the baroque twistiness of the distinctions between the two forms of trust of land, nor the pleasures (genuine, in this writer's view) of Settled Land Act conveyancing. But in the interests of plain speaking, the trust of land can only be an improvement. We now need to look at the provisions of TLATA that govern the operation of the trust of land.

THE INTERNAL MANAGEMENT OF TRUSTS OF LAND

How does joint ownership work on a day-to-day basis?

Our first case, the deliberate joint purchase, ought to self-regulate. In most cases trustees and beneficiaries will be identical. The parties have chosen joint ownership; whether the context is business or the home, they have to work out how to share. In our second case, co-ownership is asserted, or discovered, at the end of the relationship, and has had no effect on everyday life. In our fourth case, the trust will end soon after it begins. But in our case three, ownership may be complex. The trust has brought together trustees, with responsibilities, and beneficiaries with ownership rights which may conflict. There is bound to be a formal conflict of interest when there is successive co-ownership; and even when all the interests are technically identical, there may be an actual conflict. Where there are three beneficiaries with a life interest in possession, for example, who is to live in the property?

TLATA provides a framework for the management of trusts of land. The balance of power is weighted heavily in favour of the trustees, as they have all the powers of an absolute owner, so that there is no limit on, for example, the length of lease they can grant or the activities they can permit at the property. The Act acknowledges that a settlor may limit the trustees' powers, or may impose a requirement to regulate certain activities, for example by providing that a particular individual must consent before the land can be sold—it is easy to see how useful this is when land is left to a widow for life, with remainder to an adult child. The Act also gives some specific rights to beneficiaries, albeit rather heavily qualified. It states that 'in the exercise of any function relating to the land subject to the trust' the trustees must consult adult beneficiaries who have an interest in possession in the land, and give effect to their wishes—or to the majority's wish—'so far as is consistent with the general interest of the trust'. It also gives such beneficiaries a right to occupy the land, 'if the purposes of the trust include making the land available for his occupation' (think of the widow again), provided the land is not 'unavailable' or 'unsuitable'. The Act dos not say what these words mean, and we have no case law yet to give guidance. The Act enables the trustees to exclude or restrict this right to occupy if two or more beneficiaries have it; and to impose conditions on occupation, such as payment to compensate another beneficiary; but not actually to evict anyone without a court order. A more leisurely account could construct a lot of stories to illustrate these provisions, found in sections 11 to 13 of TLATA. The Act also makes provision for the trustees to delegate their functions; and for the retirement of trustees and appointment of new ones.

The point of principle to take away from this is that for an ongoing settlement where trustees and beneficiaries are not identical, TLATA does a lot of work. It lays the ground rules for the power balance, tilting it towards the trustees without being entirely one-sided. Yet by far the most common instances of trusts of land are ordinary joint ownership cases where trustees and beneficiaries are the same people and no-one has given any thought to the existence of a trust. To these people, the detailed management provisions in TLATA are irrelevant. Either they will sort things out by themselves, using whatever is their personal power balance, or they will need outside help. Equally, the personnel in our case three may find that TLATA's management provisions do not solve their disagreements.

DISPUTE RESOLUTION FOR TRUSTS OF LAND

TLATA provides as follows:

14.—(1) Any person who is a trustee of land or has an interest in property subject to a trust of land may make an application to the court for an order under this section.

(2) On an application for an order under this section the court may make any such order—
  (a) relating to the exercise by the trustees of any of their functions (including an order relieving them of any obligation to obtain the consent of, or to consult, any person in connection with the exercise of any of their functions), or
  (b) declaring the nature or extent of a person's interest in property subject to the trust,
as the court thinks fit.

15.—(1) The matters to which the court is to have regard in determining an application for an order under section 14 include—
(a) the intentions of the person or persons (if any) who created the trust,
(b) the purposes for which the property subject to the trust is held,
(c) the welfare of any minor who occupies or might reasonably be expected to occupy any land subject to the trust as his home, and
(d) the interests of any secured creditor of any beneficiary.

So the solution offered for intractable disputes is the court, and the court is given examples of matters to which it is to 'have regard'. Examples of the sort of dispute that might be brought before the court under these sections are: one owner wants to sell and another doesn't; the trustees wish to sell but the beneficiary whose consent is needed refuses to consent, unreasonably; the beneficiaries disagree with the trustees about the need to sell or mortgage the land, or the desirability of a letting arrangement. Persons with an interest in the land may include folk who are neither trustees nor beneficiaries. Any joint owner—concurrent or successive—can treat his share in the land as a separate asset, and this may involve extra personnel in the trust. He can mortgage his beneficial interest in it, for example; and in order to repossess the property, the mortgagee will have to apply to the court under section 14 for an order for possession and sale.

How does the court resolve these disputes? These two sections take over the job done by section 30 of the Law of Property Act 1925, intended for use for trusts for sale. That section gave no guidance to the courts at all; and for a few decades after 1925 the courts worked on the principle that the default option in a trust for sale was to sell. If the parties could not agree, sale was the answer. By the 1960s, however, a more subtle approach developed; the court looked at the purpose of the trust. If its purpose was over—for example because the house was bought to house a couple who had now split up—then the land must be sold.[10] But if its purpose was to be a home for the growing children of the family, who still needed to live there, then the answer would probably be that the house must remain unsold until the children grew up.[11] It can be seen that this approach has found its way into the legislation. There is still very little case law on the operation of these sections. What we still do not know is how a case will be resolved when the purpose of the trust has changed, for example where the house was bought as a home for the couple, but now granny has come to live with them. We can expect some pragmatic reasoning, driven as much by need as by principle.

When the application is made by a creditor of the joint owner it seems that the courts are occasionally willing to look at the purpose of the trust and postpone sale, but not unless the creditor is compensated for the wait; and the general trend is to favour the creditor in such a case. As will be seen, the position when application is made by the trustee in bankruptcy is rather different; and any leniency to a debtor's family under section 15 would only serve as an incentive to creditors to petition for the joint owner's bankruptcy.

One unusual tool for dispute resolution is partition. This means literally dividing the property up, physically, between the owners. Before 1925 it was the only order available to the courts in these cases, however inconvenient a physical split might be. Now, TLATA specifically

---

[10] *Jones v Challenger* [1961] 1 QB 176.
[11] *Re Evers' Trust* [1980] 1 WLR 1327; more recently, *Edwards v Lloyds TSB Bank plc* [2004] EWHC 1745 (Ch).

empowers the trustees to partition the property with the beneficiaries' consent. Equally, the court may order partition.[12]

So: a sensitive and useful provision for dispute resolution? To some extent. Again, we meet the point that joint owners come in different forms; and not all will find that TLATA goes far enough for their needs. Given that most joint ownership is by couples, it follows that most cases of dispute between joint owners are relationship break-downs and are not primarily *about* the property or the joint ownership.

So when a couple fall out, their first port of call might well be the provisions of Part III of the Family Law Act 1996, which enables the court to make Occupation Orders: swift, emergency-type orders removing one joint owner from the property, temporarily or even permanently. Typically they are needed because of domestic violence, where the dispute is not *about* the property but about the relationship and the parties' safety. But such an order is going to precipitate a property dispute. For the married couple, the solution lies not in TLATA but in the Matrimonial Causes Act 1973, and for civil partners in the Civil Partnerships Act 2004. For under TLATA the court can regulate whether or not the property is to be sold; but it cannot vary the ownership shares in the property. It can do nothing by way of adjustment of the parties' capital; and it can make no provision for support for either partner, or the children, in their day-to-day needs. It is well established that TLATA should not be used when the Matrimonial Causes Act 1973 is available, and the same must go for the civil partnerships legislation; these tailor-made statutes can adjust the parties' capital entitlements[13] and make flexible orders for the postponement of sale.[14]

So married couples involved in divorce proceedings, and civil partners bringing their partnerships to an end, are not going to use TLATA. Cohabiting couples, on the other hand, may do so, whether or not they have the need to use the domestic violence legislation first.

However, all couples have a further option if they have children, although only unmarried couples will use it: Schedule 1 of the Children Act 1989. This makes provision for property to be transferred or settled for the benefit of children. Married couples will not use it because the Matrimonial Causes Act 1973 will do all that the Children Act 1989 can do and more, as part of a package of provision for the whole family.

---

[12] A rare case in which the possibility was considered, but dismissed, is *Rodway v Landy* [2001] Ch 703.

[13] *White v White* [2001] AC 596.

[14] *Mesher v Mesher* (1973) [1980] 1 All ER 126, CA.

Unmarried couples may choose the 1989 Act. It is available to non-owners as well as joint owners, and can be used to require the owner, or joint owner, of land to settle it for the benefit of his or her child or children. Settlement in this case does *not*, according to the courts, mean changing the beneficial ownership of the land. It may involve the suspension of beneficial owner-ship—or of most of the rights in the bundle—for some years, while the house is held on trust for the use of the child concerned. This will enable one of the parents, typically the applicant, to live there with the child. It will always be followed up by a provision that the house is to be returned to its owner once the child is grown up—or sold, and its proceeds divided, if it is jointly owned. It will not lead to permanent capital provision for the child; ownership of the property will not be changed or transferred.

In effect, what the courts do under Schedule 1 of the Children Act 1989 is going to be the same as what is done under TLATA; but the Children Act will always be used if the house is not jointly owned, or if the aim of the application is to get the respondent to *buy* a house or to provide the money for purchase.

If this feels like a digression, it is. There are a number of pathways to the resolution of disputes about jointly owned property, and TLATA is not always an appropriate way to travel.

TRUSTS OF LAND IN BANKRUPTCY

In one case, however, the family-friendly provisions of section 15 of TLATA is actually a forbidden route. Here we must introduce a fifth case of joint ownership: it occurs when one of the co-owners is adjudicated bankrupt. At that point all his property vests in (i.e. now belongs to) his trustee in bankruptcy, who becomes a joint owner in his stead.

Inevitably the trustee in bankruptcy wants a sale; the other joint owner(s) may not; and so there will be an application to the court to resolve the issue. Section 15 of TLATA states that in this instance its provisions are not to be used. Instead, section 335A of the Insolvency Act 1986 operates on the section 14 application:

(2) On such an application the court shall make such an order as it thinks just and reasonable having regard to—

    (a) the interests of the bankrupt's creditors;
    (b) where the application is made in respect of land which includes a dwelling house which is or has been the home of the bankrupt or the bankrupt's spouse or former spouse—

    (i)   the conduct of the spouse or former spouse, so far as contributing to the bankruptcy,

    (ii) the needs and financial resources of the spouse or former spouse, and

    (iii) the needs of any children; and

all the circumstances of the case other than the needs of the bankrupt.

    (3) Where such application is made after the end of the period of one year beginning with the first vesting under Chapter IV of this Part of the bankrupt's estate in a trustee, the court shall assume, unless the circumstances of the case are exceptional, that the interests of the bankrupt's creditors outweigh all other considerations.

So there are two differences from section 15 of TLATA: one is that the bankrupt's own needs are irrelevant; the other is that one year after the bankruptcy, the creditors' needs become paramount. The courts have been fierce in their operation of this provision: except in exceptional circumstances, where the trustee in bankruptcy wants a sale, after that one year period has passed, a sale will be ordered. If this means that the family becomes homeless, so be it. That, the courts have said, is what debt and improvidence involve.[15] Why the severity of this rule?

It would be unfair and unrealistic to attribute it to a determination to see the family home as a capital asset in preference to its other functions, or to the law's preference for dynamic security and the wish for a fluid property market. What has drawn the legislation, and the courts, away from sympathy with the bankrupt's family is an awareness that the mortgage industry is an essential support for the supply of homes. Any reluctance to sell the family home in response to the demands of the family's creditors may, on the one hand, lead those creditors into debt and hardship; and it may, on the other hand and of wider significance, boost the costs of borrowing and make home ownership less accessible, as mortgagees try to share around the cost of the risk they incur. So the operation of section 14 on the bankruptcy of a joint owner is far more complex than a straight contest between small homeowner and big bank. Nevertheless, concerns have been voiced about the human rights implications of section 335A of the Insolvency Act 1986 and the courts' approach to it. It has been suggested that the policy of postponing sale only in exceptional circumstances may be an illegitimate interference with the bankrupt's and his family's right to respect for their private and family life and for their home. A recent High Court decision noted this argument,

---

[15] *Re Citro* [1991] Ch 142.

without finding that it influenced the outcome of the case before it.[16] But we are bound to hear more about this.

EQUITABLE ACCOUNTING

One matter not dealt with by TLATA is the business of equitable accounting. This is the name given to a set of principles built up by the courts over the years, by which joint owners may be required to make payments to each other, after sale of the property, as a result of what has happened during their joint ownership. Equitable accounting is a matter of personal obligations, not of property rights.

Equitable accounting covers four broad principles. Let us assume co-owners M and F, who own the property in the respective proportions 2/3 and 1/3. First, if M has financed an improvement to the property which has increased its value, after sale and after division of the sale proceeds F must in addition pay to M one third of the increase in value. Second, if for any period M took sole responsibility for the mortgage payments, again after division of the proceeds F must pay him one third of the total mortgage payments that he made. Third, if M lived alone in the property at any stage, he *may* be obliged to make a payment to F of two-thirds of the market rental value for that period. The old principle that rent was payable only if F had been forced out (because, of course, both co-owners are entitled to possession of the whole) has given place to a more flexible approach which regards relationship breakdown as a more realistic trigger for an obligation to pay rent. In practice, items two and three are generally regarded as cancelling each other out. Finally, if one joint owner received rent from the property without sharing it, he can be made to account to the other. So if M let the property out for part of the time while he had sole use of it, he will have to pay one-third of the rent received in that period to F when the house is sold.

The operation of equitable accounting principles is known as 'taking accounts' between the parties. It is time-wasting when some payments will cancel each other out. It is not relevant in divorce proceedings, where the court's discretionary jurisdiction is broad enough to make equitable accounting superfluous. It is scarcely necessary in proceedings under TLATA, since TLATA gives trustees the power to impose conditions on beneficiaries as a term of their being allowed to occupy the property, and the court can make an order in the same terms under section 14. The

---

[16] *Barca v Mears* [2004] EWHC 21170 (Ch).

continuing availability of the equitable accounting cases, as an alternative way of arguing about these issues, is unhelpful.

THE EXTERNAL FACE OF THE TRUST OF LAND

Finally, and squarely for the first time in this chapter, we turn to the pervasive conflict in land law: static versus dynamic security. Joint ownership has to exist behind a trust for the sake of safeguarding purchasers. How thoroughly has the law achieved this end?

Some safeguards are very simple. As has already been said, the number of trustees of the legal title is limited to four; there is a physical limit on the number of signatures a purchaser must find.

Along with that requirement goes another limitation; joint holders of a legal estate in land must be joint tenants. They cannot be tenants in common, and a legal joint tenancy cannot be severed. This is another tidying-up measure, motivated by the different tendencies of the two forms of joint ownership over time. Tenancy in common tends to proliferate, as individuals deal with their shares or pass them on to their children. Where there are originally two, there might be four after a number of years, and so on. The number of personnel involved will not get smaller unless one joint owner buys another out. Joint tenancy, however, has the opposite tendency. Every time one joint tenant dies, there will be a unification. A pair will become a singleton by survivorship. Four joint tenants will eventually become one, unless transfer is effected by the survivors at any point to themselves plus another. So joint tenancy is compulsory for the legal estate, in order to ensure that legal estates get simpler over time, rather than more complex.

But we do not want legal estates to get too simple. For if land is jointly owned, two trustees are needed in order for a purchaser to be sure that any beneficial interest he does not know about will be overreached. And here lies a difficulty; faced with a single legal owner offering to sell or mortgage land to him, how does a purchaser know that the seller is not a sole trustee?

This is to a large extent material that we have covered already; we have discussed the fact that social change, and the rise of the implied trust, mean that it is no longer possible to be sure that a sole owner is not a trustee. It *is* possible for a purchaser to be caught out, although conveyancing practice, in particular the enquiries routinely made about adult occupiers of the property, mean that instances are rare. Specifically to this chapter belong one safeguard, and one pitfall.

The safeguard relates to registered land. When joint owners purchase as beneficial tenants in common, the land registry must enter, against the register for the property, a restriction. A restriction is a direction to the effect that certain dispositions of the property cannot be registered. A restriction is entered, for example, when a bankruptcy order is made, at which point a restriction is entered forbidding the entry of any disposition; and in practice of course no purchaser will embark upon a disposition that cannot be validated by registration. The joint ownership restriction states that no disposition is to be registered if the transaction was carried out by a sole survivor of the tenants in common.

The point of this is to ensure that a purchaser is warned that he must ensure that the legal estate is sold or mortgaged to him by two trustees because overreaching will be needed. This is important because tenancy in common does not involve the right of survivorship. When one of two tenants in common dies, his share *may* vest in the survivor; but equally it may pass to someone else: Fred, say. Either way, of course, the survivor becomes the sole legal owner, because the legal estate was held on joint tenancy. Because there *may* be a Fred, the purchaser must make sure that overreaching happens. (This is very easily done; the transfer to the purchaser does two jobs, first appointing an additional trustee of the legal estate, and then transferring the property). By contrast, when the death of a beneficial joint tenant leaves a sole survivor, legal and equitable interests are united in that survivor. Thus there is no need for a joint ownership restriction, because there can be no Fred.

This does not quite work. The pitfall is that methods of severance of a beneficial joint tenancy, discussed above, mean that a beneficial joint tenancy can turn into a tenancy in common, without there being any dealing with the land register; so a restriction, which is now necessary, will not be entered. The corresponding problem in unregistered land—where the deeds will make clear that the seller is the survivor of beneficial joint tenants—is solved neatly by section 16 of TLATA, which (put simply) states that if there is no evidence of severance the purchaser can safely, and must, assume that the tenancy was unsevered. The draftsman failed to notice that the problem remains unsolved in registered land. To date, there are no reported disasters.

AFTERWORD

If this chapter feels messy, that is unavoidable. What we can see is the law's attempt to create a unitary format for trusts of land, regulated by

TLATA. The attempt does not produce a tidy body of law, for a number of reasons. First, because TLATA—in line with a great deal of English legislation—is not a codification. It does not try to state the whole of the law, and it only partially abolishes older law. What was not deemed to be broke was not fixed, and so we still have to look at quite elderly case law for the rules about severance, for example, or about equitable accounting. Another reason is that TLATA is not the answer to every form of trust. Where a trust of land runs into crisis because of family breakdown, the parties have to jump ship into the Matrimonial Causes Act 1973 and associated legislation designed with the flexibility needed for family breakdown. And in some cases the picture is untidy because of a simple mistake, as in the case of the hidden severance of a joint tenancy in registered land. A further reason for the untidiness of the picture is that provisions in TLATA are incomplete: the court is not actually told what to do on section 14 applications, merely given things to think about.

That last point is a very positive one; it is that incompleteness that gives hope for TLATA. Because the statute is not entirely prescriptive, there is room for it to adapt to different forms of co-ownership, and also to the new tide of thinking that is growing out of the Human Rights Act 1998. This is likely to be the source of major debate in land law over the next decade and beyond, particularly in the area of joint ownership, family breakdown and the balance between a joint owner's creditors and family.

BIBLIOGRAPHY

T. Allen 'The Human Rights Act (UK) and Property Law' in *Property and the Constitution* (Oxford, Hart Publishing, 1999).

H. Conway, 'Co-owners and Equitable Accounting: A Comparative and Commonwealth Analysis' in E. Cooke (ed), *Modern Studies in Property Law, vol III* (Oxford, Hart Publishing Ltd, 2005).

J. Dewar, 'Land, Law and the Family Home' in J. Dewar and S. Bright (eds), *Land Law, Themes and Perspectives* (Oxford: Oxford University Press, 1998).

G. Miller, (1999) 'Applications by the Trustee in Bankruptcy for Sale of the Family Home' *Insolvency Law and Practice*, 176.

O. Radley-Gardner, 'Chargees and Family Property' [2001] 1 Web J.C.L.I.

A. M. Prichard, 'Beneficial Joint Tenancies: A Riposte' [1987] *The Conveyancer and Property Lawyer* 273.

M. P. Thomson, 'Beneficial Joint Tenancies: A Reply to Professor Prichard' [1987] *The Conveyancer and Property Lawyer* 275.

M. P. Thomson 'Beneficial Joint Tenancies: A Case for Abolition?' [1987] *The Conveyancer and Property Lawyer* 29.

6

Mortgages

In his book *The Mystery of Capital*, Hernando de Soto asserts that the key to the prosperity of the West is our ability to unlock the capital value of our wealth. Capital, he explains, is wealth whose full potential is exploited; it is put to work rather than hoarded. If he is correct—and his book is convincing and has been extremely influential—then, after ownership rights, mortgages are the most important property right discussed in this book. They may be the key to wealth, and are certainly the key to current patterns of home ownership, in this country. We might say that the great discovery about real property in the twentieth century was this: that the home we cannot afford can itself be security for the loan that makes it affordable.

A mortgage is a security interest. We have said a lot about mortgages already; and mortgages are now (though they were not in 1925) very much part of the vocabulary and concerns of most adults. But most people use the word incorrectly, speaking of something like 'getting a mortgage for a house' to mean getting a loan to finance a purchase. In fact a mortgage is what is given in exchange for the loan. It is a property right, given to the Building Society or other lender, which makes the house liable and available to pay the loan. If the loan is not repaid on time, the lender can sell the house and take as much of the proceeds as he needs in order to recover his money. He can do this because he holds a mortgage.

Familiar to most homeowners but perhaps not to all law students are the different kinds of mortgage, depending upon their purpose and the way they are re-paid. Acquisition mortgages are part and parcel of a purchase: a loan is made to a buyer, who transfers the money lent to the seller. Two things then happen: the land (whether freehold or leasehold) is transferred to the buyer, and the lender (who made the purchase possible) acquires a mortgage as the security for his loan. A post-acquisition mortgage is when an already-owned property is used as security for a loan, whose purpose could be one of several. It could be a refinancing of the acquisition mortgage (known as a re-mortgage), consolidating one or more earlier loans, perhaps at a better rate of interest. It could be to pay for an improvement of the land, such as an extension. Or it could be for something quite different, the most common example being a loan to finance a business. And a business loan may be raised on the security of the business premises, or of the businessman's home. The most important element of the mortgage contract (since a mortgage, like a lease, is a property right and also a contract) is the arrangement made for paying off the loan. A repayment mortgage provides simply for the repayment of the loan in instalments, so that the first month's payment will be very nearly all interest while the last will be all capital. An endowment mortgage provides for the purchase, alongside the land, of an insurance policy which is calculated to pay off the loan when it matures at the end of the term of the mortgage—perhaps twenty years ahead. Meanwhile the borrower only pays off interest. The problem with endowment mortgages is that while the borrower may get a windfall if the endowment policy is larger than needed when it matures, he will be in serious difficulties if it does not grow as anticipated. Endowment mortgages are not for the risk-averse, nor for times of recession.

Finally, a property may be mortgaged several times, simultaneously, and so a mortgage may be a first mortgage or a subsequent one. Where a home costing £200,000 is purchased with the aid of a loan for £150,000, there is potential for the property to be used again as security for a further loan. In theory, there may be one or more subsequent mortgages for anything up to another £50,000. Suppose there is a second mortgage in return for a loan of £30,000, and a third mortgage for another £10,000. It is easy to see that the first mortgagee is much more secure than the second or third, and that therefore the cost of borrowing rises as the limits of the property's value are reached.

THE MECHANICS OF MORTGAGES

Before 1925, a mortgage was achieved by the borrower conveying an ownership right to the lender, on terms that the latter would convey it back when the loan was repaid. In early medieval times the estate conveyed was a lease; from about the fifteenth century onwards the borrower had to convey the fee simple (or whatever his own estate was) to the lender. Draconian rules that kept people to the very letter of the contract—so that if the money was one day late the property was lost to the borrower—were mitigated over the years by the courts of equity, but even so the transaction was objectionable. It was a legal fiction, which is undesirable in itself. Worse, it left the borrower with no legal estate in his own land. Yet the reformers of the early twentieth century found the problem difficult; there was no such thing as a mortgage, in the sense of a pure security right, and they were reluctant to invent one. Had they done so, it is unlikely that conveyancers would have been willing to use it. There was considerable difficulty, as it was, in getting conveyancers to trust the new mechanisms. Many of them insisted for some years on continuing, pointlessly, to use pre-1925 conveyancing documentation alongside the new material.

The 1925 legislation solved the mortgages problem by using a different legal fiction. Instead of the mortgagee (i.e. the lender, to whom a mortgage is granted) being given the fee simple, he would be given a lease (not an entirely new idea, of course). Moreover, there were two ways of doing this. He could be given a 3000-year lease, on terms that it would terminate when the loan was repaid; this was known as a 'mortgage by demise'. Alternatively he could be given a 'charge by way of legal mortgage', or legal charge, which meant that he had exactly the same rights and remedies as if he had a 3000-year lease whose terms stated that it would terminate when the loan was repaid. A mortgage of a lease, similarly, takes the form of a sublease, or gives the lender the rights and remedies of a sub-lessee. What was the difference between the two forms? If property rights are indeed bundles it is hard to see that the content of a 3000-year lease is any different from a bundle consisting of all the rights one would have if one had a 3000-year lease.

A lease was not what a lender wanted or needed, any more than the fee simple had been. But the new fiction had some advantages. The main one was that the mortgagor (the borrower, who grants the mortgage) could keep the fee simple. He therefore retained a property right superior to that of the lender, which was how it should be. The lender got something less than what the borrower kept. For another, the possibility of using concurrent leases meant that second, third, etc mortgages could be added into the structure without their having to be in completely different form (as was the case when the first mortgagee took the fee simple). And for another, the matter was dealt with in a way that looked as if the reformers had done it without inventing a new property right (even though they had, because this was not a conventional lease). The new conceptualisation of a mortgage also enabled a lot of the old theory to survive; in particular, just as a pre-1925 mortgagee had the right to take possession of the property by virtue of having a fee simple, so today's mortgagee has the right to possession of the mortgaged property by virtue of having a lease, or of having a lessee's rights.

The mortgage by demise, however, met its own demise in the Land Registration Act 2002, which states that a registered estate cannot be mortgaged by demise, only by a charge. This is the one restriction on an owner's powers that the 2002 Act specifies, and it means that we no longer have to accept that a mortgagee is the lessee of the mortgaged property. But we do have to regard him as having the same rights and remedies, which is just as uncomfortable and inappropriate. The registered mortgage of a registered estate is known as a 'registered charge'; and, of course, a mortgage of a registered estate is not a legal one unless it is registered (this is the effect of s. 27 of the Land Registration Act 2002).

As to formalities, it can be deduced from what has been said already about other estates and interests in land that for a mortgage to be legal (and it is one of the legal estates listed as possible in s. 1 of the Law of Property Act 1925) it must be created by deed and must be registered; failure to register generates an equitable mortgage. An equitable mortgage will also arise if the borrower himself has only an equitable estate; or where one of two or more joint owners mortgages just his own equitable interest.

Since the Middle Ages mortgages have not really been self-regulated. The courts of equity became involved at an early stage in legal mortgages, in order to protect the borrower from the consequences of having to make the wrong deal—to transfer ownership, rather than just a security right. The major intervention was in the creation of the 'equitable right to redeem'. For the common law ruled that repayment of the loan had to be made on the date set in the mortgage contract. If the borrower paid late he lost the land, but still owed the debt. This was so obviously inequitable, on any meaning of that word, that the courts of equity preserved the borrower's right to pay back the loan after the due date. This remains important; in any domestic or commercial mortgage, the date for redemption is set very shortly after the commencement of the mortgage—six months into the mortgage term, or sooner. Most mortgages provide, in addition, that if one interest payment is missed, the whole debt falls due. This is done so as to make available to the mortgagee some of his statutory rights which can only be exercised when the legal date for redemption has passed, in particular the power of sale. A homeowner taking on a domestic mortgage for a twenty-five year term would be startled to be told that, strictly speaking, he must pay all the money back in six months' time, and that his having twenty-five years in which to pay is merely a concession. This is another aspect of mortgages where what is wanted is achieved by a fiction (because if all is going well, neither party wants the loan to be paid off in six months' time).

Equity's involvement in the mortgage relationship was so significant that the term 'equity of redemption' is used to describe the sum total of the mortgagor's rights while the mortgage is in existence, including the equitable right to redeem; and this is so even post-1925 when the mortgagor's ownership remains intact subject to the mortgage. The word 'equity' is used in everyday language to describe the value of the property that is not accounted for by the mortgage debt, so that a property worth £200,000 purchased with the aid of a loan of £150,000 has an equity of £50,000. If the market falls and the property comes to be worth £140,000 it is said to be in 'negative' equity, which is a serious problem for both parties because the sale of the property will leave a debt outstanding.

So: once we get into the more technical aspects of mortgages we become aware of a number of tensions. One, already touched on, is that the way the law describes mortgages is rather different from the layman's understanding. Another is the prevalence, even today, of legal fictions: leases and contractual deadlines are used in an unusual way. And already we are seeing aspects of the need to protect one party from another. For the mortgagee is in a very powerful position. The mortgagor is dependent upon him, often for the purchase of his land and, in all cases, for the continuance of his ownership. And so a lot of the law of mortgages is about the protection of the mortgagor—the borrower—who may be very much the underdog in the relationship. But this protection exists in tension with the fact that a mortgagee takes an interest in land in exchange for money and so is a purchaser. The preference of the 1925 reformers and of the twentieth century courts is for the protection of a purchaser: and a mortgagee qualifies for all the purchaser protections incorporated in modern land law and particularly in registered land.

This means that where the law is dealing with mortgagor and mortgagee, as a duo in a continuing relationship, much has been done to protect the mortgagor, to enable him to keep his property and to prevent the mortgagee from exploiting the power imbalance between them. But if we turn the mortgagee outwards from that duo, to face the rest of the world, he becomes a favoured and protected species. Thus when the mortgagee really has acquired the ability to sell the property—when all the protections for the mortgagor have failed—the courts have taken care to enable him to sell freely, and have restricted the mortgagor's ability to dictate the terms or the timing of the sale. And when the mortgagee encounters third parties—co-owners or tenants, in particular—whose interest in the property threatens to dilute or destroy his security, the courts have done everything possible to enable the mortgagee to walk

away from them with a clean and marketable title. This gives rise to some
hard cases, because there are contests between innocent parties: mortgagees on the one hand, and, on the other, individuals whose home or
property is threatened by someone *else's* failure to repay a loan: their
landlord, or their lover.

The policy of land law is to protect the market. Protecting mortgagees
and reducing the risk they undertake stimulates the market by keeping
the cost of borrowing down. That is not a heartless commercial aim. The
mortgagee is a bank, but he finances, and stands for, countless underdogs:
ordinary people buying their homes. This is easily forgotten. Difficulties
have arisen when the courts' sympathy for the lover or the tenant makes it
hard to see the nameless millions represented by the mortgagee; but in
most cases subsequent decisions or legislation have come to the rescue
and capitalism, in the sense described by de Soto, has triumphed.

It does not have to be this way. Land ownership is not a human right,
although having a home probably is; and land ownership is not the only
way to have a home and may not be the best way. But our current society
as a whole has taken some sort of collective decision that this is the right
way for us, and mortgages have made it possible. The law's firm policy of
protecting mortgagees as purchasers is consistent with this decision.

RIGHTS, REMEDIES AND PROTECTIONS IN THE MORTGAGE RELATIONSHIP

The law's approach to the mortgagor/mortgagee relationship has been to
ask which elements are necessary as part of the giving of security, and to
be restrictive in allowing anything non-essential to that relationship.
Thus the mortgagee may control the mortgagor's use of property insofar
as that is necessary to preserve the security, but the courts will declare
void any contractual term that looks like the taking of an unfair advantage; and when the mortgagor is in default, the law is particularly careful
to give him every possible chance to put things right rather than lose the
property.

CONTROLLING THE MORTGAGE RELATIONSHIP

A mortgage, like a lease, is a contract, and contains extensive terms regu-
lating the behaviour of both parties but principally the mortgagor. Most
mortgage contracts, certainly the domestic ones and to a considerable
extent commercial ones too, are 'off the peg': they are standard deals,
available on a take-it-or-leave-it basis with no scope for negotiation. But

the terms of that standard deal are framed in the context of centuries of control of mortgages by the courts; they are made in the shadow of the law and of what the law will allow.

Most mortgages provide that the borrower is not allowed to let the property without the mortgagee's consent, overriding the provision in section 99 of the Law of Property Act 1925 that gives the mortgagor a limited power to grant leases. That contractual prohibition is backed up by a provision that there shall be a restriction on the register, preventing the registration of any dealing with the property without the mortgagee's consent. The point of this is that if the mortgagor defaults, the mortgagee will want to sell, and of course will get a better price if the property is not burdened by leases. Accordingly the cost of borrowing when a property is 'bought to let' is higher than for a normal domestic mortgage.

How far can the mortgagee go in restricting the use of the mortgaged property? A large body of law has been built up around the doctrine of 'clogs and fetters'. This is the antiquely-named principle that there should be no 'clogs' or unnecessary restrictions on the equity of redemption, nor any fetter on the mortgagor's right to redeem the mortgage, early if he wishes to. Much of the case law in this area concerns nineteenth- and early twentieth-century commercial contracts, often for mortgages of public houses. Such properties are often subject to the very obvious restriction of being tied houses: one particular brand of beer is to be sold. Where the brewery is also the mortgagee, there is potential for exploitation. So a mortgage contract that provided for the pub to sell the mortgagee's beer during part of the mortgage term was acceptable to the court. By contrast, a term that the pub was to be tied forever, even after the debt was repaid, was not, because the mortgagor has to be able to retrieve his security in an unencumbered form. More recent cases have looked at this sort of problem as one of restraint of trade, preferring to use this more up-to-date doctrine rather than the old equitable principle. The courts have been particularly fierce about deals that give the mortgagee the right, in the form of an option, to buy the mortgaged property; this is not allowed unless it can be clearly seen as part of a separate deal— even if it does not obviously disadvantage the borrower. Terms preventing the redemption of the mortgage for several years have also been declared void.

Most of these cases are remote from today's domestic borrower. Building Societies do not take options to buy the property, and they do not force commercial deals upon their borrowers. What they do force upon them is the ordinary, non-negotiable mortgage contract, which provides for the rate of interest—usually the most important, perhaps the only important, element of the deal for the borrower. It may also impose penalties for early redemption, perhaps of something like three month's interest if the mortgage is redeemed within the first three years. Surprisingly, the latter type of provision does not seem to have been attacked under the 'clogs and fetters' doctrine, even though it obviously fetters the ability to redeem. Perhaps it survives because Building Societies keep such penalties within affordable bounds; perhaps because domestic borrowers are unwilling to risk litigation with financial giants. The courts *will* in theory intervene to strike down an inordinately high lending rate, but they have not done so in standard, 'off the peg' domestic mortgage deals. The equitable doctrine of unconscionable bargain has been used to outlaw excessive rates in commercial mortgages, but only where the parties have clearly been in an unequal bargaining position. Sections 137 and 138 of the Consumer Credit Act 1974 enable the court to adjust an 'extortionate credit bargain'; but the provisions have been rarely used. They do not apply to Building Societies or to local authority lenders; and where they have been invoked, the difficulty has been that the borrowers have been in a precarious financial situation at the time of the deal, with the result that a high interest rate was seen as justified in the light of the risk the mortgagee was undertaking. Thus borrowers who are financially secure and a good risk will not need protection; it tends to be those who are in financial difficulties who resort to expensive mortgage deals, and the courts are therefore unwilling to intervene. The individual is allowed to go under, in the interests of maintaining a mortgage market for the majority.

CONTROLLING REMEDIES FOR DEFAULT

The mortgagee has a whole battery of powers, all aimed at getting his money back. Most obviously, the loan contract itself enables him to sue the debtor; and that right survives even after sale of the property, if the sale has not discharged the loan. But the whole point of a mortgage is to enable the mortgagee to take the property in satisfaction of the debt; and so he has a wide range of powers for use, in effect though not always in form, when something has gone wrong.

The most notorious of the mortgagee's rights is his right to possession of the property. This is anomalous, for it is a right not a remedy. It arises, as one old case put it, 'as soon as the ink is dry on the mortgage'. Historically this made sense, because the mortgagee was in fact the owner of the property. In practice the mortgagee is normally only going to want possession in order to sell. In the case of commercial premises, he might want possession in order to manage, and perhaps let, the property in order to maximise income from it, or to preserve its value, if the mortgagor is failing to manage it properly and where immediate sale is not a good option.

The difficulty with taking possession in order to manage the property is that the mortgagee is put under a very heavy duty of care and is strictly answerable for the profits of his possession. If he does not make as much money out of the property as he could have done, he is liable to the mortgagor. Therefore he is likely to rely not on his right to possession, but on his statutory right to appoint a receiver under section 109 of the Law of Property Act 1925. This works rather differently in that the receiver is deemed to act as the agent of the mortgagor, and is not so strictly liable for any failure to make a profit. The appointment of a receiver must be in writing, and can only be done if the mortgagee's power of sale has become exercisable (see below).

Where the property is domestic the right to possession is far more strictly circumscribed. The mortgagee will not take possession without a court order, because of the potential for violence and the risk that the mortgagee will commit an offence, under the Criminal Law Act 1977. And if he wants a court order, the provisions of section 36 of the Administration of Justice Act 1970, and of section 8 of the Administration of Justice Act 1973, state that proceedings must be adjourned or suspended if it appears to the court that the mortgagor is going to be able to clear the arrears within the term of the mortgage.

That is the combined effect of those two sections; there are two of them, because the 1970 version was inadequately drafted and appeared to state that the mortgagor must catch up his arrears within a relatively short time in order to escape an order for possession. The effect of this was dramatic where a mortgage included a provision that if two monthly instalments were missed, the whole loan became due. Repayment within, say, six months is impossible in these circumstances. Hence the 1973 qualification, extending the catching-up time to the whole mortgage period. The sections taken together probably save the right to possession from a human rights challenge, because they do allow the mortgagor a lot of leeway and ensure that the most the mortgagee can demand is the repayment of the loan within the intended term of the mortgage.[1]

---

[1] As to the use of human rights arguments as a defence to possession proceedings, see Chapter 7 at p. 163.

However, when arrears do build up it is not uncommon for a mortgagor simply to give up, move out, and give the keys of the property to the mortgagor. In these circumstances no court order is needed for possession, and the statutes and case law on the permissibility of possession are irrelevant. Whether or not this is a deprivation of possessions or an interference with the borrower's right to respect for his home is debatable; surely not, since the action is a voluntary one on the borrower's part.

The sequel to possession, then, is generally sale. It has been suggested that the mortgagee's current right to possession throughout the mortgage term, anomalous as it is, be replaced with a right to sale with vacant possession, subject to the court's discretion to postpone the sale on terms. That would then restrict possession to those cases where it is truly appropriate. As things stand, there is nothing to prevent the mortgagee from selling, in cases where he has the right to do so, without first obtaining possession; but he will not find a buyer, because a purchaser would be unwilling to 'buy a lawsuit', as we say. But when does the mortgagee have the right to sell? This is perhaps an odd question because *this* response to default may be seen as the whole point of the mortgage. Nevertheless it is not automatic.

In fact, two things must have happened before the mortgagee can sell. The power of sale must have arisen; and it must have become exerciseable. So there are two stages, and two things to check in any practical scenario.

For the power of sale to arise, the mortgage must be by deed, and the loan must be due for repayment. The latter requirement is the main point of the contractual date for redemption, fixed artificially early even in a long-term mortgage. An equitable mortgage will normally not be made by deed, of course, and the mortgagee would instead have to seek a court order enabling him to sell as if he were a legal mortgagee. For the latter, the power of sale arises without the need for an order, if both these conditions are met (i.e. the mortgage is by deed, and the loan is due for payment). But that is not enough. The power must also have become exercisable, which happens on the occurrence of any one of three things. Either notice requiring payment of the mortgage money has been served on the mortgagor and he has not paid in full within three months of service of that notice; or some interest under the mortgage is in arrears and has been unpaid for two months or more; or there has been a breach of some other provision in the mortgage, for example the prohibition on letting. This last point is rather reminiscent of the landlord's right to forfeit a lease. The twin requirements that the power of sale must have arisen and must have become exercisable are protections for the borrower, because they will deter a purchaser from dealing with a mortgagee who is not entitled to sell. If the power of sale has not arisen, the purchaser will take only the mortgagee's own interest; and if the power has not become exercisable, the mortgagor may be able to set aside the sale if he can show that the purchaser had notice of the problem.

Once the protections have all failed and sale is inevitable the mortgagee is able to take control of proceedings. He must sell the property for the best price reasonably obtainable, taking proper care to advertise it and ouchlike, and he may not sell to himself or to his agent or employee; but timing of the sale is up to the mortgagee. He need not, for example, wait for a rise in the market. This is another balancing; all the mortgagee wants and can have is his loan repaid, but he is not allowed to sell at a knock-down price that would just cover the loan and his costs. What the mortgagor wants is as much of a surplus—the financial equity—as possible; and the mortgagee's duty goes most of the way to ensuring this. Nevertheless, repossession sales do have a certain flavour; properties are likely to be cheaper than some, and there will be no 'chain' involved, but they are notorious for being in poor condition. There is no proud and anxious householder to show buyers round. The theoretical basis of the mortgagee's duty is that it lies in equity rather than in tort; the 'duty of care' is not the same as that invoked in the negligence cases. But the practical consequence of this distinction may be minimal.

Once the sale is completed, the mortgagee must apply the proceeds in a specific order; and this determines where any shortfall will lie. He must first apply the proceeds to redeem any securities prior to his own; he might, of course, not be the first mortgagee, and the first mortgagee gets first cut. Then he pays the costs of sale, and then his own loan. Next, any still-remaining proceeds go to repay any subsequent mortgagees; and finally, the surplus goes to the borrower.

Far more Draconian than sale is foreclosure. Foreclosure is the mortgagee's ability to bring the equity of redemption to an end by taking property and extinguishing the borrower's ownership. This requires a court order, vesting the mortgagor's ownership right—the fee simple or the lease—in the mortgagee (whereas before 1925, of course, no order was needed as the estate was vested already). The mortgagee may then keep the property or sell it, but there will be no surplus for the mortgagor, who loses everything. For this reason, the court order is made in two stages, allowing the mortgagor a six-month period in which to repay the loan. Forfeiture is rare today, and the court has power, on an application for Foreclosure, to order sale instead; and it is hard to imagine the court not doing so. This may be why the mortgagee's right to forfeit has not yet been the subject of a human rights challenge. If challenge comes before abolition of the right to forfeit, it is scarcely in doubt that section 91 of the Law of Property Act 1925 must be found incompatible with Article 1 of Protocol 1 to the Convention; for the legislature here is giving the lender a right that amounts to confiscation of property, in a manner disproportionate to the purpose it serves and without compensation. This must follow *a fortiori* from the decision of the European Court of Human Rights in *Pye v UK*,[2] and the more so because the alternative remedy, sale, is available and makes proper provision for the borrower to get whatever value is left for his own estate after the sale.

THIRD PARTIES, AND THE PROTECTION OF MORTGAGEES

PRIORITIES: MORTGAGEE SELLS THE TITLE HE TOOK

The tale of the law of mortgages is rather like a piece of music whose harmonic climax is the sale of the property and the consequent redemption of the loan—even though most mortgages are paid off in an uncontroversial manner and never involve an exploration of the rules relating to sale. And because this is the anticipated climax, a great deal of law is devoted to ensuring that the mortgagee has a clean title which he can pass on to a purchaser. This he will have if, and only if, he took a clean title at the point when the mortgage was granted. This takes us back to issues that are examined in Chapter 3. Anything enforceable against a purchaser at the point of the mortgage will bind the mortgagee and will therefore bind any purchaser who buys from the mortgagee. By contrast, any interest created by the borrower subsequent to the mortgage, and without the mortgagee's authorisation, will have no effect on the purchaser who buys from the mortgagee. The mortgagee's purchaser takes what the mortgagee took.

---

[2] ECtHR, Application no. 44302/02 (2005). Forfeiture proceedings could be challenged on the basis that s. 91 is incompatible with the mortgagor's right to respect for his home and/or with his right to peaceful enjoyment of his possessions, in accordance with the House of Lords' ruling in *Kay & Ors v London Borough of Lambeth, Leeds City Council v Price & Ors* [2006] UKHL 10. See Chapter 7 at p. 163.

This means that at the point of sale, if there is any dispute about burdens on the title, it is necessary to look back to the point when the mortgage was granted so as to see what is the title that the mortgagee is able to transmit.

Put like that, the answer is simple. If the mortgagor's title is registered and the charge is registered, the mortgagee is bound by any burden whose priority was, at the point when the mortgage was granted, protected by section 29 of the Land Registration Act 2002;[3] that is, by anything on the register, by any overriding interests in existence at that point, and by the obligations contained in the lease if the mortgaged property is leasehold.[4] If the mortgagor's title is unregistered, the mortgagee will be bound by any interests registered under the Land Charges Acts, and in addition by all unregistrable legal interests, and by any unregistrable equitable interests of which he has notice.

Some examples may help, both in seeing how the mechanics work and also in seeing what is the practical effect of a mortgagee being bound, or not being bound, by a given interest (and we shall limit the discussion to registered titles). Indeed, these issues bring together a number of principles that have been discussed already in earlier chapters, so what follows may be useful as consolidation. The B Building Society (BBS) took a registered charge over Whiteacre in 2000, in return for a loan to the owner, O, to finance O's business (O is the registered proprietor of a 999-year lease; but it does not matter, for any of these examples, whether he is a long-leaseholder or the freeholder). Now, O is in default and the BBS is selling. It sells, obviously, O's lease; and section 29 of the Land Registration Act 2002 makes it clear that the purchaser will be bound by all the tenant's obligations in that lease. But the A Building Society (ABS) took a first legal mortgage of the lease in 1998 when O purchased it. BBS therefore took its registered charge subject to the prior registered charge in ABS' favour, and ABS gets its loan repaid first. Moreover, in 1999

---

[3] It is perhaps worth mentioning a small complication in parenthesis here. A mortgage, being an interest in land, can be transferred; X Building Society can transfer its interest—its debt, and the security for it—to Y Building Society (YBS). If this happens, then the title that YBS takes is determined by s. 30 of the Land Registration Act rather than by s. 29. However, it is easy to see from a comparison of the two sections that the end result is the same.

[4] Another complication, again in parenthesis: if the mortgagor's title is registered but the mortgage is not registered then section 29 is of no assistance, and moreover the mortgage is merely equitable. The effect of section 28 of the Land Registration Act 2002 in such a case would be that the mortgage would take effect subject to all legal interests in the property and to any equitable interests in existence at that point.

O granted to his neighbour an easement over part of Whiteacre; perhaps a right of way over the end of the garden. It was a legal easement, created by registration in accordance with section 27 of the Land Registration Act 2002, and so as a registered burden in 2000 it bound BBS in accordance with section 29. Therefore BBS sells the land subject to the easement. We can play with variations on this theme: if the easement was acquired in that year by informal means, for example by long use,[5] there may be nothing on the register, but the easement is legal and is therefore an overriding interest under paragraph 3 of Schedule 1, and the result is the same. But if the easement is equitable it probably did not bind BBS because it is unlikely to be noted on the register and cannot be an overriding interest—because paragraph 3 is only for legal interests, and it is unlikely that the holder of an easement would be in actual occupation of the property so as to benefit from paragraph 2.

If the property is sold by ABS rather than by BBS, then whether or not ABS is bound by the 1999 easement would depend on whether or not the grant was authorised by ABS. If it was authorised, then sale is subject to the grant; if it was not authorised, then the easement disappears at the point of sale—or, rather, at the point of an order for possession of the property—and ABS can sell the property free of the easement. The effect of the easement on the value of the land is of course a factor in a mortgagee's decision whether or not to permit the grant of the easement.

Similar examples can be constructed if the interest created in 1999 is a lease. The outcome depends upon whether or not the mortgagor's statutory power to lease the property has been excluded by ABS as it normally would be; an unauthorised lease in 1999 will not bind ABS, but it remains valid between O and the tenant, and would bind BBS if it is a legal lease appearing on the register or, being too short for registration, is an overriding interest under paragraph 1 of Schedule 3 to the Land Registration Act 2002. Even an equitable lease will bind BBS if the tenant is in actual occupation so that the lease falls within paragraph 2 of Schedule 3.

That example moves us on from the preceding, relatively uncomplicated, ones which did not involve third party claimants in actual occupation of the property. Actual occupation causes, or at least has caused, greater problems, as we have seen. It is problematic because the interests

---

[5] For the law on prescription and other informal methods of acquiring easements, see Chapter 8.

of those in actual occupation tend to be substantial—they may have a
long lease, or a beneficial interest under a trust, so that the effect of their
interest having priority may be disastrous to the value of the security.
Where the occupier has a beneficial interest, it is likely to be
undocumented, and the occupier may be unaware of the nature of his
interest until the matter is litigated much later. In all cases, the interests
of those in actual occupation may be unnoticed by the purchaser if he
does not inspect properly (few of us do!) or at all (mortgagees rarely do).
And the legislation itself is defective in that it does not cater for all
possible circumstances, although the 2002 statute does better than did the
Land Registration Act 1925. Let us look at some of the permutations.

PRIORITIES: ACTUAL OCCUPATION INTERESTS

Again, O bought Whiteacre in 1998 with the aid of a loan from ABS,
and took a further loan in 2000 from BBS, each loan being secured by
separate mortgages. Let us suppose that O got married in 1999. Mrs O
had some savings, and when they got married she paid off some of the
acquisition mortgage. We are instantly in difficulties. Did she do this as
a wedding present? Or not, so that we can say she takes a beneficial
interest under a resulting trust? It is possible to construct facts and
conversations that could be interpreted as giving rise to a common
intention construction trust or even proprietary estoppel. At any rate, let
us suppose that by one of these means, in 2000 when O is negotiating
his second mortgage, Mrs O already has a 40% beneficial interest, while
40% of the property's value is still accounted for by the acquisition
mortgage. She cannot register her interest,[6] and it may not occur to her
that she has it. But she has an actual occupation overriding interest
under paragraph 2; and BBS will be bound by it, as was Williams and
Glyn's Bank by Mrs Boland.[7]

This brings us straight back to the subject matter of Chapter 3. The
Boland scenario was unforeseen by the 1925 legislators, as they did not
regard an equitable co-owner as having an interest *in the land*, only in the
sale proceeds. It took a re-conceptualisation of these property rights in
the 1970s to create the problem. It is worth pausing to consider, in more
detail than we did in Chapter 3, the context in which Mrs O's claim
comes to light and the difficulties it causes. Mrs O will make her claim
when BBS takes possession proceedings against O. She is saying: 'you

[6] Land Registration Act 2002, s. 32; see Chapter 3 at pp. 42–3.
[7] *Williams and Glyn's Bank Ltd* [1981] AC 487; see Chapter 3 at p. 52.

took your mortgage subject to my interest: and whereas you thought that the whole of the equity was available to you as security (60% of the value), your security is only 20% of the value of the property'. The consequences of this are, first, that in order to get an order for sale at all, BBS has to explore the provisions of sections 14 and 15 of the Trusts of Land and Appointment of Trustees Act 1996, because it holds a mortgage of only one co-owner's share and therefore has to obtain an order for sale of co-owned property against the will of the other owner;[8] and if it does obtain such an order, it is likely to find the security inadequate to discharge the loan.

That, as we saw in Chapter 3, is why *Boland* was seen as such a disaster for the mortgage industry and therefore for home-owning in general. The interest is substantial, and although it is visible (because para. 2 of Sched. 3 to the Land Registration Act 2002 says it must be, thus straightening out a confusion under the 1925 Act), it is unseen, because mortgagees do not usually inspect; and it wrecks the security.

However, things were not as bad as they seemed. The obvious first point to make is that the occupying beneficial owner is only a problem to a purchaser, including of course a mortgagee, if he deals with a sole owner. If there are two or more trustees of the legal estate, any other beneficial interests are overreached and will not trouble the purchaser. A mortgagee taking a charge from joint owners has nothing to fear from *Boland* (although, as we shall see, there is a different hazard to face where there are joint mortgagors).

For those who deal with a sole owner (and there is no standard practice of insisting on the appointment of a second trustee of a legal estate, although that would be a simple solution to the problem under discussion), small points have been tidied up to make the operation of the actual occupation principle cleaner. The 2002 Act states that occupation must be obvious, which will rule out some claimants. And it states that where the occupation is of only part of the property (perhaps a separate flat) the occupier's interest is overriding only in relation to that part. Moreover, it puts onto a statutory footing a decision made by the courts under the 1925 Act, namely that the time for determination of actual occupation status is the making of the disposition (what the layman calls 'completion': the day when people move house) and not registration. This is not the case for other overriding interests. Thus if a Tree Preservation Order takes effect as a local land charge between completion and registration,

---

[8] See Chapter 5 at p. 106.

the mortgagee is bound by it (because local land charges are a separate category of overriding interests). But if the owner's partner moves into the house and acquires an equitable interest in it between completion and registration, the mortgagee is not bound. Underlying this rule is a decision (made initially by the courts and now enshrined in legislation) about the sort of interests that *ought* to bind a mortgagee. If and when electronic conveyancing becomes a reality the rule will become otiose because there will be no gap, at least in theory.

However, the effect of *Boland* today is best seen in the contrast between acquisition mortgages, where interests like Mrs Boland's cannot (on the current state of the authorities) bind a mortgagee, and post-acquisition mortgages. In the latter case the combined effect of case law and conveyancing practice is that a mortgagee will nearly always be safe. Here is how the law arrived at this position.

THE RESPONSE TO *BOLAND*

(1) Acquisition mortgages and the effect of *Cann*

The charge in *Boland* was not an acquisition mortgage; the mortgagee came on the scene when both Mr Boland's legal estate and Mrs Boland's equitable interest were in place, and the precise time when those two forms of ownership came into effect did not matter. But what happens when property is bought by a sole legal owner, with the aid of a contribution from another who therefore takes a beneficial interest in the property? Can an acquisition mortgagee be bound by the equitable co-owner's interest? Initially it was thought that this could indeed happen because the logical sequence of events is as follows: first, the buyer completes his purchase; secondly, the equitable co-ownership takes effect, through a resulting or a common intention constructive trust; thirdly, the mortgage takes effect. If, and only if, during this sequence of events the beneficial co-owner is in actual occupation of the house (by design, because of an agreement that the buyer should take possession early, or by accident because keys were released too early) then his interest is given overriding status by that occupation and takes priority to the mortgagee. And the mortgagee loses priority to a third-party right arising from a deal that the mortgagee could not prevent and could not detect, and taking effect in the theoretical interval between purchase and mortgage—known, famously, as the *scintilla temporis*, which means a very brief moment, or the twinkling of an eye.

Facts following this pattern reached the House of Lords in *Abbey*

National Building Society v Cann.[9] George Cann bought a house for his
mother, Daisy, to live in. She paid most of the purchase price, but he
raised the balance, £4,000, as a loan secured by a mortgage to Abbey
National. When he defaulted on the mortgage repayments, Daisy resisted
the mortgagee's possession proceedings on the basis that her interest,
combined with her actual occupation of the house for about 35 minutes
before completion, took priority to that of the Building Society.

The House of Lords' solution to this problem was, first, to rule that
Daisy was not in actual occupation, given the particular facts. She was not
there in person, although her furniture was being moved in. This solved
the mortgagee's problem in this particular case. But, secondly, the Lords
solved the problem for the future by declaring that in any event the gap
between purchase and mortgage simply does not exist. There is no *scintilla*. The buyer acquires a fee simple already burdened by a mortgage,
and after that double and simultaneous event there is time for third party
rights to be created.

The decision in *Cann* dramatically reduces the wrecking potential of
Boland by making it virtually impossible for an acquisition mortgagee to
be bound by an unforeseen equitable interest in the property. The *Cann*
solution will only fail if there is so long a gap between the purchase of the
fee simple and its mortgage that the denial of the existence of the *scintilla*
loses credibility. How big a gap that might be has yet to be seen (24 hours?
24 days? 24 minutes?).

Cann is a heavy-handed piece of judicial law-making, a denial of logic
and of practical reality motivated by what are euphemistically called policy considerations but could perhaps be more accurately labelled socio-
political manipulation. Contrast the many cases where the courts have
refused to change the law on the basis that that would be to usurp the role
of Parliament.[10] Among their lordships' reasons for their decision was the
assertion that when George Cann acquires the freehold, purchased with
the aid of a mortgage, he never acquires anything more than the 'equity of
redemption'. This is untrue, and a harking back to pre-1925 days. He does
indeed acquire a fee simple, to be burdened not eliminated by the mortgage. Insofar as the first mortgage does not exhaust the equity in the
property he can mortgage that fee simple again. He truly does acquire the
fee simple, and could, in theory, fail to execute the mortgage. He would of

---

[9] [1991] 1 AC 56.
[10] The example seen in this book is the reluctance to use estoppel as a way of rescuing
informal contracts; see Chapter 4, p. 89

course be in breach of contract with the mortgagor, liable in unjust enrichment, and possibly also criminally liable. The fact that this is very unlikely to happen, because the conveyancing will be in the hands of a solicitor acting for the mortgagee as well as for the mortgagor, does not weaken the logical point. The decision also ignores the fact that George had an equitable interest in the property before completion day, by virtue of his contract to purchase.[11] If Daisy's money went into the deposit (it is not clear from the law report whether or not it did) her interest in the property would surely take effect when contracts were exchanged. If that were the case, then the slaughter of the *scintilla* does not affect her priority, provided she is in actual occupation before the mortgage takes effect.

Cann is simply a decision, couched in the language of reasoning, that *Boland*-type interests cannot bind an acquisition mortgagee. It fits so firmly into the political and economic ethos of the late twentieth century that it is unlikely to be reversed.

(2) Post-acquisition mortgages and the effect of *Prestidge*

Boland is therefore only really a problem to post-acquisition mortgagees, where there is clear time in which beneficial co-ownership can arise. In these circumstances, the waiver system evolved in the wake of *Boland* is the mortgagee's first line of defence, and it will almost always be effective. This has been discussed earlier,[12] and it will be recalled that mortgagees routinely inquire as to the adult occupiers of the property and secure from each of them a waiver of their rights, if any, vis-à-vis the mortgagee. The system appears to work, in the sense that its effectiveness in straightforward cases has not been challenged; and this in spite of the fact that it assumes that a mortgagor will tell the truth, and despite the fact that the available remedies if he does not do so will be worthless. The system continues despite the fact that solicitors are very reluctant to advise clients on giving such waivers (the fee chargeable being out of all proportion to the potential liability for getting it wrong), so that those who give them may well be doing so without proper advice.

Sometimes waivers are not obtained, and there is a second line of defence. It relies on the case of *Equity and Law Home Loans Ltd v Prestidge*,[13] which in turn derives from the decision in *Bristol and West Building Society v Henning*.[14] *Henning* was a pre-*Cann* decision and it said

---

[11] See Chapter 2, p. 29.
[12] See Chapter 3, p. 53.
[13] [1992] 1 WLR 137.
[14] [1995] 1 WLR 778.

this: that when a house is being purchased with the aid of a mortgage, a co-owner who knows that the mortgage is necessary to the purchase is deemed to consent to the mortgage. Although there are difficulties inherent in saying that someone consented when they did not consciously do so, there is certainly a problem with a beneficial co-owner insisting that his beneficial interest in a property take priority to a mortgage, when without the mortgage the beneficial interest (at least in *that* property) could not have existed. The deemed consent acts in the same way as an express waiver does, ensuring that the mortgagee can claim possession and realise its security as if the co-owner did not exist.

Now, after *Cann* the decision in *Henning* is not needed. But *Henning* was extended by *Prestidge*, which established the principle that where the property is re-mortgaged (i.e. a replacement mortgage granted to secure a loan used, and intended by all parties, to pay off the acquisition mortgage) then the co-owner's deemed consent to the acquisition mortgage is transferred to the re-mortgagee.

There is some logic in this. The co-owner may know nothing about the re-mortgage; but she should not obtain priority to the mortgage (in this scenario there is only one) just because the legal owner changed lenders without telling her. There are also some problems in the application of *Prestidge*, and it should not be applied unthinkingly, as if consent to the re-mortgage could be constructed automatically. If the terms of the re-mortgage are particularly harsh (and recall the comments made early in this chapter, to the effect that it is those in financial difficulties who tend to have to accept expensive loans) the cohabitant might well have refused to consent if asked. The *Prestidge* analysis does not work for a second mortgage, that is, an additional mortgage to secure an additional loan. A second mortgagee who does not protect himself by the waiver system should not be able to use this alternative protection. It is not clear whether or not it should work for a mortgage intended as a second mortgage, where the borrower chooses instead to use the loan to pay off the acquisition mortgage—this has been called the 'accidental re-mortgage'. Where *Prestidge* is appropriate the theoretical basis of its operation is unclear; there is a suggestion that it is a form of subrogation.

Subrogation is a technique used when someone who does not own the property pays off the mortgage; he is said to 'be subrogated to' the rights of the mortgagee, which means that he stands in the mortgagee's shoes and takes on the mortgagee's rights. It is easiest to see the sense in this if we imagine an unconnected individual paying off someone else's mortgage, not as a gift but as a way of—perhaps—assisting a friend who would otherwise suffer re-possession or a very high interest rate, although such a scenario is rather implausible, with a nineteenth century flavour to it. But that, without the element of philanthropy, is just what a commercial lender does when he makes a loan in order to pay off the first mortgage. Normally this lender's rights are secured by a mortgage, but if for some reason that mortgage does not take effect, the law is that the lender is subrogated to the rights of the first (now paid off) mortgagee, since otherwise the borrower would be unjustly enriched at the lender's expense.

The reasoning can be transferred to the *Prestidge*-type case, this time reversing the unjust enrichment of the co-owner, who would take a windfall benefit if she took priority to the re-mortgagee. There is no direct judicial authority for this analysis of *Prestidge*, but if correct it would appear to give a sound doctrinal basis to the case as well as to give the courts some discretionary control over these cases (in line with restitution decisions in general).

As a final point: some jurisdictions seek to avoid this type of difficulty by legislating that a sole owner of the family cannot dispose of it—by sale, gift, mortgage or whatever—without the consent of his or her spouse or (in those jurisdictions where they exist) registered partner. The non-owning partner is therefore given a veto. Such protection does not exist in this country unless the spouse has registered her right of occupation so that the purchaser simply will not go ahead unless she withdraws her registration, again producing a kind of veto.[15] It exists as nearby as Ireland and in many European jurisdictions. The consequence of proceeding without consent is that the transaction is void or voidable—the details vary. It would be possible to enact such a system in this jurisdiction. But if that were to happen, another problem would arise; what of the spouse who gives consent, but then suggests that she did so because she was lied to or pressurised? The problem would then merge with the next one we have to tackle, which concerns joint mortgagors.

JOINT MORTGAGORS AND THE PROBLEM OF PRESSURE

This final section deals, again, with the title the mortgagee is able to sell and, therefore, with the quality of title that he took when he granted the loan and purchased his security interest. Like the problem of priorities, it is discussed at this end of the chapter because it will be litigated when the

---

[15] Chapter 4, p. 75.

mortgagee comes to enforce the security and so belongs with the climax of the mortgagee's tale.

The problem is this. Greenacre was bought in 2000 by Pat and Chris. In 2005 Pat needed a business loan, and a joint mortgage was executed in order to secure a loan to Pat from the bank. Whether or not there was a prior acquisition mortgage does not matter for the purposes of this example. Pat's business goes under, the mortgage payments are not kept up, and the bank seeks possession of the property prior to sale. And at this point Chris objects to the mortgage and claims not to be bound by it.

There are two principle dangers for the bank here. The first is that Chris' signature may have been forged by Pat. This is unusual but not unknown; and on the principles applicable in unregistered land it will mean that the apparent legal mortgage is void—because Pat did not have the ability to mortgage the legal estate—although Pat's own equitable interest will be charged to the bank. The bank must therefore look to the principles in sections 14 and 15 of the Trusts of Land and Appointment of Trustees Act 1996 for a decision as to whether or not the land can be sold. The position where the title is registered is rather different. A legal mortgage will be created once the bank's charge is registered: this is the effect of section 58 of the Land Registration Act 2002.[16] Normally, however, the victim of forgery will be able to have the register altered so as to remove the legal mortgage and replicate the position in unregistered land so that only a charge of the forger's equitable interest remains.[17]

The effect of forgery in registered land is complex, as we saw in Chapter 3. It is the less common of the two dangers in joint mortgages.

The second and more common problem is where Chris claims not to have understood or really intended the transaction: specifically, that Pat lied to Chris about the effect of the mortgage, or that Pat pressured Chris into it. Chris is claiming to be the victim of misrepresentation or of undue influence. Either of these wrongs would make a transaction between Pat and Chris voidable; that is, it is not void, and remains valid until Chris claims otherwise, but Chris can apply to the court to have the transaction set aside, so that things will be as if the transaction had not happened.

So much for dealings between Pat and Chris; at first sight this does not seem to be a problem for the bank. But it is, because the courts have held that in some circumstances the bank can be regarded as involved in Pat's

---

[16] Chapter 3 at p. 41.
[17] Chapter 3 at p. 56.

misconduct, so that the mortgage executed by Chris is tainted by Pat's misrepresentation or undue influence and can be avoided by her. This means that the mortgage is void, and the register will be altered so as to remove the bank's registered charge.[18] All the bank has at that point is its debt, which can be enforced against Chris. Ultimately, it can be enforced by a charging order—a form of compulsory mortgage, which will make Chris' share in the property liable for the debt. The effect is then, again, very like that of *Boland*. The bank is going to have trouble realising its security because of the involvement of a co-owner whose share is not charged with the debt, and even so, Chris' share in the value of the house may be an inadequate security.

A considerable body of law has built up as the courts have struggled to develop guidelines about three issues. First, how can undue influence be proved? Misrepresentation is much simpler (simpler to do, and simpler to prove), being about statements rather than about pressure, and the account that follows concentrates on undue influence although issues two and three are equally relevant to misrepresentation. Secondly, when is a bank tainted by, or involved in, its client's undue influence, so as to make the mortgage voidable even though the bank did not do anything to Chris? Thirdly, how can a bank protect itself from this problem, by taking action in advance?

In the leading case on this area of the law, the House of Lords devoted a great deal of attention to issue three, because from the bank's point of view this is the most important. If the safeguards prescribed in that case are put in place by the bank, issues one and two will not trouble it. The safeguards will, incidentally, in some cases protect persons in Chris' position from entering an unwise transaction; but the purpose of the safeguards is to protect the bank. This should be no surprise from what we have seen already. It should be stressed that it would be simplistic to regard this as a preference by the courts for financial interests rather than those of individuals. At the heart of this area of the law is the courts' awareness of the financial needs of small businesses. To be avoided at all costs is a situation where the family home is not acceptable for use as business security:

If the freedom of homeowners to make economic use of their homes is not to be frustrated, a bank must be able to have confidence that a wife's signature of the necessary guarantee and charge will be as binding upon her as is the signature of anyone else on documents which he or she may sign. Otherwise

[18] Chapter 3, at p. 59.

banks will not be willing to lend money on the security of a jointly owned house or flat.[19]

As that quotation makes clear, the 'victim' in most of the many cases of this type that have reached the courts has been the borrower's wife; one of the challenges for the courts in developing this area of the law has been the need to ensure that it is gender-neutral, and that protection does not depend—as it used to—on the parties' being married. What makes this area of the law particularly awkward to explain is that it has changed rather dramatically. An approach to this kind of case was developed in a number of cases prior to 1994. That approach was to some extent disapproved, and a new approach enunciated, in the House of Lords' decision in *Barclays Bank plc v O'Brien*.[20] *O'Brien* helped lenders enormously, but generated some theoretical and practical controversy. The current law is as set out in *Royal Bank of Scotland v Etridge (No 2)*.[21] Accounts and analysis of the law are therefore beset by the need to explain how these two decisions of the House of Lords have each changed what went before them, and a layered effect is created. What follows is an endeavour to state the current law on the three issues identified above, with an explanation where necessary of how it reached its current state.

PROVING UNDUE INFLUENCE

This has caused huge difficulty because of its subtlety. Whereas misrepresentation is a matter of making an untrue statement, undue influence involves statements, tone of voice, implication and above all a relationship. What Pat says to Chris about the mortgage might cut no ice with me, but be irresistible to Chris. And of course we are all influenced by our friends, family, colleagues, children; and the law accepts this, intervening only when influence is undue in the sense of being excessive and unconscientious. Undue influence may range from threats and coercion, through bullying to pressure. The leading case suggests that there is undue influence where A trusts B to manage things for the two of them, and B 'prefers his interests to hers and makes a choice for both of them on that footing'.[22]

The courts have developed two ways of proving undue influence. The

---

[19] Lord Nicholls of Birkenhead in *Royal Bank of Scotland v Etridge (No 2)* [2001] 4 All ER 449, HL, at 35.

[20] [1994] 1 AC 180.

[21] [2001] 4 All ER 449.

[22] Lord Nicholls of Birkenhead in *Royal Bank of Scotland v Etridge (No 2)* [2001] 4 All ER 449, HL, at 33.

obvious way is for the victim to satisfy the court of what was said and done so as to demonstrate that undue influence did in fact take place. But this will not always be possible because of the subtlety of the problem and the role played by the parties' relationship. So the courts have held that if the victim can show *both* that he had a relationship of trust and confidence with the other party *and* that the transaction calls for explanation, then it will be held that there was undue influence unless the other party can provide an explanation which shows that undue influence did not take place.

The term 'relationship of trust and confidence' is unfortunate, in that it should be true of all good relationships. In this context it means something more, and something less wholesome, than the words would normally imply. It derives from earlier case law, and denotes a relationship where one party is likely to do as the other tells him or her, without enquiry or independent thought. It has been held that some relationships always have this characteristic: doctor and patient, priest and penitent, lawyer and client. Others may do in individual circumstances, and in particular, a married or engaged couple may or may not interact in this way.

So 'trust and confidence' is in this context an unexpectedly pejorative attribute of a relationship. All it demonstrates is the potential for abuse, however; it does not tell us that anyone did anything wrong. The next step towards proving that (and recall that this operation only takes place where *actual* undue influence cannot be shown) is to show that the transaction calls for explanation; that is, simply that there is something unusual about it. The fact that a member of such a couple—the one potentially abusable—has given the other a birthday present, for example, does not call for explanation. The fact that one has given the other his entire wealth does. This phrase avoids the need to show that the person claiming undue influence has done something specifically disadvantageous—something required in the pre-*Etridge* case law. That requirement was unhelpful because when a wife mortgages her share in the family home in order to support her husband's business she may well do so as much for her own benefit as for his. Obviously, a transaction to which the two were equal parties—where the borrowing was to finance a joint venture such as a holiday, or a business in which both are equal and active partners—does not call for explanation.

Once these two things have been proved (the nature of the relationship and the fact that the transaction is unusual or unexpected) then the position is this: that unless the other person actually provides that explanation, explaining away the unusual nature of the transaction, the court will find that undue influence was exerted. This method of proof is therefore known as *presumed* undue influence, rather than actual. It is so called because it involves a shifting of the burden of proof. The person alleging undue influence need not go all the way; he or she need only take these two prescribed steps, and will then be taken to have arrived unless the defendant can show that undue influence was not exerted.

This analysis is the product of the decision in *Etridge* and is simpler than that advocated in *O'Brien*, although not radically different from it.

ENTANGLING THE BANK

The more important change made in *Etridge* is in the analysis of the circumstances in which the bank will be held to have been entangled in its client's misdeed, so that undue influence exerted by Pat over Chris will render voidable the transaction between Chris and the bank. The law here has gone through some distinct stages, and it is perhaps a measure of the artificiality of what is going on here that it has gone through a number of obviously incorrect analyses before hitting upon the current acceptable one.

Before *O'Brien* the courts attributed Pat's misconduct to the bank by regarding him, in obtaining Chris' co-operation, as the bank's agent. This worked technically, by providing a way to force the bank to take responsibility for Pat's actions, but was unrealistic. Pat is the prime mover in the transaction and it is he who wants the loan; for his own sake he secures Chris' co-operation.

Conscious that this analysis was not convincing, the House of Lords in *O'Brien* said this: that the bank is bound by notice of Pat's undue influence; and that it would have notice of the undue influence if it failed to take prescribed steps to ensure that Chris received independent legal advice.

This too was unconvincing. The use of 'notice' as a tool of analysis is misleading; it is appropriate where a party to a transaction is or should be aware of a right arising through a previous transaction. But here there is just one deal. The wife's rights, against anyone, have not arisen at this stage; there is nothing to have notice of.

Etridge makes it simpler again. In all cases where the relationship between the borrower and the fellow mortgagor is non-commercial, the bank is 'put on inquiry'. And if the bank is put on inquiry, it is liable for the mortgagor's undue influence, if any, unless it takes certain steps. This means that the bank is potentially entangled in the borrower's wrongdoing in a huge range of cases—all those where the fellow mort-gagor is not a business partner. It avoids any inquiry into relationships or into emotional matters. It avoids any reference to gender or to marital status (contrast the pre-*O'Brien* cases where it was said that equity has an especial tenderness for wives, which nowadays seems endearing but inappropriate). It is not seen as a particular hardship for the lender, because the latter can protect itself simply and unambiguously by follow-ing the procedure set out in *Etridge* for its protection in cases where it is put on inquiry.

PROTECTING THE BANK

So: in certain cases the bank is 'put on inquiry'. This sounds as if it should ask questions, and in particular, 'why'? Why is this person going to be liable for the other's debt? Why is Chris doing this for Pat? But in fact those questions are too personal and are not going to produce the truth. Instead, when it is put on inquiry, the bank will nevertheless *not* be liable for any misrepresentation or undue influence on the part of the borrower if it has taken the steps prescribed in *Etridge*.

What must the bank do to be saved? It must ensure that the fellow mortgagor, to whom the loan is *not* made, has been advised by a solicitor about the implications of executing the mortgage. The advice to be given is rather thorough; it must include a breakdown of the borrower's financial situation (which therefore the bank must disclose) and a full explanation of the level of the loan, the possibility if any of the borrower drawing down further funds, and of the consequences of its not being paid. The solicitor—who may be the solicitor acting for the borrower—must certify to the bank that he has done all this. The bank need not check that he has done so. The existence of that certificate is a complete protection for the bank.

Notice that the bank itself does not have to do anything with or for Chris. It does not have to interview or advise Chris (as suggested in *O'Brien*; banks simply will not do it and the requirement has been wisely dropped by the House of Lords in *Etridge*). The onus of protecting Chris falls on the solicitor, and it is the solicitor, not the bank, who is at risk of litigation if the advice given was inadequate. The consequence for banks is one-stop litigation: the bank need have no involvement in the issues of whether or not there was undue influence or misrepresentation, it need only produce that protecting certificate from Chris' solicitor, which is then a complete answer to any involvement by the bank in proceedings arising from Chris' complaints that he was pressurised.

Notice that none of this is relevant if the loan was made to both mortgagors. In that event there is nothing to put the bank on inquiry. If there is no question of a business loan and the borrowing is claimed—truthfully or otherwise—to be taken on in order to pay for a holiday or a conservatory, then there is no place and no need for the *Etridge* rules.[23]

OUTCOMES OF THE PROBLEM OF PRESSURE

So what is the position of a post-*Etridge* Chris, who is not happy about the security he executed? If the bank can produce a certificate to show that *Etridge*-compliant advice was given to Chris, then the mortgage is valid in its entirety. Chris' options are to sue Pat for undue influence, which is unlikely to be useful; or to sue the solicitor for negligent advice. The solicitor, of course, is insured.

In the event that the bank cannot show that it followed the *Etridge* rules despite being put on inquiry, then the mortgage is voidable. But the debt, from Pat to the bank, remains. Pat must still pay it back. And if he does not do so he is likely to become insolvent; and his trustee in bankruptcy will be able to ensure a sale of the house so that Pat's share in it can be applied to pay the debt. Chris's share will be unaffected.

What we have to hope is that the *Etridge* procedure will produce real protection for borrowers, at least to the extent of making them aware of risk. It is unlikely to prevent many people from taking risks. This is one of the things that capital enables people to choose to do. What *Etridge* is certainly designed for is to prevent people from taking deliberate risks, and then, when it goes wrong, seeking to escape by saying they did not mean it, or did not know what they were doing, or were not told. The bank is given a way of proving that the risk was taken deliberately.

MORTGAGES, CAPITAL AND RISK

So: real property is a form of capital, and one of the sources of our prosperity is the ability to use it as such. The mortgage is essential to this. And a mortgage is a risk, as just remarked. The law has developed a web of protection, for lenders and borrowers. It is not all entirely logical or consistent. Much of it is about what individuals and institutions are prepared to take on, in a particular era. The evolution of the law of mortgages reflects different risk-aversions at different periods. Where an earlier age was concerned about commercial strings attached to

---

[23] *CIBC Mortgages v Pitt* [1994] 1 AC 200, HL.

mortgages, today we are willing to accept the standard form contracts imposed by banks, and are more worried about the pressures exerted by individuals. The next evolution in the law may reflect new, perhaps unforeseen, concerns.

BIBLIOGRAPHY

H. de Soto, *The mystery of capital: why capitalism triumphs in the West and fails everywhere else* (London, Black Swan, 2001).

M. Dixon, 'Consenting Away Proprietary Rights' in E. Cooke (ed), *Modern Studies in Property Law I* (Oxford, Hart Publishing Ltd, 2001), 181.

M. Haley, 'Mortgage default: possession, relief and judicial discretion' (1997) 17 *Legal Studies* 483.

J. Houghton and L. Livesey, 'Mortgage Conditions: Old Law for a New Century?' in E. Cooke (ed), *Modern Studies in Property Law I* (Oxford, Hart Publishing Ltd, 2001), 163.

M. Oldham, *Mortgages*, in L. Tee, ed., *Land Law: Issues, debates, policy* (Cullompton, Willan, 2002), at 169.

C. Sawyer, ' A world safe for mortgagees? Registering a *scintilla* of doubt' in E. Cooke (ed), *Modern Studies in Property Law I* (Oxford, Hart-Publishing Ltd, 2001), 201.

M. P. Thompson, *Modern Land Law* (Oxford, Oxford University Press, 2003), Chapter 12.

7

Leases, Licences and Commonholds

Much of what we have discussed so far has been about sharing, and relationships, and balances of power and of interests. So is this chapter. It is concerned principally with leases, but also with licences and commonholds. The law relating to leases is largely the tale of the law's endeavours to control the power imbalance between landlord and tenant. Licences are often hard to distinguish from leases, but a reason for wanting to grant a licence rather than a lease is to avoid the legal controls imposed on the landlord and tenant relationship. Commonhold was created out of exasperation with the power imbalance and the wish to create a better ownership structure for interdependent properties.

This chapter looks first at the definition of a lease, and contrasts it with the licence. We then look at features of leases in general. Finally, we look at statutory regimes designed to mitigate some of the problems of leasehold tenure; we see how security of tenure has disappeared and consider the development of leasehold enfranchisement and of commonhold.

LEASES

A lease is the grant of exclusive possession of land for a defined length of time. The payment of rent is not a necessary ingredient, although a lease is normally granted in exchange either for a 'market rent', representing the value of the property in income form, or for a low or nominal rent plus an initial capital sum (often called a 'premium'). A lease can be whatever length the parties want; but whereas a freehold estate is of uncertain duration (no-one knows when a life estate or a fee simple will come to an end), the length of a lease (known as its 'term') has to be defined at the outset. The grant of exclusive possession, and the defining of the term, are part of the contractual relationship which lies at the heart of the law of leases, or, as we also say, of the law of landlord and tenant.

The lease has its origins, like so much of land law, in medieval times. Alongside the feudal system, in which land was granted by the social superior to the inferior to be held in return for services, the use of land could also be managed by contract in return for the payment of money. The lessee, or tenant (now in the modern, landlord-and-tenant sense and not in the sense of a feudal tenant who held a freehold) did not originally have a property right in the land. He had simply a contract with his landlord, which would lose its force if the landlord sold the land. The arrangement was seen as purely commercial.

In time this changed. The lease was given increasing protection by the courts, and so it came to be regarded as a property right; like a freehold estate it came to confer ownership-type rights including the power to alienate and to exclude others. Initially it was merely personal property, so that—in contrast to real property—the remedy for dispossession was money rather than the land itself. This too changed. The lease came to be described as 'chattels real', that is, as a hybrid between real and personal property—and the distinction was very important when it came to inheritance rules, which were different for real and personal property. This distinction, too, has passed.

Leases are classified as real property. They are a form of ownership in that most lessees (or tenants; the terms are interchangeable) can say that their leasehold land is *theirs*; a lease is tenure, because it is a way of holding land, and it is an estate, because the lease determines how long the land is held for. As we have already seen, the lease is now one of the only two legal estates in land permitted after the 1925 legislation: section 1 of the Law of Property Act 1925 defines these as the 'fee simple absolute in possession', and the 'term of years absolute', normally known as a lease. It will be recalled that leases will be legal, rather than equitable, if the requirements for the creation of a legal estate are met; the requirements are discussed further below.

Let us put this into an everyday context: an estate agent's window will often advertise properties by reference to their tenure, labelling them leasehold or freehold. For reasons already indicated, and to be discussed, flats will normally be leasehold. Belinda and Ben are looking for their first home; they spend a while deciding between a freehold terraced house, and a leasehold flat. Both cost £120,000. Eventually they decide upon the flat. They find, on looking at the details, that it is held on a 125-year lease, granted in 1990 to Simon, who is now selling it. When they buy it, they take on Simon's contractual relationship to the landlord, including the obligation to pay rent and service charges; equally, they become the joint holders of a leasehold estate, derived from the landlord's freehold. The rent will be nominal, perhaps £25 per year, as the lease was granted to Simon in exchange for a premium, which is why he is selling it now for a capital sum. When Ben and Belinda buy, Simon's name is removed from the register of title for the lease, and the names of Belinda and Ben are substituted. The lease will end in 2115, 125 years after its commencement. Between now and then, Belinda and Ben can live in it, sell it, mortgage it, dispose of it by will—just as they could have done the freehold house. One important difference is that although the lease now has the same capital value as a freehold, it will depreciate rapidly, as a capital asset, towards the end of its term. This would not be a problem if the term had been 999 years.

The habit of regarding leases as tenure grew up long after the statute Quia Emptores in 1290. It will be recalled that this statute prevented the maintenance of the feudal system by forbidding any further feudal grants; but it did not and could not apply to leases, which were not at that stage a form of tenure. They are now, and there is nothing in the nature of a lease to prevent leaseholders granting leases—although a particular landlord and tenant may agree, in their lease, that this is not allowed. Thus Belinda and Ben could grant a sublease to Caroline, provided that sublease is timed so as to end, at the latest, immediately before the expiry of their own lease. Caroline, too, can sub-let, unless her lease forbids this. She might choose to grant a periodic tenancy—a lease which lasts only a week, or a month (whatever is agreed) at a time. This well-known and convenient arrangement in practice goes on, week after week or month after month, until it is brought to an end by one party giving notice to the other that the tenancy is to terminate at the end of the next contractual period.

These then are the very basics of a description of leases. There is a little more to say about the definition of leases before we discuss some details.

LEASES DEFINED

A lease is defined as the grant of exclusive possession of land for a term.[1] As can be seen from the footnote, this definition is the product of a number of decisions of the highest courts in recent years; and the various exercises in definition tend to take the form of an alleged landlord arguing that *even though* this looks like a lease, it is not, while the other party argues that certain conditions, which are met, are *sufficient* conditions for

---

[1] *Street v Mountford* [1985] 2 All ER 289, *Ashburn Anstalt v Arnold* [1989] 1 Ch 1, *Bruton v London Quadrant Housing Trust* [1999] 3 WLR 150.

the existence of a lease even though other factors, previously thought to be essential, are absent or still other factors, thought to be fatal to the existence of a lease, are present. Thus a grant of exclusive possession is a lease even if the parties have stated, in the written agreement between them, that it is not. It is a lease even if no rent is paid, and even if the landlord did not own the land. The issues have arisen, typically, where a tenant is claiming one of the add-on benefits that arise, not from the relationship of landlord and tenant itself, but from statutory protection given by the legislature to enhance the security or well-being of the tenant—in particular, security of tenure, or the landlord's statutory obligation to repair. Ironically, for most homes since 1989 security of tenure for tenants is a thing of the past, and the landlord's obligation to repair is very limited indeed unless the lease itself imposes this upon him. But these apparently peripheral issues have been used as a testing ground on which the definition of the lease has been worked out.

The most recent of these developments was the House of Lords' decision in *Bruton v London and Quadrant Housing Trust*.[2] A housing association had been allowed to use a block of flats, owned by the local authority, as temporary accommodation for homeless people pending re-development of the block. Homeless people were, in turn, given permission to live there. Permission to occupy land is known as a 'licence'; a licence may be given freely, as when you invite a friend into your house, or it may be contractual. I have permission, derived from my contract of employment, to work in an office at the University of Reading. Mr Bruton was granted a licence to live in one of the flats. Redevelopment was postponed, and he lived there for some years. Eventually, he claimed that the housing association was obliged to repair the flat, pursuant to the obligation laid upon landlords by the Landlord and Tenant Act 1985. For that argument to work, the association had to be a landlord and he a tenant, and the issue went all the way to the House of Lords.

The Lords' answer was something of a surprise. We had grown so used to regarding leases as tenure and estate that we were rather shocked to be told that neither characteristic was part of the definition of the lease. A landlord who has an estate in land will, if he grants exclusive possession for a term, have granted a lease which is itself an estate; and *that* tenant can, again, grant an estate to a subtenant. But a licensee, like the housing association in *Bruton*, can grant a lease. Such a lease will not itself be a property right, and it will have no effect on anyone other than the

[2] [1999] 3 WLR 150.

landlord—because someone who does not have a property right cannot grant one. To be proprietary, a lease must be derived from—scooped out of—the grantor's property.

Hence the rather careful phrasing of the paragraphs describing leases, above. We have indeed 'come to regard' leases as estate and 'got into the habit' of seeing them as tenure. And usually they are. It is very rare that someone who does not himself have a lease or a freehold will grant a lease, except by accident or, even more rarely, fraudulently. *Bruton* re-states the lease's contractual origins and asserts that, although a lease is usually proprietary, it does not have to be. The privileges of a tenant (in this case, getting repairs done) are available to all who have been granted exclusive possession of land, even where the grant is purely a personal one, enabling the tenant to shut the door on the landlord but not on, say, the true owner of the land (the local authority, in *Bruton*). The local authority's reaction to the House of Lords' decision was to remove the housing trust from its land, so as to enable it then to remove the *Bruton* tenants. In the ensuing litigation, the courts have stressed the tenants' non-proprietary status. Arguments that they have any rights in the land, or any security vis-à-vis the freeholder, have been firmly rejected.[3]

Leasehold law is thus a law of sufficient conditions. The grant of exclusive possession for a term is sufficient to constitute a lease; such a grant, made by a landowner, is sufficient to create a proprietary lease; compliance, in addition, with the formalities required for the creation of a legal lease (if any; as we have seen, there are none for short leases) is sufficient to create a legal lease. What the parties actually *want* to do is irrelevant. This is intentional. Few areas of land law have been so thoroughly regulated by the courts and by Parliament. To enter into a landlord-and-tenant relationship is to take on a large number of involuntary obligations and restrictions, and of course this characteristic has meant that people—especially landlords—have tried to define their way out. It is very tempting to try to create a relationship that gives them the advantages of being landlord and tenant, without actually being such. The courts have been determined that this should not work. They have been concerned about the inequality of bargaining power between landlord and tenant. The fact that a landlord does not want to grant a lease will mean that he labels the deal a 'licence', regardless of what the prospective occupier wants. Accordingly, the courts have worked on the principle that

---

[3] *Kay & Ors v London Borough of Lambeth, Leeds City Council v Price & Ors* [2006] UKHL 10. As to the security of public sector tenancies, see below, p. 171 ff.

the reality should be determined by conditions that are independent of the parties' expressed intentions.

The wisdom of this is greater in some contexts than in others. Given a political decision to have security of tenure for residential tenancies, it was obviously important for the courts to operate an anti-avoidance regime, and the courts' policy must be judged alongside the political decision. The issue is in fact nearly dead for residential tenancies, except for those in the public sector. The decision in *Bruton*, by contrast, is worrying. It was not driven by precedent; it runs counter to centuries of development that regarded the lease as a property right. Before that decision, a lease was defined as *an estate in land generated by* the grant of exclusive possession for a term—even if, on most occasions, we forgot to say the italicised words. *Bruton* affects very few situations but, where it does, the decision may be disastrous for those whom the licence agreement was intended to help. There is a world of difference between a landlord trying to avoid giving his tenant security of tenure, and a housing association trying to help as many people as possible. The precedent for the decision is unclear (the more orthodox account of leases given in the Court of Appeal decision in *Bruton* is much more attractive). The knock-on effect may be that more people sleep on the street.

Bruton affects only a tiny minority of leases. For the rest of this chapter we consider the normal paradigm where leases are proprietary, being both contract and estate. Yet another preliminary to the detail of leases is the contrast with licences, with which leases can so easily be confounded.

LEASES CONTRASTED WITH LICENCES

A licence is a permission to be on someone else's land. The friend who pops in for coffee has a 'gratuitous licence', given for free. More usual is the contractual licence, such as you grant to the man who comes in to lay the carpet, or (perhaps) to the student who rents a room and shares your kitchen. The contractual licence is usually given in exchange for payment, as in the case of a hotel room booking, or is part of a larger deal (as with the carpet man, or between me and my employer who provides an office). Least frequently encountered is the idea of a 'licence coupled with an interest'. A right to fish on someone's land, for example, is a property right in that land, and carries with it a permission to enter the land to do the fishing.

A gratuitous licence can be withdrawn at any time; you can ask your coffee friend to leave now. If a contractual licence is withdrawn there may be a breach of contract—as when my employer ceases to provide an office, or the theatre manager does not recognise your ticket and let you in. The remedies for breach of contract are damages and, occasionally, an injunction—that is, an order to the landowner to let the licensee enter. Despite this, and despite confusion in a line of cases during the twentieth century, a licence is not a property right. It is a personal right, corresponding only to a personal obligation of the landowner. It cannot normally be transferred (that is not invariable; consider theatre tickets) and it will not bind a purchaser of the land. If the theatre management sells the theatre before the performance for which you have a ticket, your right to sit in a particular seat next Thursday need not be honoured by the new owner of the land—but you can claim damages from the theatre management. Similarly, if Reading University sells its land tomorrow, the new landowner will not be obliged to let me continue to use 'my' office. Very occasionally—and the law on this is complex and not properly worked out—a licence will be enforced against a purchaser on the basis that he has undertaken an obligation to honour the licence, and therefore holds the land upon a constructive trust to that extent.[4] And a licence may be continued because the landowner is estopped from withdrawing it, because he has made assurances which the licensee has relied upon; this is part of the law relating to informal acquisition of land, since the continuance of a licence is one of the possible responses to estoppel.[5] But in normal cases, a licence is just a personal permission.

The difficulty arises with contractual licences and their closeness to leases. Look again at the student, Fred, who rents a room in a family house. He pays rent; he has a key to the house, but not to his room; but the homeowner does not enter his room. He has the shared use of the kitchen and bathroom. Is this a licence, or is it a lease: exclusive possession for a term? A term is easily derived from the intervals at which rent is payable, and so the issue boils down to one of exclusive possession. If he has it, he is a tenant. If not, he is a licensee, and this type of licensee is known as a 'lodger'.

The traditional lodger is easy to identify. He is like Fred, with the additional feature that the owner of the house provides clean linen, cleans the room for him, and makes him one or more meals each day. The owner needs access in order to provide these services, and so Fred does not have exclusive possession. But the lodger is rather old-fashioned and actually

---

[4] *Ashburn Anstalt v Arnold* [1989] 1 Ch 1.
[5] See Chapter 3, at p. 46.

quite unusual these days. Fred cleans his own room, does his own laundry and makes his own meals. His agreement with the owner is headed 'licence agreement', and gives the owner the right to enter the room, but the only time the owner goes in is when he is decorating and needs access to paint the window frame. Is Fred a tenant or a licensee? The owner does not actually want to grant him a lease but, as we have seen, intention is irrelevant and Fred may in fact be a tenant of his room. No amount of clever drafting in the agreement changes this, because the courts look at the reality of the parties' behaviour.

Even more difficult is multiple occupancy: the house or flat rented by more than one person. Do they collectively have exclusive possession of the house, and a joint tenancy, or are they each licensees, bound to share the house with whoever the owner puts in it? There is no fixed formula for determining this, but consider two contrasting cases. One is the house purchased as a 'buy to let' investment in a University town, with four bedrooms let out to a group of students. They are a floating population; when one leaves, the other three have no choice about who comes in to occupy the spare room (although they may decide among themselves who is to take over the vacated room before a new occupant arrives). They have separate agreements, and are responsible for separate rental payments. Contrast the couple renting a flat. They arrive together, they sign separate 'licence agreements', and are each responsible for half the rent. They share a bedroom. Neither would have moved in without the other. The agreement gives the landlord the right to enter, and may state that he is entitled to move another person into the flat. But he does not do so. The couple are tenants, despite the documentation; the four students are licencees.[6]

Much of the heat has been taken out of this debate because of the disappearance of security of tenure, discussed below. Whether or not Fred is a tenant, the landlord can remove him when he needs to. A landlord would probably prefer to rent a house to a group of four students as joint tenants than to deal with each individually because if they are joint tenants then each is responsible for the whole of the rent, and the landlord need not take any action if one of them moves out. We are perhaps fortunate that a good crop of cases was decided before security of tenure became a non-issue.

There are just a few formal exceptions to the rule that exclusive possession for a term gives rise to a lease. They are: when the occupier is

[6] c.f. *AG Securities v Vaughan; Antoniades v Villiers* [1990] 1 AC 417, HL.

allowed to live in the property as an act of charity; when he is a service occupier, required to live in the house as part of his job; and when he is a purchaser who has contracted to buy the property and is allowed in, pending completion. These are cases where the courts actually give effect to the parties' intention.

Now we turn back to leases, and look at the characteristics common, in one way and another, to them all.

TYPES OF LEASE

Leases can be split up formally—by length, and manner of creation; or functionally—into commercial, residential and agricultural, or alternatively into short residential, long residential and commercial (including agricultural). A commercial lease is a world away from a tenancy of a house, and for some purposes it is better to use function as the basis of classification. However, there are both periodic and fixed-term leases in all use-types, and the penalties for uncertain duration are the same whatever the function of the property, and so on; and in this basic account we shall have more to say about these distinctions than about specifically functional ones. So the more traditional method of classification is more helpful in this context.

Perhaps the most fundamental distinction between types of lease is that between periodic and fixed term. A fixed-term lease lasts for one defined length of time, specified in the contract between landlord and tenant. In the absence of specific statutory intervention (and we shall see that the law of landlord and tenant is riddled with this) the lease comes to a halt when that one period expires. By contrast, a periodic lease—or tenancy, as this type of lease is usually called—is defined by reference to a relatively short period of time. There is no theoretical limit to the size of the period, but a week, a month or a year is usually chosen. Payment of rent is specified by reference to the period: so much per week, per month etc. The duration of the tenancy operates by default: the tenancy carries on until one of the parties gives notice to the other, timed to expire at the end of a period. When the notice expires, the tenancy comes to an end. The length of notice needed may be defined contractually, but if there is no express agreement there are rules: a week for a weekly tenancy; a month for a monthly one; but six months for a yearly one. The most familiar instance of the periodic tenancy is probably domestic, where one pays rent for a house, a flat or a room on a monthly basis, but business and agricultural tenancies may equally be periodic. The yearly tenancy is

perhaps most useful to farmers. An important qualification to the notice
rules for periodic tenancies is that the Protection from Eviction Act
1977 requires that a minimum of four weeks' written notice be given to
residential tenants.

It would be an oversimplification to say that a fixed-term lease is always
granted, and assigned, for a capital sum and imposes a nominal rent,
whereas a periodic tenancy imposes a rent—normally at a level known
as the 'rack rent' or 'market rent' for that particular property. Certainly
that is the case at the extremes, and the distinction needs to be borne
in mind if one is to understand how leases function financially; but a
fixed-term lease for a few years might well impose a rent without a capital
price.

Bear in mind what was said about the conditions for a lease: exclusive
possession for a term. This means that whenever there is a periodic
arrangement for the exclusive use of land (e.g. I have sole use of your
factory, or your house, in return for a payment every month) then in the
absence of special circumstances there is a periodic tenancy, whether the
parties want it or not. That was the basis of the decision in *Bruton*, as we
have seen.

Some other, less common types of lease are again defined by reference
to time. A reversionary lease is one that gives the tenant possession of the
property not at the point when it is granted, but at an agreed future date:
for example, next Monday. A reversionary lease which gives possession
more than twenty-one years ahead is void: but there is nothing to stop
you making a contract now to grant a lease in twenty-five years' time.
This is an example—and we shall see others—of a rule which may have a
purpose (in this case, to avoid land being tied up for generations so that it
cannot be traded) but which is ill-formed and can easily be evaded. A
lease for life is another form of forbidden lease: an attempt to grant a lease
to someone for their lifetime is transformed, by statute,[7] into a 90-year
fixed-term lease, which can be brought to an end by notice after the death
of the tenant. Another statutory transformation is effected in the case of
perpetually renewable leases: such a lease is for a fixed term, but contains
a clause obliging the landlord to grant a fresh one, on exactly the same
terms, when it expires, if the tenant so requests. It is easy to see that such
a lease is perpetually renewable, unless the clause contains the words 'on
the same terms as this one *but excluding this option*' or similar. The penalty
for granting a perpetually renewable lease is that it is transformed into a

---

[7] Law of Property Act 1925, s. 149(6).

2,000-year lease.[8] Such a lease, being a single fixed term but on the same terms as the initial one, will probably not contain an adequate rent review clause (i.e. a clause enabling the rent to be raised in line with inflation) and is therefore disastrous for the landlord. The aim is to impose a deterrent to prevent such arrangements, because of the fear that they make the land commercially sterile. But if the parties really want a lease that continues forever at the tenant's option (why?), they need simply grant a 999-year term with generous 'break clauses', that is, provisions enabling the tenant to serve notice to bring the lease to an early end.

A tenancy at sufferance is what happens when a landlord has given notice to bring a periodic tenancy to an end, the notice has expired, and the tenant has not left yet. Such a tenant is really a trespasser and can be removed, by force if necessary—though the only safe way (legally and physically) to remove a tenant by force is to obtain a court order, which can be enforced by the court's bailiffs. A tenant who 'holds over', as we say, after the expiry of a lease with the landlord's permission has a 'tenancy at will'; this is a very strange entity that arises when someone occupies land as a tenant on the basis that either party may determine the arrangement at anytime. It is not at all clear how this squares with the requirement of certainty of term, or how it is to be distinguished, in practice, from a licence. It is unlikely that the concept would survive sustained analysis if it were to prove crucial in a case before the higher courts.

THE NEED FOR CERTAINTY OF TERM

As we have already seen, running through the rules about types of leases is a worry about timing: the idea that a lease must not go on forever. Put more precisely, leases must be for a certain term. Leases granted in the early 1940s 'for the duration of the war' were void, but because they were such sensible arrangements were specially validated by the Validation of Wartime Leases Act 1944. An agreement in a periodic tenancy that one party cannot ever give notice is void. A lease expressed to continue until the occurrence of an event which may never happen is void.

Since the war there have a been a number of cases that have appeared to compromise the certainty rule, and in *Prudential Assurance Co. Ltd. v London Residuary Body*[9] the House of Lords reasserted it. The London

---

[8] Law of Property Act 1922, s.145; one of the few bits of this Act that actually worked and remain in force.

[9] [1992] 2 AC 386, HL.

local authority granted the Prudential a lease of a strip of pavement, back in the 1930s, to last until the land was required by the authority for road widening. In due course, the local authority became the GLC, and later the GLC was abolished, and it became clear that the road widening was not going to happen; the landlord was now the London Residuary Body. The rent, set up in the expectation of a very short term, was now hopelessly inadequate even for such a narrow strip of commercial property in central London. The landlord therefore claimed that the lease was void because it was for an uncertain term, and succeeded. The outcome was that the land was indeed still let to the Prudential, but on a periodic tenancy: they still had exclusive possession of it, and were paying an annual rent, so the necessary conditions for a lease were present. But the periodic tenancy was terminable by notice and, presumably, after the litigation the matter was resolved by a threat in the form 'pay more rent or we give you notice to quit'.

From what has been said so far it will be seen that it is therefore very easy to let out a piece of land until you happen to want it for road-widening, residential development, a go-karting track or whatever. Grant a 3,000-year lease, include sensible rent-review provisions, and add a clause that states that if the landlord requires the land for [whatever it was] he may terminate the lease on giving, say, six months' notice. The lease would provide for the correct form of notice and would also, presumably, provide for some way of verifying that the landlord's requirement was genuine: for example, the production of a grant of planning permission.

Moreover, it is very difficult to persuade oneself that a periodic tenancy complies with the certainty rule. As a matter of fact, no-one knows when a periodic tenancy is going to end. The argument that it consists of a series of fixed terms tacked together, or that it is one single fixed term, which expands by the space of one period every time a period comes to an end without notice being given, are just word-games. So what is the point of the certainty rule given that it is child's play to evade it, and that periodic tenancies breach it in fact if not in form? It cannot be justified as a prevention of injustice, since it is indiscriminate in its benefits: the landlord was saved from an uneconomic deal in *Prudential*, but the tenant would have benefited if the lease had contained an upwards-only rent review clause (such clauses have been very common, and are extremely nasty to a tenant in times of recession).

The requirement seems to be linked with a philosophical debate about the nature of a lease. Is it mostly an estate in land, with some contractual features; or is it mostly a contract, with some of the attributes of an estate in land? Academic discussion of *Prudential* at the time of the decision was surprisingly passionate, and seem to have been linked closely with the various writers' conceptions of the nature of a lease. *Bruton* has taken much of the steam out of that debate, confirming the essentially contractual nature of the deal. That being the case, the certainty rule seems all the more arbitrary and pointless.

CREATION AND REGISTRATION OF LEASES

The practical requirements for the creation of leases follow from what has been said already about the requirements for the creation of legal and equitable interests, and for contracts to create or transfer interests in land. If a lease is basically a contract then at a minimum it must comply with the requirements for land contracts in section 2 of the Law of Property (Miscellaneous Provisions) Act 1989: all the terms expressly agreed (contrast those implied by law) must be written down, documentation must be signed etc. All leases, whether or not they are estates in land and whether or not they are recognised at law rather than merely in equity, must comply with this rule. But the rule contains an exception: leases for a term of three years or less, and granted for a market rent, need not be made in writing. They can simply be oral. Within the exception are leases for fixed terms of anything from one minute to exactly three years, and all periodic tenancies (provided the period is three years or less; and in fact in practice the maximum period is one year).

A contract for exclusive possession for a term is therefore a lease, and if it is granted by a person with an estate in land then the lease will itself be an estate in land. But if it is to be a *legal* estate then further requirements must be met. If it is for a term of more than three years it must be granted by deed; and if it is for more than seven years it must be registered (whether or not the landlord's estate is registered).[10] Otherwise it remains merely equitable. Once registered, a lease has its own title number and its own individual register, so that where both landlord and tenant have a registered title, there will be two registered titles for one piece of land, and if there are sub-leases there may be more than two. Leases for seven years or less are not registrable, but are nonetheless legal estates in land. Leases for three years or less need not be created by deed, nor

---

[10] See Chapter 4, at p. 71–2. A few leases for a term shorter than seven years are also registrable, including most reversionary leases: Land Registration Act 2002, s. 4(b), (d)–(f).

even in writing, but, again, are nonetheless legal estates if a market
rent is being charged.[11] Until the Land Registration Act 2002 the registration requirement was for leases of more than 21 years, so the new
limit represents a significant reduction. There is a suggestion that it
might be further reduced to three years to match the requirement for use
of a deed.

As well as being estates in land leases are non-ownership rights burden-
ing the landlord's title. What makes leases enforceable against a purchaser
of the landlord's estate? This, again, takes us back to what has been said
earlier. In most cases today, the landlord's title will be registered, and in
that event the enforceability of the lease will depend upon section 27 of
the Land Registration Act 2002. It will bind purchasers from the landlord
if it is registered, or if it is an overriding interest. Where a lease is
registered with its own title (because it is for a term of more than seven
years, or because it falls within one of the categories of shorter leases that
have to be registered nevertheless),[12] it will also be registered as a burden
on the landlord's title, as a result of cross-checking within the land registry and whether or not the parties have requested this. If it is not registered, either because it is an equitable lease or because it is too short to be
registered, it will bind the landlord if it is an overriding interest. Most
unregistered leases will be overriding interests: legal leases for seven years
or less are an independent category of overriding interests, and others
will often be overriding interests by virtue of actual occupation. Where
the landlord's title is unregistered (whether a lease or a fee simple), anyone buying it will take it subject to any legal lease he has granted. If he
has granted an equitable lease, then a purchaser will be bound by it if it
has been registered under the Land Charges Act 1972, as this is one of
the rights that requires registration.[13]

The picture of enforceability is thus complex, but can be worked out
steadily from principles. The point of the rules is to ensure that purchasers are not caught out by unexpected leases; but of course what
makes them enforceable is not the fact that the purchaser knows about
them, but the fact that they appear on the register or are overriding
interests.

---

[11] It is therefore quite unusual to find an equitable periodic tenancy if a market rent
is being paid; but one would arise if the landlord himself had only an equitable estate in
the land.

[12] See n. 10 above.

[13] See Chapter 3, at p. 46.

TERMINATION OF LEASES

At first sight there can be little to say here. Periodic tenancies end when notice is given, fixed-term leases expire at the end of their term. But there are qualifications to this simple picture, all arising from the basis of the lease in the landlord and tenant relationship.

First, a fixed-term lease may make its own contractual provision for early termination by the inclusion of a 'break clause', enabling one or both parties to give notice and bring the lease to an end. Usually there is some stipulation of the time when this is allowed: perhaps after a defined period, or on the occurrence of a specified event. We noticed, above, one circumstance when this might be useful. Secondly, a lease may be forfeited by the landlord for breach of covenant (i.e. breach of an obligation in the lease) on the tenant's part; we shall have more to say about this shortly. A further contractual feature is that a lease may be frustrated. This will occur very rarely when something occurs to destroy the whole basis of the letting; for example, destruction of the premises by fire or landslide.[14] This is a relatively recent development and is perhaps an assertion of the contractual rather than the proprietary nature of the lease. So is the other recent 'discovery' that a landlord's breach of covenant may be so fundamental as to amount to a repudiatory breach, so that the tenant is justified in leaving the land and ceasing to pay rent.[15] Neither of these developments has unleashed a flood of cases, and they seem more to be a reaction to individual fact patterns rather than any radical new thinking.

One very counter-intuitive rule is that a periodic tenancy held by joint tenants can be brought to an end by notice given by one tenant alone.[16] This means that one can render the other homeless. It feels odd because both tenants' signatures would be required, for example, to assign the tenancy, or to mortgage or assign a lease. It is justified by the theory that a periodic tenancy goes on from one period to another because the tenant has chosen not to give notice. Not giving notice is regarded as a positive act, in which both must participate. If one of the two gives notice, it is clear that the pair do not choose to continue the tenancy and it must end. The same rule does not apply to the exercise of a break clause, by notice, to make an early end to a fixed-term lease, because *that* type of notice is indeed a positive act in which both must participate.

---

[14] *National Carriers Ltd v Panalpina (Northern) Ltd* [1981] AC 675, HL.
[15] *Hussein v Mehlman* [1992] EGLR 87.
[16] *Hammersmith and Fulham LBC v Monk* [1992] 1 AC 478

A final qualification to the rules on termination relates to security of tenure. As has already been indicated,[17] there are instances where the law requires the lease to continue, if the tenant wants it to do so, despite the giving of notice or the ending of the term. Of the host of legal interventions in the landlord and tenant relationship, this is the most drastic. It is, however, very much a creature of politics and economics. A couple of decades ago a significant proportion of leases were subject to security of tenure, including many residential tenancies and almost all commercial and agricultural leases; but since then most of the statutory structure has been dismantled and security is very much a minority phenomenon. Security of tenure is discussed further below.

What of the argument that the termination of a lease, or for that matter of a licence, is a violation of an occupier's human rights because it takes away one of his possessions, and interferes with his home and his private life, contrary to Article 8 of the European Convention on Human Rights and to Article 1 of its First Protocol?

In principle, there is no violation of human rights. The relevant provisions of the Convention were intended to protect individuals against arbitrary interference with their possessions and their homes, in the aftermath of war in Europe. The courts have held firmly to the view that where proceedings are taken to remove someone from land in which he does not have any property or any other right, that is an interference in the public interest. It is done in accordance with the law and for the protection of the rights and freedoms of others.[18] Where a lease has been ended, in accordance with its own terms and with those of any legislation extending it, human rights legislation does not give the tenant any additional rights.

The first dent in this armour of legal certainty was made by a decision of the European Court of Human Rights, *Connors v UK*.[19] Here a local authority had evicted gypsies who had lived as licensees on a site for fourteen years, in summary proceedings. The law gave the gypsies no security and no defence. The European Court found that the gypsies' Article 8 rights had been infringed. It was swayed by their special status and needs as a minority, as well as by the fact that had the gypsies been camping on a private site they would have had some limited security.[20]

---

[17] Chapter 2, at p. 21.
[18] Reference is made to the wording of the relevant provisions of the Convention; see Chapter 1 at p. 9.
[19] Application no 66746/01, 2004.
[20] Under the Mobile Homes Act 1983.

But even here, no proprietary rights are being conferred. The decision focused on the lack of procedural safeguards for the gypsies. The direct result was the amendment of the Caravan Sites Act 1968 to enable the court to adjourn possession proceedings in such cases for up to twelve months, so ensuring that in appropriate cases the gypsies would have time to make arrangements for a move.

A more far-reaching effect of the gypsy saga was the House of Lords' examination of the potential effect of human rights upon possession proceedings in *Kay and others v London Borough of Lambeth, Leeds City Council v Price and others*.[21] Their lordships accepted that it cannot be the case that the enforcement of a right to possession in accordance with domestic property law will *never* be an interference with someone's home, or will *always* be justified under Article 8(2) of the Convention. However, by a majority they held that a human rights defence to possession proceedings can *only* be mounted on the basis that the legislation concerned is incompatible with the Convention. There can be no defence purely on the basis that the occupier's own circumstances make this exercise of the owner's rights a breach of the occupier's human rights.[22] Their lordships made clear their view that the various legal regimes under which possession proceedings might be taken (depending upon the type of lease or licence involved) would be human rights compliant. Many involve consideration by the court of the individual's behaviour or circumstances. Even where the claimant has an unqualified right to possession, the legislation will have undergone scrutiny by Parliament with a view to the public interest and in the light of the need to protect the rights and freedoms of the various parties involved. A landowner's right to recover his own property is important. In the case of a public authority landlord, a powerful consideration will be the needs of others for housing, in a context where there is not enough local authority housing or land to go round.

This is a restrictive interpretation of the Strasbourg Court's decision in *Connors*. The procedural consequences of the decision are such that human rights can only be raised in the form of a challenge to legislation. This means that unless the court can interpret the legislation concerned so as to make it compatible with the Convention, the outcome on the human rights point will be a transfer of the case to the High Court and a

---

[21] [2006] UKHL 10.

[22] The decision in *McPhail v Persons Unknown* [1973] Ch 447 is thus upheld, and that in *Harrow London Borough Council v Qazi* [2004] 1 AC 983 modified slightly, by the concession that legislation might be subject to challenge, but not overruled.

declaration that the legislation is incompatible with the Convention. This will not affect the issue in the individual case. There is therefore very little incentive for the individual to plead Article 8 in answer to possession proceedings. The decision was to a considerable extent motivated by the perceived need to prevent the wholesale complication of simple County Court possession proceedings by the involvement of human rights considerations, as well as by the view that the human rights Convention does not force a local authority to house or accommodate someone who would not otherwise be entitled to such assistance.

Normally, a judgment by a seven-strong House of Lords would be the last word on a point for at least a generation. But human rights law is as fluid as the European Court makes it, and it is unlikely that the law on this point will remain fixed for long.

LEASEHOLD COVENANTS

THE CONTENT OF THE LEASE

A lease is a collection of obligations generated by contractual promises, known as 'covenants', made by the landlord and tenant in the lease. These are undertaken by both landlord and tenant, and are crucial to the functioning of the leasehold relationship. Some are express, being written in the lease itself, and the more the professional involvement in the grant of the lease, the more express covenants there will be. Some are implied, which means that statute or case law have declared that they are among the contractual obligations set up by the lease even though neither party intended this; and these may be very important in correcting an imbalance of power. Some implied covenants are common to all leases, some only to particular types.

Thus all leases are deemed to contain covenants by the landlord to allow the tenant 'quiet enjoyment' of the property (nothing to do with noise levels or pleasure) and 'not to derogate from his grant', which means that the landlord must enable the tenant to retain possession of the land without harassment from the landlord or from his other tenants. A tenant covenants to pay the rent imposed by the lease, if any, to pay any taxes on the property, and not to deny his landlord's title, for example by paying rent to someone else. These covenants, as their terminology implies, are ancient. Further covenants may be implied in particular leases on the contractual principle of necessity: thus leases of flats in a block have been held to contain a covenant by the landlord to give access to the stairs.

Residential leases of seven years or less contain a covenant by the landlord, implied by statute, to carry out certain repairs.[23] These are carefully defined, being: to keep the structure and exterior of the property in repair; to keep in working order the installations for the supply of gas, water, electricity and sanitation; and to keep in working order the space heating and water heating. It is easy to see how important this is in short residential leases. A tenant in such cases is very unlikely to have a capital investment in the property (the vast majority of these leases will be at the very short end of the category, being periodic tenancies) and really should not have to pay for items such as structural repair and central heating. But without the statutory implied covenant, there is nothing to stop the landlord imposing this obligation if he has the bargaining power. When a lease falls outside the scope of the statutory covenants, the only arrangements for repair will be those made expressly. They are vital to almost every lease, but may be non-existent or inadequate. They need to be particularly complex in a shared building: a block of flats or offices. Sometimes a landlord sets up a management company to take over the landlord's obligations; where there is a group of residential flats there is a statutory right for the tenants to form a company to do this.[24] And there has been endless litigation over the meaning of the word 'repair' and related expressions. Does an obligation to repair mean that one has to replace a component that is beyond repair? Or to replace features of the building that have not actually gone wrong but are badly designed? The answer to both questions is 'no', but argument on this is endless because of the variety of things that can go wrong in buildings, and the variety of wordings in express covenants.

Express covenants may relate to the use of the land. This is simple enough in a block of flats, where the main concern on the landlord's part will be to prevent business use, but complex in a shopping centre, where tenants will expect the landlord to ensure that their fellow shopkeepers stay open for business, and do not carry on competing trades. It is common to restrict the tenant's ability to assign his lease without the landlord's consent (and there is a whole raft of law relating to the landlord's ability to withhold consent, which could otherwise be exercised tyrannically). There may be similar provisions restricting or excluding the ability to sublet. It is unheard of for a lease to contain a restriction on a landlord's ability to assign his own interest in the land (known

---

[23] Landlord and Tenant Act 1985, s.11.
[24] Commonhold and Leasehold Reform Act 2002, Part 2, Chapter 1.

technically as his 'reversion' because the land reverts to him at the end of the lease). Other common covenants include one to permit the landlord to enter and inspect the premises; obligations on one or other party to decorate; and restrictions for the benefit of neighbours relating to noise, parking etc.

All covenants, express or implied, generate incomes for lawyers in disputes about their meaning and scope. This is perhaps one of the few areas of underregulation in leases, where the parties might be better served by some imposed definitions.

REMEDIES FOR BREACH

Another earner for lawyers is the law surrounding remedies for breach of covenant. Again, we start in the law of contract: the primary remedy is damages. There is a degree of protection for tenants, in that damages for a tenant's failure to repair are limited to the loss in value of the landlord's reversion—usually this will be rather less than the cost of having the work done.[25] A landlord, too, may have to pay damages for failure to carry out *his* repairing obligations. Moreover, despite the courts' general reluctance to make an order forcing someone to carry out work, a tenant may be granted an order for specific performance: i.e. an order requiring the landlord to carry out the repairs on pain of being in contempt of court. Other breaches of covenant are less easily translated into money— breach of a covenant relating to use of the premises, e.g. or to noise—and more readily translatable into a court order restraining the behaviour concerned.

Unpaid rent can still be recovered by the ancient remedy of 'distress', that is, by the landlord entering the property and seizing the tenant's goods, so as to sell them to pay the rent. There are restrictions as to what can be seized, and upon the timing and method of carrying out the distress; and certain residential tenancies are exempt. Even so, distress is about intimidation rather than debt management, and would seem unlikely to survive a challenge on the basis of the tenant's human right to peaceful enjoyment of his possessions. It is hard to see that there is any public interest in the continued availability of this remedy, given that there are other more effective ways for the landlord to protect his interest. Mention of distress does, however, provide the opportunity to tell the story of *Walsh v Lonsdale*.[26]

[25] Section 18 of the Landlord and Tenant Act 1927.
[26] (1882) 21 ChD 9.

Lonsdale agreed to let land to Walsh for seven years, but no legal lease was drawn up or executed. The agreement stated that the rent would be payable annually in advance. Walsh paid quarterly in arrears; and so Lonsdale distrained. Walsh claimed that the distress was illegal because the rent was not yet due. He claimed that he held a legal periodic tenancy (arising from his exclusive possession and periodic payments). But by virtue of the agreement, Walsh had an equitable seven-year lease. Which prevailed? It was held that the equitable rules prevailed; and so the distress was legitimate. So although we have regarded equitable interests as consolation prizes, where a legal interest could not be achieved, this case shows that this is not quite an accurate picture. Equitable leases give rise to problems of enforceability against purchasers of the landlord's interest; but between the original parties there is nothing second best about them.

Another notorious remedy is forfeiture, available to the landlord in response to any breach of covenant provided that the lease includes a 'forfeiture clause' (any properly drafted lease will have one). Forfeiture means simply bringing the lease to an end. It is a drastic remedy if the tenant paid a capital sum for it, and the law has devised numerous safeguards with the aim of ensuring that it is carried out only as a last resort and only after the tenant has had ample notice of the threat and time to put right the breach of covenant where that is possible. These safeguards are not as tight as one might wish. In particular, if the lease is not residential, it is still open to the landlord to forfeit the lease by 'peaceable re-entry', that is, entering the property when no-one is around and taking possession of it.[27] Despite calls for a number of years to outlaw this practice, it remains available. The tenant may apply to reverse the forfeiture after it has taken place (whether by court order or by peaceable re-entry)— 'relief from forfeiture' is the technical term— by remedying the breach of covenant. So may his sub-tenants and mortgagee, whose interests otherwise disappear when forfeiture takes place.

Remedies for breach of covenant have a flavour of ancient law, including very physical self-help, pasted over with modern safeguards of varying adequacy. This remains an area where the landlord is more powerful than the tenant. There is still no straightforward right, for example, for a tenant to withhold rent when the landlord has failed to carry out repairs.

---

[27] The Protection from Eviction Act 1977 prevents the landlord from forfeiting a residential lease without a court order; and the Criminal Law Act 1977 makes it an offence to use violence to enter premises without lawful authority (and 'lawful authority' would not include a right to forfeit).

But in one case the law is particularly generous to tenants: where the landlord, in breach of his covenant for quiet enjoyment, harasses or threatens the tenant to try to make him leave. In this case, the tenant is entitled to damages calculated by reference to the value of vacant possession to the landlord, which is likely to be considerable.[28]

LEASEHOLD COVENANTS AND THE TRANSMISSION OF LIABILITY

Obviously, either party in the landlord and tenant relationship can sell: the tenant his lease, the landlord his reversion. What happens to the parties' obligations when either one sells on? The first and vital point to make is that a new tenant, or a new landlord, will take on his predecessor's obligations automatically. The covenants in the lease 'run with the land'. The only qualification to this is that the covenants must relate to the property and not to specific individuals. A covenant that the tenant shall buy groceries from the landlord's shop will not pass to a new tenant; a covenant to pay rent or to repair the property does.

This is so simple and obvious that one might think it hardly needs stating—but it does, because there is no similar mechanism for freehold land. Purchase a freehold, and you will be bound by any restrictive covenants your predecessor (or his) entered into, provided they are properly registered, but positive obligations (to repair; to maintain a fence; to keep a shop open in normal business hours) drop off the land when it is sold. The person who imposed the covenant, or who now has the benefit of it, cannot make the buyer of the land observe it. This means that where land is shared by a number of separate, but practically interdependent owners—a block of flats or an office complex—the individual properties must be leasehold, not freehold, because a complex of this kind cannot function efficiently without properly enforceable positive, as well as restrictive, covenants.

There is some terminology to go with this. Look at any lease; no matter how many times the lease or the reversion have been sold, the *current* landlord and tenant are said to be in a relationship of 'privity of estate' and are liable to each other, as landlord and tenant, for the performance of the landlord's and the tenant's covenants in the lease, express or implied.

The big issue arises in connection with a different form of privity. Look at that lease again, and at the very first landlord and tenant. *They* set up the lease and were the original parties to the contract; they are said to

---

[28] Sections 27 and 28 of the Protection from Eviction Act 1977.

be in 'privity of contract' with each other. When the tenant sells, contract law dictates that he does not cease to be a party to that contract unless the landlord expressly releases him; and normally the relative bargaining power of the parties is such that he will not do so. Moreover, the benefit of that contract is automatically transmitted to any subsequent landlord for that lease. Putting those two factors together, if the current tenant—whether T2, or T22—fails to pay the rent or to renew the roof, the landlord (whether the original one or a purchaser of the reversion) can sue two people: the current tenant, with whom he is in privity of estate, and the original tenant, with whom he is in privity of contract. The original tenant is liable, moreover, even if the rent has increased since he sold, because of a rent review clause. The clause was part of the contract to which he was a party, so. . . . And in fact the landlord may be able to generate further alternative defendants to an action for the rent (or to enforce any other covenants). Most leases will contain a covenant not to assign without the landlord's consent, so that the landlord has some control over the identity of the new tenant. As a condition of giving his consent, the landlord may require the new tenant to enter into a direct covenant with him to observe the covenants in the lease. Thus the current tenant at any point is in a relationship of privity both of estate and of contract with the landlord, and the contractual relationship will not come to an end if he, in turn, sells on.

Transfer that scenario into a recession, where tenants' businesses are failing, rent review clauses are in 'upwards only' form, and rent is not being paid, and it spells financial disaster for the original tenant on a long or longish lease of business property. Such disasters, in the early 1990s, prompted reform of the law relating to transmission of leasehold covenants in the Landlord and Tenant (Covenants) Act 1995. Clearly privity of contract operated unfairly to tenants, who might be held liable for huge sums of money payable on a lease with which they had long since parted. Privity of contract also applied to landlords, but aroused far less concern, probably because landlords' obligations tend to be less extensive than those of tenants. Equally clearly the privity of contract rule represented a valuable asset for landlords by providing them with additional parties to sue. To deprive existing landlords of that asset was felt to be illegitimate, and so the 1995 Act set up two separate reforms: one for pre-1996 leases and one for post-1995 ones.

For pre-1996 leases, the fairy godmother cannot remove the wicked fairy's curse on original tenants, but she can soften it a little. For such leases, the Act provides, first, that the landlord must give notice to the original tenant of any sum he is going to seek to recover from him, within six months of it becoming due, so that he will not be taken by surprise by a huge liability. Secondly, it provides that if the original tenant is forced to take responsibility for the current tenant's breach of covenant, he may require the grant, to himself, of an overriding lease. In other words, he can be slotted in as a tenant between the landlord and the current tenant. He becomes the head tenant, the defaulting tenant becomes *his* subtenant; and he can take enforcement proceedings against that current tenant— for example, forfeiting the sublease so that at least he gets the right to take possession of the property that he is being forced to pay rent for.

But the original tenant on a post-1995 lease can sleep more soundly at night. The basic rule for such leases is that liability ends when he sells his lease, providing the sale was not itself a breach of covenant. The exception to the release of tenants (original and subsequent) is that they may each be required by the landlord, as a condition of his giving consent to the assignment, to enter into an 'authorised guarantee agreement', that is, to guarantee the performance of covenants by his assignee. But the guarantee extends to that one assignee only, and when *he* assigns, his predecessor's liability ceases. So tenants cannot quite walk away from privity of contract, but their position is considerably better than the open-ended liability in pre-1996 leases. There is no automatic release for landlords from their contractual obligations, but the Act enables the landlord to apply to the tenant for that release. The statute does not prevent the parties to a lease from agreeing a more generous rule. A clause that states that the original landlord or tenant's obligations will cease when either assigns his estate is valid, because the statute is intended to provide an additional escape route from liability, and not to prevent the parties from agreeing their own, whether for the tenant's benefit or for the landlord's.[29]

STATUTORY REGIMES FOR THE PROTECTION OF THE TENANT'S INVESTMENT

The idea of power imbalance has been a theme of this chapter. Perhaps the ultimate imbalance in leasehold law is that the tenant, in paying rent, or in buying a lease in return for a premium, is investing in property which ultimately—in the long or the very short term—belongs to the landlord. In return the property is his for a while, perhaps for many years, or perhaps for a few years or a few weeks. There are a number of points of view as to whether or not this is fair, and points of view in this context tend to be political. Whatever one's views, it is easy to see the hardship for the residential tenant whose total payments of rent, over most of an adult lifetime, amount to the value of the freehold; or the business tenant who takes a ten-year lease of a shop (because that is the longest the landlord would grant him), builds up the business, and then has to walk away after ten years; or for Belinda and Ben who bought a 125-year lease, right at the beginning of this chapter, for something close to the price of the freehold of a similar house, and find that 60 years later it is unsellable, because unmortgageable, because the end of the lease is in sight.

The law has found ways to protect the tenant's investment in the leasehold property. For most of the twentieth century this took the form of security of tenure, turning a short-term use right into a long one. Recent politics have frowned upon this because of its adverse effect on the landlord's investment. More recently, the tenant's right to buy, in public sector housing, and the right to leasehold enfranchisement in the private sector, constitute new ways of protecting—perhaps rescuing—the tenant by giving him a capital asset.

SECURITY OF TENURE

Most people have heard the expression 'sitting tenant'. It signifies a tenant who cannot be got rid of, so that his landlord is not able to sell the property with vacant possession. In legal terms, such a tenant has security of tenure; and for much of the twentieth century he may have been residential, agricultural or commercial.

Security of tenure for residential tenants in the private sector was generated by the Rent Acts, which operated on lettings of houses below a certain rateable value, but where the rent was above two-thirds of the rateable value. Thus long leases granted for a premium were excluded, as was the upper end of the market, and the Acts bit primarily on periodic tenancies of relatively low value. They restricted, stringently, the circumstances in which the landlord could remove the tenant. The landlord's notice would indeed terminate the contractual tenancy, but transformed the tenant into a 'statutory tenant' with a personal (not proprietary) right to remain there. If he paid his rent and observed all the tenant's covenants he might stay there for his lifetime. The legislation even allowed members of his family living with him to take over the statutory tenancy after his death. Similar protections in the Housing Act 1985 operate to protect public sector tenants—in particular, those renting council houses. The Rent

Acts applied only to tenancies and not to licences, and were therefore the source of the litigation that thrashed out the sufficient conditions for the existence of a lease. The other role of the Rent Acts was control of rents. The idea was to restrict rents for certain properties—limited by rateable value—at a level below what could be obtained on the open market. Rent control remains today for the remaining Rent Act tenants (see below), but in a much diluted form that is scarcely a disadvantage to the landlord.

Security for business tenants—again, licensees were excluded—derives from the Landlord and Tenant Act 1954. It took rather a different form: it prevented the ending of a business tenancy except in accordance with the terms of the 1954 Act. So whether the tenancy was periodic or fixed-term, it would not come to an end in the normal way—by expiry or by the giving of notice; it could be ended if the tenant so desired, or by the tenant's application for a new tenancy, or by the landlord's giving notice and establishing one of the grounds for possession set out in the Act. These grounds included breach of the tenant's obligations, and a limited range of possibilities for the landlord to recover possession of the land in order to redevelop it or to occupy it himself. The Act sets out a minefield of procedural requirements for the various notices. It enables the court to determine the provisions of a new tenancy, if either of the parties so requests. These will depend to a considerable extent on those of the old one, but the maximum term is fourteen years. There was provision to have a lease excluded from security, subject to the approval of the court, but the statute provided no criteria for the court's approval or otherwise of exclusion. Thus whether or not the lease was excluded from security came to depend largely upon the bargaining power of the parties.

Meanwhile quietly in the background successive Agricultural Holdings Acts gave security of tenure to agricultural tenants and licensees, converting most of them to yearly tenancies, requiring at least a year's notice to quit, and ensuring that they could not be ended against the tenant's will except on the basis of one of the grounds specified in the Act.

Today, security of tenure has largely been dismantled. Residential security went first. It made investment in property to let extremely unattractive, and was of course inimical to Thatcherite politics. The Housing Act 1989 enabled landlords to choose whether to grant an Assured Tenancy—which gave the tenant security—or an Assured Shorthold Tenancy which gave the landlord full rights to terminate the lease on notice, after the expiry of a short initial fixed term (usually six months). Following the Housing Act 1996, residential tenancies are Assured Shorthold Tenancies in the absence of specific provision to the contrary, and it is hard to think why a landlord would voluntarily adopt the secure regime. Thus residential security is no more, in the private sector, for tenancies granted from 1989 onwards. Its death was virtually unnoticed by the Press and seems to have attracted no protests.

Existing secure tenants have not lost their rights in this sequence of reforms: it is just that there will be no new secure tenants in the private sector. There are, of course, Rent Act tenants still; they and their successors will be around for another generation yet. They have been a godsend for family law and human rights. Out of litigation to decide who was a 'member of the tenant's family' and who has been 'living with [the tenant] as his or her husband or wife' have come decisions as to the nature of the family and the value of partnerships, and the recognition that a same-sex partner, unable to marry the deceased, is nevertheless to receive the same succession rights as the tenant's spouse. The draftsmen of the Rent Acts did more good than they could have dreamed of.

Business and agricultural security took rather longer to die. The Agricultural Tenancies Act 1995 designates all agricultural tenancies granted from that date onwards as 'Farm Business Tenancies', without security of tenure. For other business tenancies, a regulation made in 2003 enables landlord and tenant to contract out of security for leases granted after that date, provided the landlord has met the requirement to give a notice to the tenant explaining the security he is foregoing. Thus unless a tenant has exceptional bargaining power, business security is no more.

The one context where security of tenure is alive and well is that of public sector residential tenancies, that is, those where the landlord is a local authority or other public sector landlord. Such tenancies are regulated by the Housing Act 1985, and do give security. It is possible, nevertheless, for such a landlord to grant a very short-term 'introductory tenancy' in order to assess whether or not a tenant should be retained. The difference is obvious; the whole point of the provision of housing by such landlords is the provision of housing, and not the making of an investment or the receipt of income. It has been suggested that this is what marks out public ownership of land from private ownership: the right, or the absence of it, to act in a self-seeking way.

THE RIGHT TO BUY, AND LEASEHOLD ENFRANCHISEMENT

Security of tenure for public sector tenants was originally introduced by the Housing Act 1980. That same statute also introduced the 'right to

buy', that is, the right for public sector tenants to compel their landlord
to sell their house to them, at a discount determined by the number
of years the tenant has been paying rent. The motivation behind this
legislation is complex. It arises to some extent from the feeling that it is
unfair for someone to pay rent without getting a capital return, but also
from the very political view that it is in some senses 'better' to own than
to rent.

The right applies only to periodic tenants and, of course, only to public
sector tenants. Private landlords can be subjected to a similar form of
expropriation, but only in the case of long leases. The Leasehold Reform
Act 1967 gave to tenants holding leases of houses of over twenty-one
years, which they occupy as their homes, the right to 'enfranchise', that
is, to covert their leasehold tenure to freehold tenure (to 'enfranchise' is to
'make free') by buying the property from the landlord. The 1967 Act is of
no assistance to tenants of flats, who cannot become freeholders because
of the impossibility of enforcing vital covenants. The Leasehold Reform,
Housing and Urban Development Act 1993 tackled this by giving tenants
of flats, acting together, a right of collective enfranchisement by acquiring
the freehold of the block. If they do so they can grant themselves leases so
long that their expiry is not an issue. They can then together as owners
of the freehold take over the management or, rather, adopt the usual
structure of delegating this to a management company. The Act also
allows individual tenants to purchase a new lease of their own flat—
relevant where a majority of tenants cannot be found to enfranchise collectively. The system has been further reformed by the Commonhold and
Leasehold Reform Act 2002, which removed the residence qualification
from the right to enfranchise, and also enabled collective enfranchisement
by 50% of qualifying tenants.

The price for enfranchisement is subject to two different regimes.
Tenants of low value houses under the 1967 Act are able to pay a very low
price, supposed to be the site value without the building. Others—tenants
of higher value houses, and tenants of flats—pay a higher price, including
(unless the lease has more than 80 years to run) one half of the property's
'marriage value', that is, the additional price payable on the open market
by *this* tenant because he lives there and is the only one capable of
merging the lease with the freehold. This results in something near to a
market price, and represents a less Draconian deal for landlords.

Leasehold enfranchisement—the private sector version of the right to
buy—has been subjected to challenge on the basis of human rights; and
the European Court of Human Rights ruled, in the case of *James v United*

Kingdom,[30] that enfranchisement legislation did not contravene Article 1 of Protocol 1 to the European Convention, because its goal was to remove social injustice. Injustice is a notoriously moveable concept, but at the root of the enfranchisement legislation, in its private law context, is the idea that one should not be paid twice for something. A landlord who receives a premium for a long lease should not be allowed at the end of that lease to regain possession and do it again. The right to buy is the public law parallel, and here the motivation is much more benevolent: it is not merely that a landlord should not be paid unfairly but rather that a public sector landlord should be actively facilitating homeownership by the tenant, giving a discount on capital price as a response to rent paid.

COMMONHOLD

Commonhold is a response to the same problems that enfranchisement addresses; and it solves the problems that beset enfranchisement in the case of flats. It is a form of freehold ownership for interdependent properties, where leasehold is objectionable both because of the wasting nature of the lease as an asset, and because of the potential for oppression, in the form of poor management, by landlords. Conventional freehold ownership is impossible in such cases because it is imperative to have enforceable positive obligations between owners. Commonhold is not restricted to flats, but is available to any group of properties: houses on an estate; business units, whether divided horizontally or vertically; or a pair of maisonettes.

Commonhold was created by the Commonhold and Leasehold Reform Act 2002. It consists of, first, a number of unit holders (two or more) and, secondly, a commonhold association. The latter is a limited company, of which all the unit holders are members. Title to the whole of the land involved must be registered. Unit holders hold their own unit, and the association holds the common parts of the property (staircases, roofs, car parks etc; the parts that would be retained by the landlord of a block of leasehold flats). The obligations of all are regulated by the Commonhold Community Statement—registered along with the property holdings— which sets out a 'local law' for the group. Some of its contents are prescribed by statute including—thank heavens—the repairing and maintenance obligations. Others are variable by the association, including rules about the use of the property and the rights of holders to grant

---

[30] (1968) 8 ECHR 123.

leases. As to the latter, there are severe restrictions by statute. The theory of commonhold is that it should be a system of self-regulation by occupiers, and therefore unit holders may not grant leases of more than seven years, nor may they grant a lease in return for a premium. There may be further restrictions in a particular commonhold association. Obligations, negative and positive, run with the unit, and enforcement of covenants is not a difficulty. Unit holders will pay a maintenance charge to the commonhold association to pay for the upkeep and management of the common parts.

This apparently simple and obvious arrangement has a great many parallels in the law of apartment ownership worldwide, and there has been a corresponding industry in comparative academic analysis. The key to comparison, however, has to be the fact that in this jurisdiction the leasehold structure has been the norm, whereas in other jurisdictions this may not be an option. The introduction of commonhold had to be done in a form that was at least as attractive to developers, and to potential mortgagees, as leasehold, and the devising of such a form proved controversial and time-consuming. What we now have may or may not be a success. The huge limitation on its adoption is that existing leasehold developments can only convert to commonhold if all the holders of leases over twenty-one years consent. Unanimity may be hard to organise. New developments should be the most fertile source of commonhold registration, but so far only a handful of commonholds have been registered.

CONCLUSIONS AND REFORM

It is perhaps possible to work one's way through an account of leasehold tenure and conclude that nobody wants it, particularly in the light of the development of rights to enfranchise, and of commonhold. But that would not be a safe conclusion. There is certainly a dislike of inequality, and of unequal sharing, which makes the landlord and tenant relationship problematic. And the purchase of a lease as a capital asset is almost a contradiction, since it is a wasting asset. But given our society's use of land as capital, leasehold tenure is an ideal structure both for landlords wanting to maximise the potential of their land, and for tenants who do not have and cannot raise capital. Business and agriculture cannot function without the ability to rent land or office space, and almost a third of the population of England and Wales rent their homes.

So leasehold tenure is essential to our economy and as a way of housing people. Given that, perhaps the greatest problem with it is the multitude of ways in which successive governments have tried to help with its admitted disadvantages. Successive security regimes in the public and private sector have left us with far too many different types of tenancy—protected, statutory, assured, assured shorthold, introductory and so on, with a number of different succession regimes, and with parallel regimes coexisting because legislation has not been retrospective. The law is widely recognised to be a mess.

With that in view, the Law Commission has been working since 2001 on a project designed to simplify the law for those who rent their homes and to make it more consumer-friendly. They plan to sweep away the current multitude of types of tenancy and to replace it with two forms: public sector and private sector, the former carrying security of tenure, the latter not, but both involving some succession rights. Most radically, the terms of these two types of occupation agreement will be prescribed by statute, rather than left to individual negotiation (and therefore to individual bargaining power) as at present. It will be possible to vary prescribed terms, but only in favour of the occupier. Whether or not the Commission's proposals become law is a matter for government. Such a simplification can only be an improvement and it is to be hoped that reform will be swift.

BIBLIOGRAPHY

S. Bright, *Landlord and tenant law: the nature of tenancies* (Oxford, Clarendon, 1995).

S. Bright, 'Uncertainty in lease: is it a vice?' (1993) 13 *Legal Studies* 38.

D. N. Clarke, *Commonhold, The New Law* (Bristol, Jordan Publishing Ltd, 2002).

M. Dixon, *Modern Land Law* (London, Cavendish, 2005), Chapter 6.

Law Commission No. 297, *Renting Homes: The Final Report* (2006).

N. Roberts, 'Two cheers for commonhold' 2002 152 *New Law Journal* 338.

P. Routley, 'Tenancies and estoppel—after *Bruton v London and Quadrant Housing Trust*' [2000] 63 *Modern Law Review* 424.

P. Sparkes, *A new landlord and tenant*, (Oxford, Hart Publishing Ltd, 2000).

P. Sparkes, 'Certainty of leasehold terms' (1993) 109 *Law Quarterly Review* 93.

8

Land Obligations

'Land obligations' could have been the title of Chapter 7. Leases, being contracts, are a form of tenure whose essence is a collection of contractual obligations controlling the use of land. By contrast, freehold tenure is a feudal relationship, in origin composed of obligations much more stringent than those in a lease, but the relationship is now almost content-free and involves no substantive obligations at all. Nevertheless, the term 'land obligations' refers to obligations involved primarily in freehold ownership, arising not from the nature of the ownership, but from the owner's dealings with his neighbours.

'Land obligations' is an optimistic title; it expresses the hope that at some stage our land law might come to regard such obligations functionally in one category, rather than dividing them into easements and freehold covenants as it does at present. That division is a conceptual one, springing from the origins of different sorts of obligation. Roughly: an easement arises from a grant, to another landowner, of a right over one's own land, whereas a covenant is a promise, given to another landowner, to do or not do something on one's own land. This gives rise, as we shall see, to unwelcome complexity.

EASEMENTS

WHAT IS AN EASEMENT?

Easements are to some extent familiar already. We have mentioned the right of way as an obvious example of a non-ownership right over someone else's land, and we know that an easement is one of the few possible legal non-ownership rights.[1] An easement is usually a right to do something specific on another person's land, for example to walk across a path, or to drive down a roadway, to enter the land for a particular purpose such as repair of one's own property or access to pipes, to use storage space, or

[1] Section 1 of the Law of Property Act 1925.

to park a car. The right might not involve personal presence: it might be the right to have one's drains or sewers run underneath the neighbour's garden. Most easements, and all those just described, are positive: they give a positive right to the owner of another piece of land to do something, directly or otherwise. A negative easement is a right to prevent the owner of the burdened land from doing something. So an easement of support, such as the right for my semi-detached house to lean against yours, prevents my neighbour from demolishing his building, and an easement of light prevents him from obstructing my window (but note that an easement of light must be a right for light to pass through a defined aperture; there can be no right to a lovely view).

Similar to easements are *profits à prendre*. A profit, as it is briefly called, is the right to take something from someone else's land, typically fish, sometimes other game or crops. Profits behave, technically, very similarly to easements in the way they are created and in their enforceability, and this chapter will have very little to say specifically about them.

Any formal definition of an easement tends to start with the old case of *Re Ellenborough Park*,[2] in which the court worked out what sort of right *could* be an easement if correctly created. The case concerned the garden in the middle of a square of houses, which the residents in the square were able to use for recreation. Did they therefore have an easement over the garden? The court came up with four conditions for an easement. First, there must be a dominant and servient tenement. A tenement means a piece of land. The dominant one has the benefit of the easement, and the servient one is the object of the right. This is perhaps unexpected, because it means that it is not quite true to say that my neighbour has a right of way over my back yard. Rather, *his land* has the benefit of a right of way, so that he and anyone who buys the land from him can walk across my yard. The right of way is a property right, but it is not separable from the ownership of my neighbour's land. Not all jurisdictions have this rule. In civil law countries an easement, or its equivalent, can be held 'in gross', that is, separately from the ownership of another piece of land. That is not possible for easements in England and Wales; but it *is* possible for *profits à prendre*. As we have seen, the benefit of an easement should be noted on the land register as part of the description of the property, that is, in the property register of the dominant tenement. It should also appear on the 'Charges' section of the servient tenement, as a burden on that title.

[2] [1956] Ch 131.

Easements thus have a debit and a credit entry, one on each of the two titles involved.

Secondly, the right must be one which 'accommodates the dominant tenement'. This links the easement more closely with neighbouring ownership, because it means that the easement must be a right which makes the dominant land a better property. Typical is the English terrace of houses, where there is no access from back garden to front without going through the house, which is inconvenient for someone wheeling a bicycle or a lawnmower. A terraced house is a better property if it comes with a right of access across the neighbours' back gardens to the end of the terrace.

Thirdly, the two pieces of land must be in different ownership. If a servient owner buys the dominant tenement, in theory the easement is extinguished—although in practice this is often ignored. The land registry, for example, would not automatically remove the note of the benefit and burden of the easement from the two titles, if they were kept as separate titles rather than being united as one; and if it is a legal easement, its validity is guaranteed. So this rule is no longer absolute.

Finally and infuriatingly, the Court of Appeal ruled, in *Re Ellenborough Park*, that an easement must be 'capable of forming the subject matter of a grant'. It is unfortunately difficult to say that this means anything except that the right must be 'the sort of thing that can be an easement'. This fourth condition seems simply to leave the courts leeway to rule out something which does not feel like an easement. We can give it substance by pointing out examples of things which have been held *not* to be so capable. Anything which requires the servient owner to spend money, for example the right to draw on a hot water supply—although, anomalously, an obligation to maintain a fence may be expressed as the grant of a right to the neighbour, in which case it is an easement. If the obligation to fence is expressed as a promise to do so, it is a covenant—the behaviour of the right depends upon the wording used in its creation. Anything which amounts to taking exclusive possession of the servient land and preventing the servient owner from using it will amount to 'the wrong sort of thing'. This last one is tricky and has generated some inconsistent decisions about storage spaces. It also means that a right to park in a single space any time is not an easement, whereas a right to park at restricted times, or in any one of a number of spaces in a car park, can be. Of course, if a particular right cannot be an easement, it can still be granted by one landowner to another; but it remains a contractual right, not an interest in land, so that it should not appear on the land register and cannot be alienated, nor be enforced against anyone other than an original party.

So the rules we have as to the nature of easements are rather complex, and not entirely logical. A few anomalies have been mentioned already. Another is the easement of support: the owner of land has a natural right to have his land—i.e. the earth itself—supported by his neighbour's, but not to have his buildings supported. Thus while he has bare land, his neighbour may not dig up against the boundary, but as soon as he builds on it, he effectively loses that right because there is nothing to prevent his neighbour digging so as to threaten the building, until it has stood for twenty years and acquired an easement of support by prescription (see below).[3] This has been a difficulty in the law for a long time, but in recent years it seems that the neighbour who undermines a building will be liable in tort, and equally that the Party Walls Act 1996 will give neighbours a degree of protection from each other's activities. Another tricky area is rights of access to neighbouring land for the purpose of repairing one's own, or for inspecting services. Some properties have it, by express grant when they were divided by a single owner; some have not. All benefit from the Access to Neighbouring Land Act 1992, which imposes a pragmatic solution to this common problem by setting up a system of notices, access and compensation. Again, the law of easements has not been tidied up in order to take account of this development in the law.

CREATION OF EASEMENTS

(1) Express creation

How do easements happen? The theory in all cases, and the reality in most, is that they are granted deliberately by one landowner to another. Usually easements are created when part of a landholding is sold; and they may be either granted to the buyer, or reserved for the seller. This is easy to imagine for a pair of houses, originally owned together. When one is sold off, the seller grants the buyer a right of way over his half of the shared driveway, and reserves for himself a right of way over his new neighbour's half. Occasionally an easement is granted as a separate deal, without a sale. In either case, because an easement is an interest in land, the grant must be in writing in accordance with section 54 of the Law of Property Act 1925. If an easement is to be legal it must be granted by deed (s. 52 of the same) and registered against the servient owner's

---

[3] *Dalton v Angus* (1881) 6 App Cas 740.

title (unless that title is unregistered). Easements that fall short of these requirements—just created in writing, without a deed, say—will be equitable provided that they meet the requirements of section 2 of the Law of Property (Miscellaneous Provisions) Act 1989; so will any easement granted by someone who only has an equitable ownership right.

Creation by a written grant, usually followed by registration, is conceptually easy. More difficult is the fact that there are so many other ways in which easements can be created. They fall into two groups: creation by implication and creation by prescription.

(2) Creation by implication

We have met a number of contexts now where the law implies things: for example trusts of land or covenants in leases. When this happens the law is saying that the parties did something, even though they did not. Similarly an easement is implied when the parties did not create one expressly but the law says they have done. An easement will be implied 'by necessity' when A buys part of B's land and then finds that he cannot get access to it because it is completely landlocked. This is going to be rare, and probably accompanied by an action in negligence against the conveyancer. It will not work if access is possible but difficult, for example if the land is bordered by a public road, but there is a natural barrier such as water or a cliff face in the way; the law is not generous about necessity. Another category of implication is 'by common intention', when it is clear that the parties must have intended there to be an easement when land was sold off. The example usually given is of the ground floor of a building, let for use as a restaurant. A leaseholder claimed that he had an easement enabling to him to fix a ventilation shaft to the upper part of the building so as to allow cooking smells to escape; because the owner of the building had leased the land specifically for this use, the court held that there was an easement arising from the intention they must both have had, that the requisite ventilation shaft be fixed to the wall, since without it the tenant would not have had health and safety clearance for the restaurant.[4] (This latter case is a useful example of the fact that a tenant may have an easement over his landlord's land or, equally, over a neighbour's land). As in most cases where the law implies something because of the parties' intentions, it is a complete fiction; the best that can be said is that the law is filling in what the parties *would* have intended if they had thought of this situation and sorted it out in good faith. But perhaps the

---

[4] *Wong v Beaumont Property Trust* [1965] 1 QB 173.

owner of the building *did* think about it, and consciously did not want the ventilation shaft, and did not care that the tenant would not be able to operate his restaurant without it? After all, he remains liable for the rent. Implied intention, in these cases, is really a matter of what the parties *ought* to have intended, regardless of whether they did or not.

A further context for the implication of easements is where two areas of land have been owned together, but have to some extent functioned as two separate properties, whether just by being physically divided (two fields next to each other with a fence between) or in a more complex way—for example where one has been in the possession of a licensee or tenant while one person remains freehold owner of both. In such situations it may *look as if* there are two 'tenements' and an easement, even though that is not possible because the land is in the same ownership. For example, the farmer always drives across his own, fenced, field to get to the main road; or the person running the shop (whether a tenant or a licensee) always uses the yard at the back to get to the service road; or the lodger hangs out his washing in the garden. Problems arise when part of the land is sold, where before the sale, it looked as if it had the benefit of an easement, although it did not. Should it *actually* benefit from an easement when it passes into separate ownership? If the shop manager takes on a lease of the shop (a new lease on the expiry of an old one, perhaps, or a lease instead of an earlier licence) he might want to carry on using the landlord's yard for an extra means of access. Ideally he would negotiate for this and get it written into the lease. If he forgets, or did not persuade the landlord, will the law let him have the easement nevertheless?

The law does so, making use of a statutory provision that was not designed for this purpose. Section 62 of the Law of Property Act 1925 states, roughly, that certain words are written into conveyances by magic. 'Conveyances' means any deed creating or transferring a legal estate in land: a transfer of registered land, a lease, a mortgage. The magic spell says that the deed "shall be deemed to include and shall . . . operate to convey, with the land all buildings, erections, fixtures, . . . fences, liberties, privileges, easements, rights and advantages whatsoever appertaining or reputed to appertain to the land . . ., or, at the time of the conveyance, demised, occupied, or enjoyed with . . . the land". The section derives from a nineteenth century statute. The intention was, first, to ensure that with the land is conveyed the house that stands on it, and the garden shed; hardly necessary, given the statutory definition of land,[5] but the

---

[5] Chapter 1 at p. 6.

draftsmen were careful souls. In addition, it ensured that if the land had the benefit of an easement, that benefit was transferred to the buyer, without the need for the conveyance to include a paragraph to say so. Also, where a buyer had, for example, been allowed access across the seller's other land during the period between contract and completion, the section was supposed to convert such informal permissions into easements for continued use after the sale. The latter was the most intrusive of the section's purposes, as this might not have been the seller's intention; but if it was not, he was of course free to explicitly exclude the operation of the section from the conveyance.

However, the section was used by the courts to go two steps further. First, it operates where the two pieces of land, although in common ownership, are occupied by different people before the 'conveyance', as we have imagined with the shop manager or the lodger, and has some sort of permission to use the owner's other land. In that case, section 62 will write that permission into the conveyance. If it is the sort of thing that *can* be an easement (i.e. we have to look at the *Ellenborough Park* requirements first) then by dint of being (magically) set out in a deed it will become a legal easement. The shop manager's lease will have an easement over the landlord's yard; if the lodger formalises his situation by taking a lease of part of the house, he will acquire with it an easement to hang washing. So will anyone to whom he transfers the lease.

Secondly, section 62 operates where both plots of land are owned and occupied by the same person, but there is visible evidence of something that looks like an easement, benefiting one plot by the use of the other. The obvious example is a path; moorings for boats might be another. The name for this is a 'quasi-easement'; something that would be an easement if the two plots had different owners. When the owner sells what we can call the 'quasi-dominant' land, section 62 will write into the conveyance the 'liberty' or 'advantage' of being able to walk across, or moor boats on, the other plot of land, or whatever, and if it is a right that *can* be an easement (as can those just mentioned), it will be. This trick with quasi-easements can also be achieved using the authority of the case *Wheeldon v Burrows*[6] in the few fact-patterns where section 62 will not work (e.g. where the 'quasi-dominant' plot is sold or leased, but the interest granted is equitable rather than legal).

---

[6] (1878) 12 Ch D 31.

(3) Creation by prescription

Prescription is the acquisition of easements by process of time. Roughly, if you walk across your neighbour's back yard once a day, for twenty years, without her permission, you will have a legal easement. This may sound very like the process of acquisition of title to land by adverse possession (discussed in the next chapter), and the two processes do indeed look alike, but to the lawyer they are conceptually distinct.

Adverse possession works on the basis that possession of land gives title (i.e. a species of ownership); the longer that possession goes on, the stronger it gets; once the limitation period expires the person dispossessed loses their title. At that point the squatter's is the best title there is and so he is the owner of the land. By contrast, for the whole of the twenty years during which you walk across your neighbour's backyard, you have no right whatsoever. But at the end of twenty years the law says 'you have been doing that so long that your neighbour must have granted you an easement. Therefore you have an easement.' This is, at least, overt fiction rather than any pretence about intention.

In order for prescription to take place, the right claimed must be the sort of right that can be an easement; back to *Re Ellenborough Park*[7] and its four conditions. It must be claimed by a fee simple owner against a fee simple owner. Moreover, it must be exercised openly, peacefully and without permission. Walking across the neighbour's yard only at night, or breaking his gate in order to do so, will not do, and a claim will fail if he writes to give you his permission, or if he nods, smiles and says 'go ahead' whenever he sees you. All these are inconsistent with the fiction that he has at some point actually granted an easement, and so will defeat a claim to prescription; the point used to be expressed by the pleasantly rhythmical Latin phrase *nec vi, nec clam, nec precario*. A further requirement is that the two parties involved—the person claiming the right and the owner whose land is to be the servient tenement—must both hold the land in fee simple. If the claimant is a leaseholder, he can only make the claim on behalf of his landlord (assuming the latter is the freeholder).

If these requirements are met, there are three procedures that can be used to make the claim, known as 'common law prescription', 'lost modern grant', and claims under the Prescription Act 1832.

Common law prescription works only if the claimed right has been exercised 'since time immemorial'; and the courts regard themselves as capable of remembering everything that has happened since Henry II's

---

[7] Note 2 above.

last voyage to Normandy in 1189. Why this method is not officially obsolete is a mystery. If it is clear that the behaviour concerned cannot have gone on for so long—for example if it involves a building of more recent construction—the claim will fail. Perhaps the only real use of common law prescription now is to explain why the courts invented the doctrine of 'lost modern grant'. This is the idea that, since 1189 is a bit distant now, if the claimant proves that he has been exercising the 'right' for twenty years, the court will find—despite clear evidence to the contrary—that he was granted the right claimed, at some point in the past, and must have lost it. There was a grant, at some point in modern times, but it has been lost. Evidence that no grant was made will make no difference at all, but evidence that the supposed grantor did not have capacity to grant it (e.g. because he was a child) will prevent a claim from succeeding.

In order to regularise this mess of fictions, the Prescription Act 1832 was enacted. It is even more badly drafted than the Land Registration Act 1925, and is not a pleasant read. It sets up three methods of claiming an easement: a claim for an easement of light; a claim for any other easement where the claimant has never been given permission; and a claim, again not for light, where the claimant was given oral (i.e. spoken not written) permission. The periods of use necessary for these three situations are respectively twenty years; twenty years; and forty years. There is provision in the Act for the use, on which the claimant relies, to have been interrupted for anything up to a year, so it may be that the claimant has only been using the pathway for nineteen years. What he must prove, however, is that his use of the pathway (or whatever), whether interrupted or not, has taken place in the *last* twenty years before he brings his action—whether that action is litigation in the courts, or an application to the land registry for the entry of an easement. If he is relying on something more distant—something he used to do, and did for twenty years, but the neighbour has kept him out for the past two years—he will have to use 'lost modern grant'.

There are other details that distinguish the three methods and that need not detain us here. The point to be aware of is that there is indeed a lot of detail, and that much of the art of claiming easements by prescription lies in working out which method will fit the facts. This is a time-waster; and it bears little relationship to the purposes behind prescription. One of these is to confirm behaviour and arrangements that have suited people for long periods and which they have come to value and rely upon. Another is to ensure that land benefits from rights that are really essential for its use, whether for access or for the provision of services. Another is to avoid litigation over stale claims, where memories and evidence have faded: this is, as we shall see, one of the traditional justifications for the law of adverse possession. We have to ask whether or not we should retain prescription on its current basis, particularly where title is registered and guaranteed, at least so far as non-essential easements are concerned? Prescription has always been open to the criticism that it penalises altruism or neighbourliness. Someone who has made no objection to next-door's car being parked on his bit of waste land perhaps does not deserve to have his land subjected to a legal right for his neighbour to use the parking space. On the other hand, prescription has some essential functions: hidden easements, particularly for drainage and other services, are vital to land use, and prescription can fill in the necessary rights when they have not been formally granted. It is probably fair to say that prescription requires some dramatic tidying, but not abolition.

ENFORCEABILITY OF EASEMENTS

So: once an easement has been created, does it remain enforceable once the servient land is sold? A sells part of his land to B, but keeps and lives on the rest. The transfer to B gives B a right to walk over A's back yard. If A subsequently sells his land to C, must C continue to give access?

Assuming A's land is registered: ideally, the burden of the easement will appear on A's register, because A and B will have created the easement expressly and completed the disposition by registration. Registration guarantees both validity and enforceability; there is no doubt that the easement will bind C because we know that a purchaser is bound by everything that appears on the register, and by overriding interests. But implication and prescription will create legal easements which will not appear on the register until someone claims or otherwise discovers them. Occasionally, legal easements created before registration of title to the servient land are not registered, by an oversight. Nevertheless these unregistered legal easements will normally bind C, because legal easements are, in most cases, overriding interests.

It is unfortunate that we have to say 'in most cases'. Paragraph 3 of Schedule 3 to the Land Registration Act 2002 is drafted so as to give some protection to the purchaser from rights that he could not have discovered—even though overriding interests bind a purchaser because of their status as such, and *not* because he knows about it (this should sound familiar from what we have said about paras. 1 and 2 of the Schedule).[8]

---

[8] See Chapter 3, at p. 43.

It provides that legal easements are overriding interests *unless* three conditions are all fulfilled, namely; the easement was not obvious on reasonably careful inspection; the purchaser did not actually know about it; and the claimant cannot show that the easement has been used in the last year. This means that an unseen, but daily used, drainage easement will bind a purchaser. So will an easement to pass over someone else's property via a fire-escape, rarely if ever used but clearly visible. But a right of access of which there is no visible clue, and which is used once every couple of years, can be lost when the servient land is sold.[9]

Moreover, equitable easements that are not recorded on the register of the servient land's title will not bind a purchaser. Most equitable easements are equitable precisely because they have not been completed by registration; some, however, are equitable because the grantor (the owner of the servient land) only has an equitable estate in land. The only way to preserve such an easement in case of sale is to record it on the register of the servient land; as an equitable easement it is not a registrable estate and so its validity is not guaranteed by registration, but its priority is preserved by the register.[10]

Finally, if title to the servient land is not registered, the enforceability of easements depends on the old rules: legal easements bind all the world. Before 1925 equitable easements bound a purchaser if he had notice of them; but since then, equitable easements have been registrable under the Land Charges Acts,[11] and so will be void against a purchaser if unregistered.

COVENANTS IN FREEHOLD LAND

A covenant is a promise in a deed. When A sells part of his land to B, the transfer imposes on A the obligation to let B walk across the back yard, as we have seen. It also imposes on both A and B the duty to use the land only for residential purposes and not to run a business on it. This and other stipulations are common in sales of part, because seller and buyer are going to become neighbours and so have an interest (in the non-technical sense!) in the way the other uses the land. They are standard when an estate of

---

[9] This account is incomplete because it does not discuss the transitional provisions, for easements which were overriding interests under the Land Registration Act 1925 but do not qualify under the 2002 statute. The reader is referred to the statute itself, and to conventional textbooks.

[10] See Chapter 3, at p. 42.

[11] See Chapter 3, at p. 46.

freehold houses is built, each of which is to be under an obligation to all the others not use the property for a business, and suchlike.

But while the right of way is created by a grant, made in the transfer to B, the right to control the use of the other's property is created by a promise given in the transfer. The grant is an easement. The promise is a covenant. The grant creates a property right. The promise may or may not create a property right for the person to whom it is made. The rules about the enforceability of covenants are much more unpleasant than those relating to easements. Easements and covenants are different animals that look the same—both give rise to obligations between landowners—but their genetics and behaviour are different. We have to look a little further at the characteristics of covenants, and the rules for their enforceability, before we see if we can bring easements and covenants together so as to create one species.

CHARACTERISTICS OF FREEHOLD COVENANTS

Two parties are needed to make a covenant: the one who makes the promise and the one to whom it is made, or the promisor and the promisee, or the covenantor and covenantee. One has the burden of the promise and one has the benefit.

Two distinctions need to be borne in mind. First, covenants are said to be either positive or restrictive. Positive covenants are promises to do something: to keep a fence in good condition, for example, or to contribute to the cost of maintaining a shared driveway. Negative, or restrictive covenants are promises not to do something: not to use the land for business purposes, not to keep animals on the land, not to build on it, etc. Whether a covenant is positive or restrictive depends on its substance, not its wording. A promise not to allow the fence to fall down is positive; a promise to use the land for residential purposes only is negative. Substance may be easier to see if we ask whether or not keeping the promise involves expenditure or effort; if it does, it is positive.

Secondly, a covenant may 'touch and concern the land'; or it may be merely personal. We met this in the context of leasehold covenants where the same distinction is relevant. A covenant touches and concerns the land if it has an effect on the value of the land, or changes the way one occupies it. Restrictions on its use are obvious examples.

Covenants are created expressly; they do not arise by implication and cannot be generated by time alone. So the space devoted to methods of creating easements is not needed here. Armed with the distinctions just discussed, we can look at enforceability.

ENFORCEABILITY OF FREEHOLD COVENANTS

Oliver sold part of his land to Percy, who promised to maintain the fence dividing the two plots, and not to use his new property for business purposes. One covenant is positive, the other is negative; both touch and concern the land. Percy now sells the land to Quentin (or perhaps leases it or mortgages it; Quentin needs simply to be a purchaser in one of the many possible forms); can Oliver enforce those promises against Quentin and subsequent owners? If not, they are now valueless. If he can, they are in some sense property rights because they are enforceable beyond the original parties to them.

The situation is more complicated if Oliver, too, has sold his land, because then we have to ask if his purchaser, Raffles, is able to enforce the promises, even though they were not made to him. So whenever action is needed to enforce covenants, and the folk involved are not those who made or received the promises, we have to ask: has the benefit of the covenant passed to the person who now wants to enforce it? And has the burden passed to the person against whom action is being taken?

None of this is necessary in the case of leasehold covenants. The passing of the benefit of covenants in leases, from the original landlord to his successor, is well-established by ancient rules; and the passing of the burden is managed by the doctrine of privity of estate. The current landlord and the current tenant are always liable to each other for the covenants made by landlord and tenant in the lease. As we have seen, the problem with leasehold covenants was that *too many* people may in the end be liable, and rules have had to be devised for getting people off the hook. Nor is there any problem about the passing of the benefit and burden of easements. Easements are indisputably property rights. The benefit of an easement sticks to land, in accordance with section 62 of the Law of Property Act 1925; a more visible expression of this is the noting of the benefit of an easement on the proprietorship register for an individual title. The burden of an easement—the fact of being a servient tenement—passes to a purchaser of land only in accordance with section 27 of the Land Registration Act 2002, if the title is registered, and there is no difficulty here if the easement is on the register or is an overriding interest. But covenants between freeholders are, in origin, just contractual promises. And while the contract lawyers have ways of getting the benefit of contractual promises to pass to other people, this cannot be done with obligations to keep promises. Contractual promises are personal obligations.

Again, equity rides to the rescue. Decisions in the courts of equity in the nineteenth century transformed covenants into something far more substantial. Substantial enough to cling to the land, so that in some circumstances, but not all, subsequent buyers of the land must keep these promises even though they did not make them. The covenant can be enforced, and the usual remedies—damages or an injunction—are available. But equity's capacity to rescue the covenant was limited, indeed chopped in half, by one factor: the covenant must be negative. Positive covenants—those which, however worded, involve a promise to do something rather than to refrain from doing something—do not stick to freehold land. If you promise to maintain the fence between your property and mine, and then sell your land, I cannot make my new neighbour keep your promise.

That paragraph hides a hornet's nest of detail. It is not intended here to expound the detail sufficiently to enable the reader to operate the rules, only to explain enough detail to demonstrate what is wrong. To that end, two preliminary points and then enough of the nightmare to alarm, but not enough to induce despair.

The first preliminary point is about method. In any action to enforce a covenant between freeholders, it is worth looking at the two sides and asking: does the defendant actually carry the burden of the covenant? And does the claimant have the benefit of it? If the answer to either of those questions is 'no', then the action will not succeed. The second point is an easy one: anyone who is a party to the original covenant will carry the burden, or bear the benefit, unless there has been a further agreement assigning the benefit to someone else, or explicitly releasing the burden.

(1) Does the defendant have the burden?

Looking, then, at the covenants made to Oliver a few paragraphs ago: if they are to be enforced, we have to ask if the defendant has the burden of them? And if the defendant is Percy, the answer is obviously 'yes'; and it remains 'yes' even if Percy has sold the land, although there are few examples of this happening. Because freehold covenants do not involve the payment of rent, the liability of the original covenantor has never been the massive problem that it became for leasehold covenants.

If the defendant is Quentin, or another later owner, the answer bifurcates.

If the covenant is positive, the answer is 'no'. The covenant to maintain the fence cannot be enforced against anyone other than Percy. We shall see later that there are some indirect methods of achieving enforcement in some cases; but in general the burden of positive covenants does not pass. This is why flats must be leasehold or commonhold, because their interdependence is such that the observance of positive covenants is essential, in particular ones to repair, or to pay a maintenance charge to cover the upkeep of the common parts of the building and land. There has been some debate as to whether or not section 79 of the Law of Property Act 1925 makes the burden of positive covenants pass in any event; the answer appears to be that although the section reads as if it does, it was not intended to do so (only to widen the original covenantor's liability), and does not do so.

If the covenant is negative, the answer may be 'yes', if certain conditions are fulfilled. This is because the landmark case *Tulk v Moxhay*[12] decided that, under these conditions, the courts of equity would enforce the burden of covenants against successors in title; and although what was said in *Tulk v Moxhay* seemed to apply to both positive and negative covenants, later cases discovered or decided that only negative ones had been intended. *Tulk* was about the green patch in the middle of Leicester Square, and the court's decision has kept it green (we should give thanks when we picnic on it or queue for the cinema). Later cases also attempted a rationale: it is said that once the right to, say, build on land has been taken away from it, the land will be passed on to others, shorn of those rights. The right to build just is not in the bundle. This does not make sense, because it is only under certain conditions that equity allows the burden to pass, and where those conditions are not met the right stays in the bundle. It makes more sense to say that the courts are reluctant to pass to a purchaser the burden of a covenant that involves expense, such as maintaining a road. But this does not worry anyone in leasehold land. . . . The issue has been addressed by the House of Lords relatively recently, in *Rhone v Stephens*[13] and, although it is difficult to find any logical basis for the distinction, it was held that it has to stand, because of the chaos that would be caused if the law were changed now by the courts. Careful legislation, with some transitional provisions, would be another matter.

The actual conditions for enforceability are: that the covenant must touch and concern the land; that the covenant was imposed in order to benefit land held by the original covenantee (promisee); that the burden of the covenant must have been intended to run with the land of the

---

[12] (1848) 2 Ph 744.
[13] [1994] 2 AC 310, HL.

original covenantor (and s. 78 of the Law of Property Act 1925 ensures that this is the case unless it is clear from the sale by Oliver to Percy that this was not the intention); and that the covenant must be recorded as a burden on the defendant's land (or, if the latter is unregistered, as a charge under the Land Charges Acts). For pre-1926 restrictive covenants, the latter condition is expressed as a requirement that the purchaser have notice of the covenant. As to the second of those conditions, it is interesting to note that it is very much like the requirement of a dominant tenement for easements. Restrictive covenants can only be property rights if they benefit land, not just a person. Thus if Oliver sold *all* his land to Percy, Quentin and other later owners could not be forced to observe Percy's covenants.

(2) Does the claimant have the benefit?

The rules on enforceability thus cut out a great many covenants once land has changed hands; none of the positive covenants can be enforced directly against successors in title to the covenantor. But if the action is taken against Percy, or against Quentin and for the restrictive covenant only, we have to ask if the claimant actually has the benefit of the covenant.

If the claimant is Oliver, the answer is 'yes', obviously. He can sue on the covenant forever—although it is doubtful if he would be awarded a remedy if the land was no longer his, because in that case he would not have sustained any loss as a result of the breach of covenant. Moreover, section 56 of the Law of Property Act 1925 widens the field a little, making it possible for the transfer from Oliver to Percy to join in others, perhaps neighbours, as parties to the deed and as covenantees, so that they too can enforce the covenant. Section 56 is a little like section 79, mentioned above: its wording is obscure, and it can easily be read as if it does rather more than this. But it seems reasonably well-established that it does not.

If the claimant is Raffles, or any later owner of Oliver's land, then there are two sets of rules, evolved by the two sets of courts and maintained as alternative routes to enforcement even after the courts united. Each route consists of a set of requirements, which can be summarised as follows.

For the benefit of a covenant to run to a successor in title at law:

- the covenant must touch and concern the land;
- the benefit of the covenant must have been intended by the original parties to run with the land (and so the drafting of the covenant by Percy to Oliver must demonstrate this intent);

- the original covenantee (Oliver) must have had a legal estate in land; and
- the current claimant must have the same legal estate as had Oliver.

And for the benefit to run in equity, again the covenant must touch and concern the land, and then one of three things must have happened:

- either the transfer from Oliver to Percy must have annexed the benefit to the land (again, this is done by wording in the transfer from Oliver to Percy, and only certain forms of words will do the trick);
- or the benefit must have been expressly assigned by Oliver to Raffles (again, special words are needed, attaching the benefit to a person rather than to land);
- or the deal between Oliver and Percy must have been part of a 'building scheme'—not, that is, just any new development, but one conforming to conditions set out by the courts.[14]

A wealth of detail attaches to each of these conditions, and a multitude of cases. There has been extensive litigation and academic debate as to whether or not section 78 of the Law of Property Act 1925 does the job, for the legal rules, of determining (in the absence of contrary intention) that the benefit of the covenant was intended to run and, for the equitable rules, of annexing the benefit to the land. It seems reasonably well-established that it does both these jobs.

Given two sets of rules for the passing of the benefit, which does one choose? It is not entirely clear whether or not it matters; but it would seem that if one is enforcing a restrictive covenant against a defendant who is not the original covenantor, the equitable rules for the passing of the benefit should be chosen. So they should if the claimant is seeking a specifically equitable remedy, in particular an injunction to order the defendant to do or not to do something. The proviso must be added that there is always a risk attached, because equitable remedies are discretionary and may, in theory and occasionally in practice, be refused if the claimant's conduct has been less than honourable.

Enough has been said, missing out swathes of detail, to establish that the rules about the enforceability of freehold covenants are unacceptably complicated. There should not be two sets of rules, one at law and one in equity, for the passing of the benefit and burden. A single set of much simpler rules would be a great improvement. The rules as they stand are

[14] In *Elliston v Reacher* [1908] 2 Ch 374.

the subject of so much uncertainty that a change, to clearer law, could not be said to damage any vested interests.

(3) Other Methods

There are other ways, direct and indirect, of ensuring that covenants can be enforced.

Sometimes, an obligation is linked to a benefit. You pay to maintain a private road, and you get to use the road. In *Halsall v Brizell*[15] it was decided that one who accepts a benefit must also accept a burden linked to it. This sounds like rather a good way to enforce positive covenants, but it does not go very far. Some covenants, such as fencing, are not linked with a corresponding benefit. And subsequent cases have refined the rule; the link must be a very close one, so that observing the positive obligation is actually a condition of receiving the benefit; moreover, it must be a benefit that the person concerned can choose whether or not to accept. A road which is the only access to a house, for example, will not be maintained by this method.

Another method, very indirect and unreliable, is the chain of indemnity. Take Percy, who has promised to maintain a fence, and is liable on that covenant forever. So when Percy sells, he may require his buyer, Quentin, to promise—by a covenant in the transfer deed—that *he* will observe positive covenants and will indemnify Percy (i.e. compensate Percy for any damages he has to pay) if they are broken. The covenant may be repeated with each sale, from Raffles to Selina to Tipsy, so that a chain of indemnities is created. The hope is that it will therefore ensure performance by the current owner, at the end of the chain, who knows she will be sued by her predecessors if she fails. Unfortunately a chain of indemnities does not ensure performance of the covenant, as it becomes worthless when one person in the chain dies or becomes bankrupt.

Another method of ensuring that a positive obligation sticks to land is for Oliver to impose a rentcharge on Percy, rather than requiring a covenant from him. A rentcharge is a monetary payment attached to freehold land—an unusual property right, mentioned only briefly in our introductory account of legal interests.[16] It can take the form of a maintenance payment, for a shared road for example. If it is not paid, the freehold is forfeited. Legal rentcharges are registrable estates, and if protected

---

[15] [1957] Ch 169.
[16] See Chapter 3, p. 37.

by registration they will bind a purchaser on the usual principles. Such obligations are very little used, perhaps because purchasers are unwilling to accept an obligation where breach carries such a Draconian penalty.

Finally, if there is any difficulty with the running of the benefit of the covenant, it may be that in some circumstances the Contracts (Rights of Third Parties) Act 1999 may help, in enabling a claimant who was not actually a party to a contract to sue on it; but as yet there are no decisions on the effect of that Act in this context.

GETTING RID OF LAND OBLIGATIONS

Both easements and covenants may be released, expressly; in effect, the person who has the benefit of them says 'I don't want this any more'. This rarely happens. Both may be impliedly released, by behaviour that makes it clear that the person entitled to the benefit does not want it any more. This is quite hard to prove. Where, for example, a passageway behind a row of terraced housing has been blocked off by one or more of the households that are allowed to use it, by fences or sheds or the like, it may eventually be concluded that the easement is not wanted. 'Eventually' may take a long time. Twenty years' use of a pathway may generate a right of way, but twenty years' non-use is not sufficient to get rid of it (although, as we have seen, one year's non-use of an easement that is not obvious to inspection will make it unenforceable against a purchaser of the servient land).

Many covenants are now extremely old, having been imposed in the nineteenth century when the industrial revolution was the motivation for land being sold off, by the landed gentry for new housing. At the time, it was a valuable form of private planning control. Now, the covenants may be meaningless—a promise not to build a house worth less than £200 is obviously pointless now—or it may be entirely unclear whether anyone has retained enough of the covenantee's original land to be able to enforce the covenant, or that it would benefit them if they did. Accordingly section 84 of the Law of Property Act 1925 gives the Lands Tribunal the power to modify or to discharge a restrictive covenant when it has become obsolete in one of these ways, or if the person entitled to the benefit of the covenant consents.

REFORM? LAND OBLIGATIONS?

NEED FOR REFORM

So: what is wrong with land obligations as the law stands? So much is unsatisfactory that it is hard to know where to begin. Some of the issues stick out, and seem ripe for piecemeal reform, but it will be suggested that this would not be a wise approach.

For one, there is the problem that there are too many ways of creating easements. Recent case law has made the operation of section 62 of the Law of Property Act 1925 more complex. The rules relating to prescription are complex, badly drafted in the case of the statutory method, and come in too many variant forms. What is the purpose of having three sets of rules? Another issue relates to the acquisition of land obligations. To what extent should it be possible for them to be acquired by implication? So far as the servient owner is concerned, acquisition by implication is tantamount to acquisition by accident. In particular, is the current operation of section 62 acceptable? Given that it is certainly wrong that three different methods of prescription are possible, do we want to retain one (properly drafted) method and, if so, for which rights should it be available? At minimum reform should deal with the current anomalies linked with rights of support for land and buildings.

Just as importantly, consistent rules are needed for the discharge of obsolete obligations. There are obligations that no-one wants or uses; there are some that impose an obligation disproportionate to the benefit conferred; and some that prevent land being used. At present covenants are well-catered for in this respect, both procedurally and substantively, but easements are not. This would seem to be an easy reform to effect.

The issue that perhaps looms largest is: should the burden of positive covenants run with land? No-one has come up with a convincing reason, other than precedent, why they should not, and any consideration of the problem is almost certain to come up with the answer 'yes'. The real difficulty lies in deciding which of the people with an interest in the land should bear that burden. The range of potential bearers includes not only freehold owners, but people who are purchasers from them, not outright, but of a lesser interest such as a lease or a mortgage, as is the case with easements and restrictive covenants. Certainly a freeholder should observe positive covenants, and certainly a 99-year leaseholder—both have unambiguous ownership rights. But where land is burdened with an obligation to carry out expensive maintenance, a weekly tenant should not have to bear this. The solution chosen in Northern Ireland, which has effected this reform,[17] is to provide that covenants are enforceable against a fee simple owner or the holder of a life estate. The correct answer may depend upon the nature of the obligation. A weekly tenant might reasonably pay for services he uses, but not for major repairs. The practical answer is probably to link positive obligation to capital payment. Someone who has an interest in the land for which he has paid a capital value (in particular a long leaseholder) should have to observe the positive covenants just as the freeholder does. A weekly tenant paying rent should not, although the charge for services he uses can easily be factored into his rent.

Another discrete problem is that as matters stand there are just too many sets of rules for the enforceability of covenants. Whether or not the burden of positive covenants is to run with the land, the whole mass of rules on enforceability needs to be boiled down. If I want to enforce a covenant, I must make a whole series of decisions, and get them right, before I can be sure of success: do I have the benefit of this covenant? Shall I go for the equitable rules or the legal rules (and why should one system of courts use two sets of rules? Can the courts not simply decide when it is right for the benefit to run, according to one set of principles?). Can I satisfy either set of rules?—this largely depends not upon me, but upon the drafting of the transfer that set up the covenant. Would the Contracts (Rights of Third Parties) Act 1999 help me here? If I have the benefit, does the defendant have the burden? If he is not the original covenantor, there is no point in suing him unless the covenant is negative (but if it *is* positive, would the rule about linked benefits and burdens be of any assistance? Or shall I sue the original covenantor and hope that the chain of indemnities is in working order and provides an incentive for the current owner to mend the fence?). If the covenant is indeed negative, has the burden run to this defendant?—again, much depends upon the original draftsman. If the folk involved when the covenant was set up used the wrong words, all may be lost. The making of all these decisions is a waste of time—and indeed millions of pounds and hours have been wasted on the litigation that gave rise to the cases that made the rules so complicated. Litigation uncertainty is made much worse than usual by the presence of statutory provisions, in particular sections 56, 78 and 79 of the Law of Property Act 1925, whose meaning is unclear. Another problem is the continuing liability of an original covenantor for

[17] Property (NI) Order 1997, art. 34.

breaches of covenant by the current owner, after he has parted with his interest in it. The contractual rules should be changed, but more decisively than has been done in leasehold land, to ensure that only the current owners of the land can sue and be sued for breaches of obligations, or interferences with rights. The mass of rules on the running of benefit and burden should be erased and replaced with simple rules attaching the benefit and the burden of obligations to land. And the rules must not require a claimant to decide whether to opt for law or for equity. The claimant should be able to rely on the court to administer one set of rules in response to his evidence, and one range of remedies.

It is tempting to try to reform one or perhaps all of these issues. But they are in fact micro issues. Any reform must tackle the big issue, on pain of being justly seen as a waste of an opportunity. The big issue is that, officially, we do not have land obligations. The successful operation, and in particular the enforcement, of easements, *profits à prendre* and covenants depends on their being correctly classified as such, even though all generate obligations associated with the ownership of land. And it may be difficult to know which is which. To the layman it is wholly unclear why the right to prevent his neighbour from building a wall in front of his window should operate in a different way from the right to prevent his neighbour from running a business on his property. The fact that one right is an easement and the other is the benefit of a restrictive covenant is largely a historical accident, so that form has triumphed over substance. The fact that an obligation to fence may arise from an easement or from a covenant depending on the drafting of the document creating it is equally unacceptable. This problem should be made to disappear, and classification should be redrawn along functional lines.

And having got land obligations under one roof, it would be possible to tackle afresh the subsidiary problems of creation, discharge and enforceability. Should implied creation be possible at all, or should creation only be express? If implied creation is to be allowed, which methods are appropriate; and are there obligations which it should only be possible to create expressly? And what should be the conditions for enforceability? Easements, which are enforceable without the convoluted combinations of conditions required for covenants, provide a good model for all land obligations. Extra rules could be provided to regulate the enforcement of positive obligations, i.e. those that require action or expenditure.

Can this be done? There have been some attempts, and it may be that another one is about to happen, with a good chance of success.

THE LAW COMMISSION'S CONTRIBUTION

There have been several reports and recommendations for reform of this area of the law from the 1960s onwards. The most significant have been those of the Law Commission, which has produced two suggestions, and is in the process of producing another.

The first was contained in a Working Paper in 1971.[18] The suggestion was that easements, covenants and *profits à prendre* be brought within a unified scheme, and that they be known as land obligations, of a number of different types. The scheme distinguished neighbour obligations, where only two properties were involved, and development obligations used for a number of properties. Only certain types of obligation, corresponding to positive easements and to *profits à prendre*, would be capable of being created other than expressly, for example by prescription.

The second was contained in a Report in 1984.[19] The Report's suggestion was restricted. Again a unified scheme was proposed, enabling the burden of positive covenants to run, and again distinguishing between development obligations and neighbour obligations.

These two suggestions have remained on the shelf for so long because attention was diverted, after 1984, to commonhold and was focused on developments of interdependent properties. It was believed that the solution to the problem of the running of freehold covenants was the invention of commonhold, so that flats would not have to be leasehold any more. But of course commonhold is not the happy ending to the problem of the running of positive freehold covenants, let alone to any of the other problems inherent in land obligations. Most existing developments of flats will remain leasehold (unless there is unanimous enthusiasm for conversion to commonhold). New commonholds are not, for the most part, being constructed (although that may change with time), and many freehold properties need to be able to enforce positive covenants, without having other elements of interdependence that make them suitable for commonhold. The vast majority of properties look set to remain freehold or leasehold for the foreseeable future.

But with commonhold on the statute book, it may be that there is space to look again at land obligations; indeed, to look at easements and covenants as land obligations and to see if rationalisation is possible. The Law Commission announced in its Eighth Programme of law reform an

---

[18] Law Commission Working Paper No 36, 'Transfer of Land: Appurtenant Rights'.
[19] Law Commission No 127, 'Transfer of Land: The Law of Positive and Restrictive Covenants'.

examination of 'easements and analogous rights, together with a possible
system of land obligations'. How far should it go? Clearly 'analogous
rights' includes *profits à prendre*. Covenants are not expressly mentioned,
but they are part of the core of land obligations in the 1971 Working
Paper, while the 1984 scheme of land obligations related only to covenants. The Commission is therefore free to look at land obligations as
a whole; perhaps to consider in detail a number of issues relating to
easements—in particular prescription and rights of support—and then to
pick up the ball dropped after 1984 and bring the whole together again,
as it did in 1971. In doing so it would have to decide whether to recom-
mend a scheme that would work for groups of properties, as well as for
pairs of neighbours, or to leave the issue of groups of properties to be
dealt with using commonhold. This is a tricky one. On the one hand,
commonhold is not yet working and there is as yet no possibility of its
adoption on a large scale. On the other hand, there would be political
difficulties ahead of any legislation that openly admitted defeat on commonhold. Whatever the answer on that one, another essential difficulty
will be the problem of retrospectivity: how would any new scheme interact with existing rights? It is probably not right, nor practicable, to do
what the House of Lords refused to do in *Rhone v Stevens* and make the
burden of existing positive covenants run with the land. This aspect at
least of any reforming legislation would have to be prospective only.

At the time of writing, a Law Commission Discussion Paper is awaited.
Eagerly awaited, in view of the horrible messiness of this area of the law.

BIBLIOGRAPHY

A. Dawson and I. Dunn, 'Negative easements—a crumb of analysis' (1998)
18 *Legal Studies* 510.

N. Gravells, 'Enforcement of Positive Covenants Affecting Freehold Land'
(1994) 110 *Law Quarterly Review* 346.

Law Commission No 127, 'Transfer of Land: The Law of Positive and
Restrictive Covenants' (1984).

L. Tee 'Metamorphoses and s. 62 Law of Property Act 1925' [1998] *The
Conveyancer and Property Lawyer* 115.

Whatever Happened to Relativity of Title?

This chapter concerns relativity of title, which used to be an important concept, but is no longer. We need to explore why this is. Closely linked with relativity is the law relating to adverse possession; again, this used to be central to land law, but is no longer. Nevertheless, it has sparked off considerable excitement within the period in which this book was written, by engendering the biggest incursion of human rights law into land law that we have yet seen. That excitement—and the story is not yet finished—is a fitting way to end this chapter and this book, because it concerns the nature of ownership of land and forces a re-examination of some of the concepts with which we started.

RELATIVITY AND LIMITATION

To get the idea of relativity of title, remember what was said in Chapter 3 about deeds. Where title is unregistered, ownership of land is proved by producing a stack of deeds, which when read through from the top down tells the story of the ownership of that land. Apart from being on paper rather than oral, this is conceptually no different from peasant folk proving title to land by reciting a genealogy: this land is mine because I inherited it from my father, who had it from his father, etc. The idea being expressed is: 'the land is mine, not by virtue of one single indisputable transaction, but because I live here and I [and my predecessors] have been here longer than anyone else'. What is being asserted is not an absolute title, but a relative one: the best available right to possess the land.

Why did English land law develop so as to depend upon proof of relative rather than absolute title? After all, in the early Middle Ages it was still possible to prove a right to hold land by pointing to a Crown grant, whether documented or by appealing to witnesses and to memories. The answer to this question lies in medieval court processes. Of the numerous ways of recovering land in the Middle Ages, two procedures seem to have steered the substance of this part of the law. One was the 'writ of right' (a writ was a document summoning the parties to court), the *breve de recto tenendo*. Such a writ required proof of the best possible entitlement to the land—something like absolute title—and it was tried by battle. It was not therefore to be undertaken lightly. Even when trial by battle became obsolete, the writ remained procedurally and evidentially inconvenient. The other way of doing it was to use the 'assize of novel disseisin'. This was tried by producing witnesses before a jury; and it was relatively quick and easy. What had to be proved was simply that you were in possession of the land before your opponent—who was supposed to be a recent trespasser, hence the 'novel'. Accordingly, the action in trespass came to be used always in preference to the writ of right, as a general way of asserting title to land, and English law did not bother to develop any other way of proving title absolutely. Thus it has been said that all an English landowner can ever prove is a relative title, an entitlement that is better than that of whoever is disputing it, rather than an absolute title indisputable by anyone at all.

The trouble with relative title, of course, is that, logically, proof is never complete. The weakness of a title going back 100 years might be that someone else could prove a chain of title going back 150 years, and so on. Surely the system requires us to prove ownership all the way back to 1066, or as far back as we can get? It does not, and the reason it does not is the concept of the limitation of actions. There is a policy that court proceedings should be brought reasonably promptly, so that evidence does not go stale and so that people can be reasonably confident that what they hold will not be challenged after a while. This applies as much to the law of obligations as to the law of property. You can sue for a breach of contract up to six years after a breach, and after that there is nothing you can do about it. And so it goes for land as well. If someone else sets up home in your house or starts grazing horses in your spare field, you cannot put off forever the day on which you take court proceedings to throw him out. The principle of limitation of actions means that, at the end of the limitation period—twelve years—you will simply lose your title to the land.

The logical outcome of this is that when proving ownership of land, where title is unregistered (where title is registered, the law is now quite different, as we shall discuss), all one really has to do is to prove that one has been in possession of the land for longer than the limitation period: the last twelve years. And this puts a convenient limit on the size of the heap of deeds that one has to keep.

In practice, in unregistered land the requirements for proof of title take one a little further back than that, for the avoidance of doubt and in order to ensure that good quality evidence of title is available. The stack of deeds is supposed to start with a document at least fifteen years old (thus a little longer than the limitation period). That document must be a 'good root of title', namely one which gives comprehensive information about the land, and must be a transaction for value rather than a transmission after death. Thus the landowner whose family acquired a farm, or perhaps a stately home 200 years ago, would keep at the bottom of his heap of deeds the conveyance to his ancestor 200 years ago, plus all the documents transmitting the land down the generations since then, plus any documents dealing with the land in the meantime; mortgages, leases, grants of easements, records of sales of part of the land, etc. Jones, selling his ordinary suburban house, bought and sold every few years, would simply trace title back to the last conveyance more than fifteen years ago. That small stack of deeds says: 'this land is mine because I bought it from Bloggs ten years ago, and he bought it from Biggs twenty years ago. Since you can see that I am in possession of the land, there is no chance that it has been acquired by a squatter in the course of the last twenty years. So you can safely buy it from me.' Notice the importance of possession in that analysis: the claim is not watertight without it, because if Jones is not in possession of the land someone else might be, and might have been, for all we know, for more than twelve years, because Bloggs may not have bought a good title from Biggs.

Suppose someone else—Sam the squatter—*did* take possession of the land, or of some of it, nineteen years ago. The land is now his. How does that work?

SQUATTER'S TITLE

Let us embroider the story a little; and for the sake of understanding how adverse possession and relativity of title *have* operated, let us assume that all the titles in it are unregistered despite the fact that, in real life, compulsory registration would have changed that, and let us ignore, for now, changes to the law of adverse possession caused by human rights legislation.

Bloggs bought the land twenty years ago. It is not an ordinary house, but a large farm and Bloggs was not a careful farmer. Nineteen years ago his neighbour Sam, who had been trespassing by grazing his goats on an unfenced area belonging to Biggs and then to Bloggs for some time, put up a fence around that area, separating it from Bloggs' land and joining it on to his own. The goats grazed on quietly. Ten years ago Bloggs sold to Jones, who did not notice the discrepancy between the land on the plan and the fencing on the ground. Jones now wants to sell; and *his* purchaser has noticed that Jones is not in possession of the goat field. Investigations are made. It turns out that Sam can prove the date on which he put the fence up, and can show (from a mixture of documentation, photographs and the evidence of his wife and the neighbours) that he has been in possession of the field ever since. If he can also show that he intended to possess the land and to exclude others, including the 'true' owner, so far as was practicable, then he has proved, first, that Jones ceased to be owner of the land seven years ago, at the point when Sam clocked up his twelve years' possession.[1] Secondly, the evidence he has collected is equally proof that he is the owner of the goat field. He can produce that evidence to the land registry and his title can be registered, on a voluntary basis. He is not obliged to register, but a purchaser is unlikely to accept his title unless it is acceptable to the registry.

The detail of what a squatter must prove in order to grow a title to the land in this way has been evolved over the years in the courts. The courts have analysed possession as having both a physical element—the squatter must, as a matter of fact, be in possession of the land—and a mental element—he must actually intend to be there and to use the land as his own, and to keep others out so far as practicable, and his actions must make that clear. Mending a fence around an area in order to keep live-stock in it will not necessarily do this; fencing an area and padlocking the gate will. He does not have to show that he intended to become the owner, nor that he meant to steal it, nor that he thought the land was his, nor that he would not have been unwilling to pay rent for the land if asked. There is no need for him to have actively evicted Bloggs, nor for his activities on the land to have been interfering with Bloggs or Jones. But he must not be there with permission; permission makes him a licensee, and a licensee cannot be in adverse possession. This means that one easy way to defeat a claim by a squatter is to give him permission to stay.

Before 1833, successive limitation statutes required that the squatter's possession be *adverse*, in the sense that it must be inconsistent with the way the paper owner intended to use the land. The 1833 statute dropped that requirement. The courts revived it in *Leigh v Jack*[2] in 1879, holding that if a squatter was using land for which the paper owner had no

---

[1] Limitation Act 1980, s. 17.
[2] (1879) 5 Ex D 264.

current use, and was not actually interfering with anything the owner wanted to do, he was not in adverse possession and the limitation period could not run against the owner. That decision was not clearly overruled until 1990.[3] Notice that a consequence of these developments is that it is possible for a landowner to lose land inadvertently, by carelessness about the activities of a trespasser during a period when he had no use for the land but intended to develop it in the future. This sounds like the legitimisation of theft, or, at least, like a very harsh penalty for understandable slackness. We shall have more to say about this shortly.

The squatter's title arises, not from the ending of the entitlement of the paper owner of the land after twelve years, but from his own possession. It works like this. At the point just before Sam takes possession of the field (it is not clear when that is: but it happens, at the latest, when he puts the fence up), Bloggs has a legal fee simple estate in it. Just after Sam takes possession, so has Sam, purely because he has possession of the land.[4] There are two fees simple in the land at this point, and for the next twelve years. Someone who has taken possession of land has a fee simple in it because of the status of possession in legal proceedings. If all that is needed to remove another person from land is proof that you were in possession of it before he was, then possession is a strong right, and so, over time, possession itself came to be regarded as an estate in land, provided the possessor is not on the land by permission. And the law allows this estate to be transmitted to one's heirs, so that it can be called a 'fee'.[5] If Sam dies after five years' possession, his heir (by his will or intestacy) will take over that five years' credit, as it were, and can carry on squatting. There is no particular restriction on its duration, so it is a fee simple. By section 1 of the Law of Property Act 1925, it qualifies as a legal fee simple.

So for the first twelve years of Sam's possession there are two legal owners of the land; but one owner has a stronger right than the other. Both Bloggs and Sam have the right to keep others out of the field. But while Bloggs has the right to remove Sam too (he could take down the fence and chase off the goats or, if that does not work, he can sue in trespass), Sam has the right to eject anyone who enters the land against Sam's will *except* Bloggs. Bloggs still has the best available right to possession of the land; but in legal proceedings between Sam and another, later

[3] *Buckinghamshire CC v Moran* [1990] Ch 623.
[4] *Asher v Whitlock* (1865) LR 1 QB 1, Exch Ch.
[5] Chapter 2, at p. 18.

passer, Sam will win, because he has a better right to possession—he as been there longer—than anyone else except Bloggs. Title is thus relative. What matters in any given set of proceedings is having a better title than one's opponent, not being the 'true' owner of land. If this all sounds medieval, it is. But it has been fiercely defended by lawyers because it has the virtue of pragmatism. It enables the purchaser of land to start from the assumption that whoever has possession of land is supposed to be there, and it ties ownership of land to the truth about what is happening on the ground.

Sam's squatter's title is therefore not one that he has taken from Bloggs or Jones. His title is acquired by possession. It is always a fee simple title, even if Bloggs and Jones happen to be leaseholders rather than freeholders.[6] If that is the case, their right to the land ceases at the expiry of the limitation period just as it does if they are freeholders. Suppose they held, successively, a 99-year lease granted by Fred the freeholder in 1951. In 2050, their lease would have ended anyway. Sam has by then been enjoying a fee simple for a number of years. But when the 1951 lease ends, Fred becomes entitled once again to take possession of the land. And from that point onwards, Sam can be evicted by Fred for twelve years, because Fred has the right to sue in trespass until the limitation period expires against him, as it did decades ago against the successive leaseholders.

The law of adverse possession is particularly useful in the context of mistakes about boundaries. I build a garage at the edge of my land. I make a mistake about the boundary, so that the garage encroaches onto your garden by about 20 cm. Neither you nor I notice. I have physical possession of that 20 cm; I certainly intend to use the land as my own, it being part of my garage. For twelve years, if you notice what has happened you can make me move the garage. After twelve years the mistake does not matter because the law of adverse possession has brought ownership into line with possession and I am now the sole owner of the 20 cm strip. If anyone notices the discrepancy between the land and the plans, we can check the date when the garage was built and we can re-draw the plans. This avoids litigation and ensures that documentary title can easily be brought into line with what is happening on the ground.

That, then, is the background; and that is still the law in the rapidly reducing number of instances of unregistered title. But the Land Registration Act 2002 dramatically reduced the circumstances in which title can be acquired by possession where title to the land is registered. This

---

[6] *Fairweather v St Marylebone Property Co Ltd* [1963] AC 510.

will now be so very rare that it is no longer realistic to say that title is in any sense relative in registered land.

THE REVOLUTION: ADVERSE POSSESSION AND REGISTERED LAND

In a number of jurisdictions, acquisition of title by adverse possession is not possible when title is registered. Indeed, it was not possible under the early English registration statutes in the nineteenth century. The limitation of actions is not needed as a way of avoiding trials of very old disputes with stale evidence if the only evidence of title needed is the register itself. But the Land Registration Act 1925 allowed it, because of its usefulness in dealing with boundaries. Experience with the early registration statutes, where boundaries had to be determined precisely, indicated that it would be much easier to leave boundaries rather loosely indicated on land registry plans, and to allow adverse possession to operate to resolve difficulties when they arose.

Working out the mechanics of adverse possession when title is registered is not straightforward. Suppose, in our example above, Biggs' title were registered. Bloggs would have become the registered proprietor ten years ago, and his title would have included the goat field. What happened seven years ago, when he ceased to be the owner of the goat field? He did not, of course, notice this happening (neither did Sam, unless he was unusually well-informed), and no change was made to the register. Bloggs remained the registered proprietor of the goat field and that means, as we have observed,[7] that he still held the legal title to that land, even though adverse possession is supposed to have taken away his title. The solution to this problem adopted by the Land Registration Act 1925 is to say that from the point when the limitation period expires, Bloggs holds the registered title upon trust for Sam. If Sam eventually registers his squatter's title, Bloggs' legal title to the goat field will disappear. The same analysis works for the boundary mistake, where eventually the land registry plans for the two titles will be amended.

This meant that the Land Registration Act 1925 did not truly abolish relativity of title. It substituted a registered title for a deeds-based title. But it did not eliminate the possibility of a concurrent and unregistered fee simple by adverse possession, growing quietly in the background, maturing after twelve years into one that defeats the ownership of the

[7] Chapter 3, at p. 41.

registered proprietor. Proof of possession, as well as reference to the register, remained an essential part of the proof of title.[8]

The use of a trust to manage the discrepancy between paper ownership and the truth of ownership on the ground is ingenious, but uncomfortable. Sam is supposed to have a legal title from the point at which he takes adverse possession; is it converted to an equitable one when the trust takes effect? If Bloggs owns the land jointly with his wife would Sam's interest be overreached when Mr and Mrs Bloggs sold the land? If so, would Bloggs hold the sale proceeds on trust for Sam? In any event it is unnecessary, because Sam's interest was an overriding interest[9] and would bind a purchaser just as could other legal, unregistered interests such as an easement or a short lease.

At a more general level, the idea of having more than one fee simple in registered land was upsetting to land registration theory. Can there be more than one registered freehold estate, as in the case where Biggs and Bloggs were leaseholders and they have lost their titles but their landlord has not? The practice of different land registry offices differed in such cases.[10] And what, at a higher level still, about the idea of the guarantee of title? If registration means that one's title is guaranteed, does it make sense to have the possibility of losing it to a squatter?

The answer to that last question is actually 'yes', if land has been abandoned, and for boundary problems. But in other respects, adverse possession is not relevant to registered land, because it is not needed as a way of controlling the proof of title. All the business about restricting the age of deeds one needs to keep and produce in order to show title is irrelevant when title is seen simply by looking at the register. So much of the need for adverse possession is gone, even though some of the practical justification remains.

---

[8] Just a few cases may still be decided under the Land Registration Act 1925, where it is claimed that title was actually acquired by a squatter before 2003 and remains valid because of the transitional provisions of the Land Registration Act 2002. These cases have now been radically affected by the decision in *Beaulane Properties Ltd v Palmer* [2005] EWHC 1071 (Ch): see below, at n. 13.

[9] The 1925 Act included an overriding interest: 'rights acquired or in the course of acquisition under the Limitation Acts'. This meant that Sam's years of adverse possession still counted in his favour when Bloggs became owner; and that once he became absolutely entitled as against Bloggs, his ownership remained enforceable against purchasers, even if he was not in actual occupation of the land. That overriding interest is not found in the 2002 Act.

[10] In *Spectrum Investment Co. v Holmes* [1981] 1 WLR 221 the squatter was given a leasehold title, becoming a tenant under the lease that the dispossessed leaseholder had held, but with a different title number.

ADVERSE POSSESSION AFTER THE LAND REGISTRATION ACT 2002: TITLE BY REGISTRATION

Section 96 of the Land Registration Act 2002 abolished the limitation period for registered titles. It did so, because the Law Commission was persuaded by the technical conveyancing point just mentioned, by the argument about guarantee, by the fact that limitation is not needed to prevent stale evidence of title, and by one further issue: the need to encourage voluntary registration. One of the aims of the Land Registration Act 2002 was to get rid of unregistered title and ensure that all land gets on to the register. As we have seen,[11] land is forced on to the register when it is sold or mortgaged, or when it is transmitted on death. Some land never goes through these processes, because it is held on a family trust, for example, or owned by a University or a local authority. One way of persuading such entities to register their land voluntarily is to make registration attractive: and so by providing that there is no limitation period with respect to registered titles—i.e. there is no restriction on how long one can delay before evicting a trespasser—the Land Registration Act 2002 has made registered titles squatter-proof. Subtract five years from the figures in the story of Sam, Jones, Biggs and Bloggs. Now, at the point when Sam has been in possession of the land for twelve years, the Land Registration Act 2002 is in force. There is no limitation period for registered titles, Bloggs does not automatically lose to Sam, and Sam has no right to registration.

This means that proof of title has been divorced from proof of possession just as surely as the Land Registration Act 1925 divorced it from deeds. All that is needed to show ownership of land is the land register. And that is why it no longer makes sense, except for those areas of land whose title is not yet registered, to say that title to land in England and Wales is relative. Legal ownership is by registration alone. Although, technically, a squatter can still be growing a fee simple by adverse possession, that fee simple will never, by itself, mature into true ownership and so it is not a significant interest. There are some very limited circumstances, to be discussed below, where Sam can become the registered proprietor of the land; but adverse possession alone is never sufficient. And in those limited cases, the title Sam acquires on registration is the

[11] Chapter 3, p. 40.

title that the dispossessed proprietor lost. It is a takeover; if Bloggs was a leaseholder, Sam will take over the lease so far as it relates to the field. The squatter's fee simple, acquired by adverse possession, disappears.

Now that, in the vast majority of cases, the squatter's interest in the land can no longer turn into true/sole ownership, it may be that we shall in time cease to regard it as a fee simple (since most land law concepts have been defined by reference to their practical effects). So it would be a short step to a legislative redefinition of the squatter's interest during the qualifying period. All the rigmarole about his ability to evict later trespassers is scarcely necessary; he need not be regarded as having a property right during this period. Limitation starts to look much more like the prescription of easements.

So that is what has happened to relativity of title. But there is more to say about adverse possession, and about its surviving role.

ADVERSE POSSESSION AND HUMAN RIGHTS

The statutes of limitation can be said to deprive landowners of their property without compensation. English law has never regarded them in this light. We have always viewed them as a necessary rule of litigation and a component in conveyancing practice. As we have seen the necessity for the limitation of actions to recover land is considerably weaker once title is registered. And alongside the growing appreciation of the inappropriateness of limitation in registered title there is a new awareness of the human rights difficulties inherent in the principle.

Against that background come two landmark decisions on adverse possession, *Pye v Graham*[12] and *Beaulane Property Ltd v Palmer*.[13] Both concerned farmland, specifically fields used for grazing. In both cases the fields were not currently useful to their registered proprietor, but were supposed to be developed in the future. In both cases the registered proprietor was a property developer and the land, with its development value, was extremely valuable. And in both cases it would have been very easy for the owner to turn the squatter off the land. The squatter was inoffensively taking advantage of the owner's failure to object to his presence. In both cases he would have left if asked. Eventually, the two squatters realised the strength of their position and claimed a title by adverse possession, before the coming into force of the Land Registration Act 2002.

---

[12] [2002] UKHL 30.
[13] [2005] EWHC 1071 (Ch).

The two cases were unconnected, but their stories overlap. Pye (Oxford) Ltd lost its land after appeals as far as the House of Lords. The decision was seen as an uncomfortable one, in that the loss of so much land was an excessive penalty for the owner's laziness. But human rights considerations were dismissed by the Court of Appeal on the basis that the Limitation Act 1980 does not take away the owner's land, but simply forbids him access to the courts to recover it. This is surely, quite simply incorrect, because of the fact that the owner's title is also extinguished; but in the House of Lords, surprisingly, Pye conceded that human rights arguments were not relevant because the dispossession took place before the coming into force of the Human Rights Act 1998.

Pye then made a claim in the European Court of Human Rights on the basis that the UK government, by maintaining the limitation of actions to recover land, had deprived it of its possessions, otherwise than in the public interest and without compensation, contrary to Article 1 of the First Protocol to the European Convention on Human Rights. And it was while the European Court's decision was awaited that the first instance decision was given in *Beaulane Property Ltd v Palmer*.

It was held in *Beaulane* that the landowner had apparently lost title to the squatter, and was therefore holding the registered estate in trust for him. But the judge was troubled by the human rights aspect of the case. Article 8 of the Convention allows a deprivation only 'in the public interest and subject to the conditions provided for by the law and by the general principles of international law', and those principles are generally taken to mean that there should normally be compensation, even if the deprivation is in the public interest. Where title is registered, that public interest loses the force it has in unregistered land. Adverse possession is not needed for certainty of title once title is registered. Nor is it needed to control conveyancing procedure. So it was concluded that Beaulane had indeed been deprived of its possessions, and that there was no public interest in favour of this deprivation. The reasons justifying the operation of the limitation of actions to recover land are largely specific to unregistered land—in particular the promotion of certainty and the facilitation of conveyancing—as indeed the Law Commission argued, in its consultative document,[14] in favour of the reforms it proposed.

Moreover, the judge noted that the Land Registration Act 1925 was enacted during the period (which extended from 1879 to 1990) when adverse possession had to be incompatible with a landowner's present use

[14] See p. 211 above.

of the land, so that it was going to be very difficult to lose his title by inadvertence. Adverse possession would operate primarily in boundary cases or where land had been abandoned, and in both cases there was an obvious public utility for it even where title was registered.

Given a situation where adverse possession seemed to be operating in a way that was incompatible with human rights legislation the court was obliged either to operate section 3 of the Human Rights Act 1998 and to interpret the relevant statutory provision in such a way as to make its operation compatible with the Convention, or to declare the legislation incompatible, under section 4. The judge opted for section 3, and held that section 75 of the Land Registration Act 1925 was to be interpreted in accordance with the case law in existence at the time of its enactment: namely, as if *Leigh v Jack*, from 1875, remained authoritative. This meant that the squatter's claim failed, because he had used the field for grazing for a period during which the registered proprietor had no use for it. Accordingly his possession was not adverse and did not establish a title for him.

The judgment given in *Beaulane* was intended, the judge said, to assist the European Court of Human Rights in deciding *Pye*, and the case was referred to in the European Court's judgment.[15] Here, of course, the parties were different: Pye had lost its land already, and the defendant was the government, on the basis that the legislation caused the deprivation of Pye's possessions.

The government's argument against the Article 8 point was that there was no deprivation, because the Limitation Acts are part of the conditions of landholding in this jurisdiction. It is a given that if you allow a trespasser on to your land and fail to take action for twelve years, your title is lost and his is confirmed. The European Court's view was that ownership simply cannot be qualified in that way. In so holding, the court showed its very European concept of land-ownership. The government's position was much more in tune with the common law concept of ownership as a bundle of rights, and perhaps still not fully divorced from the feudal idea of landholding as a privilege exercised upon conditions. The government's argument was fatally weakened by the fact that it had already legislated to reform adverse possession in registered land. The European Court's judgment appears to have been very much influenced by the changes made in the Land Registration Act 2002, as if the issue had already been decided by the government against itself. It was

---

[15] *Pye v UK*, Application No. 44302/02 (2005).

unmoved by the argument that Pye was responsible for its own loss—and Pye had indeed been very careless, given that the squatter had on more than one occasion requested a grazing agreement and would have paid rent if asked. It seems that whatever the extent of the landowner's inadvertence or carelessness, the court regarded Limitation Acts as the cause of the loss.

The European Court declared that the loss of Pye's land was not in the public interest, in view of the fact that its title was registered. The court expressed approval of the changes made in the 2002 Act—as had the English judges in *Pye v Graham*—and so gave the impression that the human rights problem in the 1925 statute has in fact been solved for the future. That may not be entirely true, as we shall see. Moreover, the European Court's decision leaves the government with a potentially serious liability for compensation in the event that future claims are brought under the 1925 Act. Worse, the decision is set to cause serious upheaval in Ireland and Northern Ireland, whose title registration statutes are modelled on the English 1925 statute and allow the acquisition of title by adverse possession. At the time of writing, the government is seeking leave to appeal the decision in *Pye* to the Grand Chamber of the European Court of Human Rights.

THE RESIDUAL LAW OF ADVERSE POSSESSION

Adverse possession remains a live concept, for two principal reasons.

First, and most obviously, it is alive and well where title is not registered. Landowners whose title is not registered may still lose it to a squatter.

The next episode in the story of a squatter on unregistered land is likely to be either that the problem is discovered on sale, as it was in our story of Bloggs, Jones and Sam, or that the squatter applies for registration of his title. In either case, the outcome is likely to be that the squatter's title is registered, with or without litigation. If Sam simply applies for registration, independently of any transaction, Jones will not even know about the registration. It may be years before he discovers that his deeds are no longer proof of ownership of that particular part of his land. That outcome has in the past been beyond dispute once the squatter's factual case is made out. The European Court's judgment in *Pye* was not, apparently, intended to impinge upon unregistered land, but it is not hard to see that it may do so, because the loss of title may take place without the landowner's knowledge and without any provision for compensation.

Is the public interest in maintaining the law of adverse possession in unregistered land so strong as to justify these two factors? If such an argument were to prevail, it is equally easy to see that the reinterpretation of adverse possession in *Beaulane* might be extended to the unregistered land context also.

An alternative outcome for the story of Sam the squatter in *unregistered* land is that Jones, or a purchaser from Jones, applies for registration of title to the land. We have said little about first registration, apart from the fact that it is triggered by certain transactions, and that it is also available on a voluntary basis—owners might register because they have lost their deeds, or with the intention of making their land squatter-proof, as discussed above. Section 11 and Schedule 1 of the Land Registration Act 2002 set out the interests that will bind the land on first registration and for the most part the intention is to replicate whatever was the position just before registration. But section 11(4) states that, on first registration, the land is subject to any interests on the register, any interests listed in Schedule 1, and any interests acquired under the Limitation Act 1980 *of which the registered proprietor has notice* [emphasis added]. Schedule 1 is a list of interests that override first registration; contrast Schedule 3, which is the list of interests, already repeatedly discussed here, which override registered dispositions. There are some interesting differences between the two lists, but one element they have in common is paragraph 2. The details in the two paragraphs 2 are different; but the effect is that if Sam is in actual occupation of the land still, his interest survives registration. He can, when forced to do so by a challenge from the newly-registered proprietor, or on his own initiative, apply to have the register altered so that he becomes the registered proprietor. But it is possible that after clocking up his twelve years, Sam left. He holds an unregistered fee simple in that land, nevertheless. There was some concern in Parliament while the 2002 Act was being debated about squatters who acquire title and then abandon the land. So the effect of the provisions of section 11(4) is that if Sam is not in actual occupation, Jones' newly-registered estate will only be subject to Sam's interest if Jones has notice of him. Constructive notice is presumably included.

Accordingly, an unregistered title can be lost to an adverse possessor without the dispossessed proprietor knowing anything about it. The squatter can get his title registered, ditto. But if the dispossessed proprietor happens to apply voluntarily for first registration, not knowing that he has lost his title already to a squatter who, however, is not currently occupying the land, the dispossessed proprietor will actually regain his title, and the squatter will lose what he gained. This is far-fetched, but possible. It demonstrates the potency of registration. It also demonstrates an alarming tendency for ownership to be lost, without the owner knowing. The potential for a human rights challenge is obvious, and the counter to that challenge is the public interest in not allowing unregistered title to be lost to a squatter who then abandons the land but retains title to it. It is arguable that for the sake of certainty and marketability (not to mention individual desert) in such a case paper title should prevail, and that it certainly should do so once registered.

The second reason why adverse possession remains a live concept is that it still plays a restricted role in registered title, as follows. For one thing, there may still be cases where title to land was registered under the 1925 Act and was lost to a squatter before the Land Registration Act 2002 came into force in October 2003. Transitional provisions were designed to ensure that there should be no difficulty in the squatter applying now for his title to be registered. As we shall see, there is now a considerable difficulty. The decision in *Pye v UK* does not actually change domestic law, but it leaves the government liable to compensate those who have lost their title in this way, or at least will do so if it stands following an appeal. In that event, it may be that the reinterpretation of adverse possession in *Beaulane* will solve the problem by ensuring that no claims are successful—there can, as just stated, only be a few more such cases. If not, the government faces claims for compensation by those whose land is lost to a squatter under the provisions of the Land Registration Act 1925.

The 2002 Act, of course, makes things very different. It accepts the possibility of Sam and his adverse possession of the goat field. It states that there is no limitation period with respect to registered title, so that there is no point at which Bloggs loses his title automatically by operation of law. But there are two ways in which Sam can acquire land by adverse possession nevertheless. The Act provides that after ten years' adverse possession, Sam can apply for registration as the proprietor of Bloggs' registered title (not, notice, for registration of *Sam's* title acquired by adverse possession). When he does so, the registrar will inform Bloggs. If Bloggs responds within 65 working days, stating that he objects to Sam's registration, then Sam will not be registered as proprietor. Bloggs then has a further two years to evict Sam. If Bloggs does not reply to the notice, or if Bloggs fails to get rid of Sam in the next two years, then Sam has a right to apply to be registered, and to take over Bloggs' title to the goat field.

So the first way in which Sam can acquire title to the field is if the land has been abandoned by Bloggs—demonstrated by his not replying to the registrar's notice, or not bothering to follow up the notice by evicting Sam.

The Act provides that even if Bloggs makes objection Sam can be registered if he falls within one of three exceptions. Two of them actually have nothing to do with adverse possession; they occur when Sam is entitled to the land because he has an equity arising from an estoppel,[16] or otherwise, for example under a registered proprietor's will. The point about both of these is that adverse possession is irrelevant; Sam could have applied to the court to be registered as proprietor of the land. But the law gives him a little reward for having also been in adverse possession of the land for ten years: it enables him to use the procedure appropriate to adverse possession, namely an application to the land registry Adjudicator,[17] instead of having to use the court system. The Adjudicator is cheaper and quicker.

But the third exception is about adverse possession: it is the case where there is a genuine mistake about boundaries, as in the example of my garage, given above. This is therefore the second way in which Sam can acquire title by adverse possession.

So the draftsman of the 2002 Act did cater for the cases where there is still a practical need for adverse possession, namely abandoned land, and boundary problems. Unfortunately there is still room for challenge, following *Pye*. First, is there sufficient provision, in the Land Registration Rules as they stand, for a registered proprietor to be warned that a squatter has applied for registration? What of the proprietor who is away from home, in prison, in hospital, or just too busy—or too old, or too scared—to reply? Some thought may need to be given to this, in view of the fact that the very conspicuous carelessness of Pye (Oxford) Ltd did not sway the majority in the European Court of Human Rights, who took the view that the operative cause of Pye's losing the land was the terms of the statute. A dissenting minority of judges in *Pye v UK* disagreed on this point, and therefore this is the argument that may be successful on appeal to the Grand Chamber. As things stand, and if the appeal is unsuccessful, there is a potential problem. The European Court of Human Rights approved the three exceptions in the 2002 Act, but said nothing about the fall-back position whereby the registered proprietor who fails to make objection following the registrar's notice, or who objects but

---

[16] Chapter 4, p. 81 ff.
[17] Land Registration Act 2002, s. 107.

then fails to take proceedings against the squatter, will lose his land without compensation.

EVALUATION

An initial concern about the 2002 Act was that it might not have left sufficient room for adverse possession. The Act fails to allow it as a resolution for boundary disputes where there has been no mistake. I might have deliberately encroached on your land to build my garage: even there, there is something to be said for a limit to the length of time in which my garage is at risk of legal proceedings. If it has stood happily on the land for fifty years without the neighbour minding, and then I apply to have the land registry plan brought into line with possession on the ground, it may not be right to have to litigate about states of mind at this distance. But the adverse possession provisions of the Land Registration Act 2002 help only the virtuous squatter, who is saving land from abandonment, or who genuinely got the boundary wrong when he built his garage.

On a more general level, there was some doubt as to whether or not the law had been improved by the abolition of the limitation period for registered titles. It has certainly had some of its desired effect, in that since the Act came into force a number of local authorities have registered their titles. The register has been made more powerful. The uneasiness that remained, before the decision in *Pye*, was the divorcing of title from possession. There is a risk that at some stage, too much land will be rendered unusable, even if not actually abandoned, by the non-application of the limitation period, or that legal ownership may be out of synch with physical possession to an uncomfortable extent. This has happened in other jurisdictions; it is not unimaginable that there may have to be a re-think.

Yet now, post-*Pye*, concern may need to be expressed in the opposite direction. The provisions for registration of a squatter in the limited circumstances that the 2002 Act allows may themselves be violations of the registered proprietor's human rights. The Act may not have gone far enough in eliminating adverse possession.

These two trains of thought apparently cannot stand together. We feel we *need* the limitation of actions for the recovery of land. But that law of limitation is to be seen now as a violation of human rights.

What can bring these two factors back together is compensation. A deprivation of possessions in the public interest *is* permissible if it is

'subject to the conditions provided for by the law and by the general
principles of international law', and in much of the Strasbourg juris-
prudence that has meant compensation. Recall what was said in Chapter
3 about the indefeasibility of registered title, and English law's compromise solution to this problem, which regards possession as a decisive factor.
The registered proprietor who is in possession, and who is not at fault in
the generation of the mistake that gives rise to the need for rectification,
has a veto. He can keep his title, leaving the victim of the mistake to the
land registry's indemnity fund. The law of adverse possession could take
a similar turn. The registered proprietor who loses his land to a squatter
could be compensated. If it is agreed that adverse possession has some
public utility—as has been suggested here—then it is not unreasonable
that the public purse, in the shape of the registry's fund, should compensate those individuals who carry the cost of the law's operation. The
right to compensation could be duly restricted, in cases of true abandonment despite generous warning provisions, and would not generate
large claims in cases of boundary mistakes. Reform in this direction
might then leave space for the limitation of actions to be restored in
some contexts if its removal in the 2002 Act is eventually seen to cause
problems.

   If such a re-think proves necessary, it may be worth bearing in mind
that in civil law jurisdictions, acquisition of title by possession is managed
without relativity of title. A squatter is not regarded as having a (defeas-
ible) ownership right during the initial years of his possession. Once the
limitation period has expired, the squatter takes over the dispossessed
owner's title. We are part-way there. The law now provides that in the
exceptional cases where a squatter can become the registered proprietor
of the land, he takes over the old registered title rather than having a new
one. It would be a small step to legislate out of existence the squatter's fee
simple insofar as it exists before the expiry of the limitation period, and to
regard him as having an inchoate claim like that of anyone who is in the
course of acquiring an easement by prescription. The public interest
in keeping land ownership in line with possession—seen so vividly in
English law's version of indefeasibility—could be combined with a step
taking our insular land law a little further into Europe.

BIBLIOGRAPHY

M. Dockray, 'Why do we need adverse possession?' [1985] *The Conveyancer
   and Property Lawyer* 272.

The Law Commission and H. M. Land Registry, *Land Registration for the Twenty-First Century; a conveyancing revolution* HC 114 (Law Com No 271) (London, The Stationery Office, 2001), Part XIV, p. 299 ff.

D. Rook, *Property Law and Human Rights* (Blackstone Press, 2001).

A. W. B. Simpson, *A History of the Land Law* 2nd edn, (Oxford, Clarendon Press, 1986), Chapter II.

Index